A HISTORY OF ITALIAN FASCISM

A HISTORY OF ITALIAN FASCISM

FEDERICO CHABOD

Translated from the Italian by

MURIEL GRINDROD

WEIDENFELD AND NICOLSON
20 NEW BOND STREET LONDON W1

945.091

© 1961 Giulio Einaudi editore S.P.A., Torino
English translation © 1963 by George Weidenfeld and Nicolson Ltd.

Printed in Great Britain by C. Tinling & Co. Ltd.,
Liverpool, London and Prescot

CONTENTS

Preface   7

PART ONE
AFTER THE FIRST WORLD WAR

Chapter 1 DELUSIONS OF VICTORY   15

Chapter 2 ECONOMIC AND SOCIAL CONSEQUENCES OF THE WAR   21
    I Poverty and economic ruin of the middle classes   22
    II The peasants and the struggle for land   26
    III The rise of the industrial proletariat   29

Chapter 3 THE PARTIES AND THE GOVERNMENT   33
    I Politics in Italy up to the First World War   33
    II Changes in Italian political life: the elections of 1919   35
    III The political crisis: its causes and manifestations   39

PART TWO
FASCISM

Chapter 1 THE RISE OF FASCISM   47
    I Mussolini and the beginning of Fascism   47
    II Causes of the Fascist success   51
    III Deeper reasons for Fascism's rise to power   55

Chapter 2 THE FASCIST RÉGIME   62
    I The establishment of the dictatorship and its institutions   62
    II Consolidation of the régime   69
    III The Abyssinian War and its consequences for the régime   76

CONTENTS

PART THREE
ITALY TODAY

Chapter 1 THE WAR AND THE COLLAPSE OF THE FASCIST RÉGIME: THE RESISTANCE MOVEMENT	87
I *The political framework of the struggle against Fascism*	88
II *The fall of Fascism: the political situation in a divided Italy*	94
III *The resistance: military organization and political action*	101
IV *The political situation at the time of liberation of all Italy*	117
Chapter 2 THE POLITICAL PARTIES IN REPUBLICAN ITALY	123
I *The first elections in free Italy*	123
II *Politics after the election of June 1946*	134
III *Distribution of political forces in post-war Italy*	143
Chapter 3 THE ECONOMIC SITUATION	151
I *The economic and financial consequences of the war*	151
II *Economic development: 1945-9*	153
III *Unemployment and the population problem*	157
Conclusion	159
Bibliography	163

PREFACE

IN A COMMEMORATION of Gaetano Salvemini, Franco Venturi emphasized how Salvemini, like so many great historians, wrote the history of his own times. In the same way Federico Chabod in this series of thought-provoking lectures delivered in the University of Paris in January 1950 reconstructed the history of the times through which he had lived.

In these lectures of Chabod's the story of the Fascist régime is told with unquestionable impartiality, although, even when dealing with the more successful aspects of Fascism, the author never disguises his own deep-rooted anti-Fascist convictions. He examines the reasons which, despite the feelings of moral revolt and loss of confidence temporarily aroused by the Matteotti murder, ensured wide support for the Fascist dictatorship; and the reasons which, in course of time, caused that support to wane. He recalls earlier misfortunes—such as the catastrophic failure of the harvest in 1920, due in part to natural causes but also to social conflicts in the countryside—and the fears they aroused (including the retrospective fear of a Bolshevik revolution in Italy), and assesses their significance in facilitating the success of the Fascist movement. He shows how certain actions of Mussolini's Government, in particular the reconciliation with the Vatican, helped to consolidate the régime. All this he does in a manner which is truly penetrating in its objectivity and precision. Many Italians began by approving of Fascism for what they hoped it might become; but Fascist policy became gradually, and at the last completely, divorced from those expectations. The sanctions applied by outside countries during the Abyssinian war generated the last wave of sympathy for the régime, and after that people began to feel they could no longer approve of the totalitarian direction in which it was developing. Professor Chabod's exemplary account conveys the significance of this whole period.

The years 1936-7 marked the opening of the phase of 'definite breach between the régime and the country' (p. 83). In 1939, when, after the prestige success of Munich and Franco's victory in Spain, Fascism appeared to be at the height of its power, it no longer had the whole nation with it, as Chabod shows. The world war merely enlarged 'the profound abyss that had opened up between the country and Mussolini' (p. 84). This could not have happened if, as Chabod notes, the support which had previously upheld the Fascist Government had not had, as far as the great majority of those supporters was concerned, limitations which only a small group of fanatics could ignore. But we could not fully estimate the importance of those limitations if Chabod had not explained and recognized realistically the extent and nature of the support which Fascism had won for itself in the period of its ascendancy.

Against this background, Professor Chabod's account of the Italian Resistance is much more than a mere commemoration of its exploits—understandable though that would have been in him, for the Resistance was very close to the heart of this historian who himself joined the Action Party and became a courageous partisan leader in one of the politically most important areas of the war of liberation. It is not as a concession to neo-Risorgimento rhetoric, but rather in order to show 'how the Italian *bourgeoisie* had become detached from Fascism', that Chabod stresses the point that in 1940, unlike the Risorgimento or the 1915-18 war, there was no sign of a widespread volunteer movement such as had always, up to 1918, been a marked feature of the participation of Italian patriots in any warlike venture (p. 87). Instead, the volunteer made his reappearance in the Resistance, drawn from the ranks not only of the middle classes but also of the industrial workers and peasants; this last was something of a novelty, though workers had also had a share in the Risorgimento (pp. 109-10).

A by no means negligible part of this volunteer partisan service, Chabod goes on to say, was purely military. There were a number of officers and men who, despite the catastrophe of the armistice, wanted purely and simply to remain loyal to the Italian flag; and that signified the duty to fight against the Germans occupying their country. They therefore joined the 'autonomous' non-political bands, some of which did extremely well (p. 111).

But the majority of Resistance volunteers, especially those from working class or peasant backgrounds, went into bands which were both military and political. 'This showed that the active and definite participation of the masses in political life... was by now an established fact, which it had never been during the years between the achievement of Italy's unity and the First World War. This alone would suffice to explain why political life in Italy after 1945 was different from that of the pre-1914 period' (pp. 110–11).

The political volunteer bands of the partisan war were naturally associated with the political parties which supported them. Chabod follows the logical course in prefacing his account of the Resistance by a description of the anti-Fascist parties which managed to survive though banned, or were reconstituted underground, even before 1943. He lays his finger on the fundamental point in the Action Party's programme, a point held in common by all its trends and which was to 'give it considerable importance politically' and cause it to play 'a foremost role in 1943–5': this was the conviction, derived from twenty years of underground democratic struggle against Fascism, of the 'need for a fundamental change in the whole life of the State, beginning with the institutional framework.' And he shows how this particular question in the long run became, in one way or another, the dominant problem for the other political parties too, while it also contributed, in combination with the Action Party's own internal dissensions, towards eliminating that party from the scene at the very moment of success of the Republican view for which it had fought (pp. 93, 127).

For the historian, the political significance of the Resistance lies—notwithstanding the share of many brave monarchists in the struggle for liberation—in the change-over from monarchy to a republic. Chabod's study shows particular acumen in his analysis of the varying conditions, whether military, political, social, or above all psychological, which pertained in the three different parts of Italy. The South brought forth the first insurrection, that of Naples, but almost at once found itself under Anglo-American administration. Rome, a special case because of the presence of the Pope there, and some of the central provinces had to endure German occupation and fought against it gallantly, but always in the expectation that the British and Americans would soon be there. The North, including Romagna (and in certain respects Tuscany), had the time, the opportunity, and the will to organize

A*

a genuine partisan war in opposition to German domination and the so-called Fascist Republic of Salò. The North constituted the main strength of the struggle for liberation, but after its victory, apart from the institutional question, more moderate political methods prevailed—methods evolved in Rome but in which the less advanced, more sceptical, or more traditional attitudes of the South also had some influence.

One may not agree entirely with some particular judgements of Chabod's, for example with the view that, from the standpoint of the new outlook represented by the militant wing of the Resistance, and despite the diplomatic success of its negotiations with the Allies, the Northern Liberation Committee's agreement to act as a representative of the Italian Government—which meant in effect acting under the control of the Allied Supreme Command and the Rome Government—contributed towards splitting the revolutionary impetus politically (pp. 114–16). In point of fact, the revolutionary developments, both political and social, in North Italy were much more pronounced after the signature of the agreements of December 1944 than before it. This was obviously due in part to the growing strength of the partisan political formations, both in the towns and in the mountains, as the struggle became more intense and its victorious conclusion more certain. But it was also due to the fact that, as a result of the representative powers accorded to them, the CNLs (including also, by virtue of the CNLAI's overall agreement, the local, provincial, communal, district, trade, and factory CNLs, in which latter the revolutionary impetus was much stronger) were able to present themselves as legitimate authorities in the conduct of the struggle against Nazism and Fascism and in the subsequent purge policy. If the revolutionary impetus failed, it was not because of the agreements of December 1944 but for much deeper and more complex reasons, among which must be included the strong pull exercised by the British and Americans in the traditional and therefore anti-revolutionary direction. Moreover the whole picture has to be viewed within the wider framework of that division of Europe into spheres of influence which not only the British and Americans but (as Chabod does not fail to point out) also, and more importantly, Stalin and his collaborators desired and regarded as inevitable.

On the subject of the anti-Fascist purge, which was at the very heart of the political struggle in 1945 (and in Rome as early as

1944), Chabod has little or nothing to say, perhaps because at the time when he wrote documentation was lacking on what was then still a burning topic. But he attaches due importance to the tremendous hidden influence of the bureaucracy in curbing the movement towards revolutionary change (p. 120). Similarly, he does not disguise the fact that the Socialist and Communist parties failed to support Ferruccio Parri's Government when it got into difficulties at the end of 1945 through the action of forces seeking a more conservative solution (p. 121). This does not prevent him from giving an impartial estimate of the Communist Party's tactical skill and political flexibility, and of the importance of its penetration into the countryside, first in the Po Valley and Central Italy and later in the South, or from recognizing the significance of the Socialist Party's electoral successes in 1946, when they did better than the Communists in Lombardy and Piedmont.

The solution of the problems of post-war reconstruction during 1947 and 1948 is lucidly illustrated by Chabod on a basis of both economic and electoral statistics. National unity emerged victorious from the terrible trial of a lost war. Italy has been rebuilt thanks to her workers and administrators, and also to international circumstances, but her traditional economic and demographic problems—the latter, according to Chabod, the more serious of the two—remain unsolved. From the political angle, Christian Democracy, the party of the great Catholic masses, has taken the place in the democratic Republic which the Liberal Party (or, more exactly, the liberal political class) held under the constitutional and parliamentary monarchy between 1861 and 1922. Christian Democracy is now more closely linked to the Church than formerly inasmuch as the Concordat of 1929 has been given a place in the new Italian Constitution; it is also powerfully assisted by the Catholic Action movement, which has developed on an immeasurably wider scale than in the days of the Partito Popolare. Government under the Christian Democrats is very different from what it was under the Liberals, not only in the nature of its structure and mentality and in its political, administrative, social, and cultural aims but also because of the different times in which it has to function. Christian Democracy's outstanding victory was due in the first place to the fears entertained by the *bourgeoisie*—and not by them alone—in relation to Communism in 1948. But the result, in any case, has been the complete transformation, by comparison with 1870, of the whole orientation of the Italian State, which nevertheless has stood firm despite the unprecedented crisis through which it has passed (p. 159).

The continuity of the State despite changes in its institutional form, in the character of its political leadership, and in the scope of its activities; and the rise of the Catholic forces with the Church as their spiritual guide—these seem to Chabod to be the two main developments emerging from the thirty-year struggle between 1918 and 1948 in this country which has nevertheless revealed 'a quite astonishing capacity for recovery' (p. 159).

LEO VALIANI

PART ONE

AFTER THE FIRST WORLD WAR

1 DELUSIONS OF VICTORY

MY SUBJECT IS TO BE the history of modern Italy. This task, I must say, rather alarms me. This is partly because I shall have to discuss events that are still close to us—too close, perhaps, for the historian to be able to see them as a whole. But it alarms me even more because it involves the reconstruction in a few lectures of thirty years of Italian history, a history which during those last thirty years has been extremely complex, often dramatic, and sometimes tragic.

The march of events, indeed, became increasingly rapid and complex from 1919 onwards. That is the date which we must take as our point of departure, the moment at which we become aware of a profound change in Italian life as compared with pre-war days. Yet by 1919 the war had come to a victorious end with the collapse of Austria-Hungary and the Hapsburg Empire, the great enemy of Risorgimento Italy. But that very collapse raised problems and debates—the first problems and debates that we shall be called upon to examine.

The collapse of the Hapsburg Empire had been Mazzini's dream. He saw the Italian Risorgimento, and the unification of Italy, as the beginning of a general revolution which would liberate not only Italy but also the other oppressed nations and cause to disappear from the face of Europe 'the two monsters', as Mazzini called them: the Hapsburg and the Ottoman Empires. On the eve of his death, in 1871, when speaking of international politics Mazzini used still to reiterate those same ideas which he had preached to Europe for forty years.

Thus 1919 saw the disappearance of the Hapsburg Empire, the enemy in the face of which Italian unity had perforce been created and Italy's political renaissance had come into being. What more could the Italians want? Their fellow-countrymen of Trento and Trieste, hitherto separated from them, were now reunited to Italy.

Nevertheless, during the last months of the war and the winter of 1918–19 it was precisely the question of the succession to the Hapsburg Empire which aroused the most violent discussions and disputes; reading certain newspapers or listening to certain speakers in Parliament one might almost have had the impression that the Italians were the vanquished, not the victors. Such disputes centred round Dalmatia and Fiume, to which Yugoslavia put forward claims against Italy, with 'Italian nationalists' contending against 'Yugoslav nationalists', the latter showing themselves no less proficient than the Italians in the matter of exaggeration.

Italy's situation did not improve at the Paris peace conference. Discussion of the 'Adriatic question' (i.e. Fiume and Dalmatia) proved so bitter that the Italian Prime Minister and Foreign Minister, Orlando and Sonnino, left Paris and returned to Rome in April 1919, though they soon went back again to Paris.

What lay beneath this dissatisfaction and these explosions of extreme nationalism on both sides?

Let us begin by examining the Italian Government's policy. And when we say the Italian Government we mean in fact the Foreign Minister, Sonnino. It was Sonnino who had conducted the negotiations with the Allied Governments which had brought Italy into the war under the Treaty of London (26 April 1915), and he had directed Italian foreign policy throughout the war. But Sonnino had not been aiming at the downfall of the Hapsburg Empire. His whole policy can be summed up thus: to fight Austria and the Hapsburg Empire in order to obtain for Italy the 'unredeemed territories' still under Hapsburg rule—just that and nothing more. Why was this so, we may ask? Why not aim also at the downfall of the Hapsburg Empire, which was in any case inevitable? We find ourselves up against the tenacious obstinacy of a man who was certainly of no mean intelligence or character. Sonnino was a highly cultivated man, of great rectitude and possessed of considerable qualities. Why then did he remain up to the last moment deaf to all the voices raised around him, even to those of some of his collaborators?

I mentioned just now the revolutionary tradition of Mazzini; but there was also within the Risorgimento another tradition, which had found clear and shining expression in the famous book of the Piedmontese Count Cesare Balbo, *Le speranze d'Italia* (Italy's Hopes), published in 1844, which expounded ideas, schemes and programmes diametrically opposed to the 'general revolution of nations' preached by Mazzini. On the contrary, there should be no general revolution, according to Balbo: Austria was necessary to Europe; she represented a fixed point in the vanguard of Christian civilization; her function, far from being at an end, was destined to grow, with the Danube valley and the Balkans as her sphere of action. To this end, Austria should abandon her Italian possessions which acted merely as a deadweight and a restriction upon her, and should turn her surplus energies eastward. Thus, while Italy would be freed, the interests of Christianity would be protected by this great Empire which was indispensable to the balance of Europe.

This thesis of Balbo's was the inspiration behind Italian policy from 1866 onwards. It would have been impossible at that time to envisage a complete collapse of Austria or to speak of a 'general revolution' as conceived of by Mazzini; apart from anything else, such an idea would have come up against the monarchist and conservative convictions of the men in the government. Consequently, the dominating factor in Italian policy between 1870 and 1914, and the factor which explains the Triple Alliance, is what we may call the 'Balbo idea'. In other words, Italy must try to go ahead in agreement with Austria; Italy could not start a war for Trento and Trieste on her own; she must therefore wait in patience and the day would come when perhaps by a friendly agreement she could regain her lost territories without disturbing the balance of power in Europe by overthrowing the Hapsburg Empire.

This was also the view, after 1880, of such a man as Crispi. Yet Crispi was an old follower of Mazzini, a former revolutionary; not a man who had emerged from government circles in Turin, but an ex-republican converted to monarchy: a parliamentary deputy, then a minister, and finally, in 1887, Prime Minister. Now Crispi, after 1880, had publicly declared in Parliament that the Hapsburg Empire was a necessity. Like many political writers in Western Europe around the 1840s, he feared the Slav peril, in other words Russia; and Austria served as a bulwark against Russia. But there was more to it than that: Crispi, who certainly could not be suspected of hostility to Germany, still thought it better that there should be other countries—Austria-Hungary, Switzerland—between Italy and the great newly-formed Empire of Germany, in order to avoid too close proximity.

We find this conception reflected on the diplomatic plane. It is relevant here to recall Article 7 of the Triple Alliance, the fundamental article on which the whole diplomatic action of Sonnino and the Italian Government in the winter of 1914-15 was to be based. That article established an agreement between the Governments of Vienna and Rome in accordance with which neither of the two Powers—which in practice meant Austria—might proceed to the occupation of territory in the Balkans without the previous agreement of the other party, which in that case would have the right to compensation for any such acquisition of territory. And the Italian politicians were well aware of the form that compensation would take.

Thus we find in Sonnino's policy an epitome of the experience of Italian diplomacy throughout the previous fifty years. He had himself lived through that experience and had been among the advocates of the Triple Alliance in 1882; he belonged to the circle of politicians who had governed Italy between 1880 and 1914. When he became Foreign Minister he was already an old man, his mind closed against voices from outside, addicted to solitude, stubborn and obstinate; he had completely ceased to listen to those who might have modified his convictions, and in his actions as Foreign Minister he inevitably drew his inspiration from that conception framed fifty years before.

Thus the policy of 1914-19 was a policy after the fashion of 1866; but what suited excellently in 1866 was completely outmoded by 1914. It was no longer possible to ignore the fact that within the Hapsburg realm the national movements in the north and south, in Croatia and even more in the Czech regions, represented something of much greater significance than in 1866, foreshadowing the prospect that a fresh conflict would be a life-and-death struggle for Austria-Hungary. It was no longer possible to envisage a world conflict which would end, in the event of a defeat for the central Powers, without the downfall of Austria. Thus if Italy wanted Trento and Trieste, which meant war, she must also accept the logical conclusion. Consequently it behoved her to evolve new conceptions adapted to this situation; to follow a fresh line of policy. But Sonnino never believed this, not even in 1917 and 1918; and when people warned him: 'Keep an eye on national movements: it is to Italy's interest from now onwards to act in agreement with the Slav nations and establish relations of confidence and reciprocal collaboration with them which will

DELUSIONS OF VICTORY

guarantee the future', Sonnino would reply, 'Those nationalities aren't anything serious, they're just propaganda subjects'. Within the Government itself, he encountered the opposition of another minister, Bissolati, a Socialist who had been expelled from his party shortly before the war (at the Reggio Emilia congress in 1912) and had become leader of the Reformist Socialists. Bissolati favoured a policy based entirely on the idea that Austria was on the verge of collapse and that Italy should try to come to an agreement with the peoples who would create the new successor states.

Between these two policies, that of Bissolati looking towards the future and that of Sonnino still anchored in the past, the latter prevailed.

At the peace conference, Sonnino from the very beginning came up against that reality which till then he either could not or would not recognize: he had clung tenaciously to the Treaty of London and refused to budge from the 'written tablets of the law'. Hence the difficulties surrounding the discussions on the Italian frontiers, poisoned by increasingly bitter disputes between the Italian and Yugoslav nationalist groups, the latter no less vociferous than the former. Wisdom was equally absent from both these manifestations of nationalism on either side of the Adriatic.

A mistaken policy on the part of the Government, which in a period of profound crisis in the history of Europe attempted to apply long outmoded political and diplomatic criteria, thus led to what may be described as the 'crisis within the victory'. True, mistakes were also made at the peace conference by the Allied Powers, and especially by Wilson, who at a certain point seemed to wish to apply his famous 'principles' solely in relation to Italy. All in all, many Italians had the feeling that their whole effort in the war had been disregarded. A significant phrase began to be bandied about and heard on the lips of students and officers back from the front: 'the mutilated victory'.

National feelings became increasingly exasperated. This was the first disappointment of the hopes that had been based on the end of the war. People had come to believe, as so often happens, that the late war would be the last war, and that, once ended, peace and tranquillity would return and life would become serene again. We shall see the consequences of this state of mind later on when we come to discuss the masses, the peasants and workers, and the social composition of Italy at that time. The whole country had been repeatedly told: 'This is the last effort. When you fight 3,000 feet up in the mountains, in the wild Carso, on Monte Grappa or on the Piave, you must put everything into the effort, because victory will follow and then the country's longings will be satisfied.'

The nationalist propaganda of such men as Federzoni and Corradini thus fell on fertile ground for stirring up national resentment. And that produced a phenomenon to which it is worth while drawing attention: it even succeeded in impelling army officers and men, in September 1919, to take part in D'Annunzio's march on Fiume and the occupation of that town. I only mention the episode here because of its internal repercussions, which were quite serious. Nitti, who was then Prime Minister, made the significant comment that this was the first time that the spirit of sedition had entered into the Italian army, even if for a noble aim. He was right. Up till then the army had never shown disobedience of any kind towards the State. The generals in command may have been only mediocre, but that is another question; the commanding officers may not have always been quite up to their job, but that had nothing to do with the traditionally good and solid qualities of the Italian soldier. And, in any case, the army had always obeyed.

But not now. Every Italian school-book was wont to recall Garibaldi's famous answer in 1866 when, having laid at his country's feet all the military laurels of a campaign which, as far as the army was concerned, had gone quite well, he was checked by a telegram from the king ordering him to halt. His sole response was: 'I obey.' This time nobody answered: 'I obey.' D'Annunzio marched on Fiume and occupied it against the Government's orders; and, though this was not the case everywhere, he found officers who were ready to follow him, even in a picked corps like the Sardinian Grenadiers, and others of high rank who encouraged him.

All this meant that the Adriatic problem, and questions of foreign policy, represented an element capable of disturbing profoundly the internal order of the life of the State; it meant that, like a faulty gear, something had gone wrong in the State itself.

2 ECONOMIC AND SOCIAL CONSEQUENCES OF THE WAR

THE PATRIOTIC RESENTMENT of which we have spoken was a wave which certainly stirred up great depths, but it touched only a relatively restricted surface. The anxiety and irritation aroused by the interminable discussions on the new Italian frontiers, on Fiume and Dalmatia, undoubtedly affected a great number of young men, students and officers, of the middle and lesser *bourgeoisie*; but those feelings alone would not have sufficed to cause an upheaval in the whole life of the State. The truth was that the upheaval had already taken place; the repercussions of the international situation were only one of many elements which were beginning to stir up a storm in Italian life. What were those other elements?

At this point we have to consider the internal upheavals which Italy's social and political structure had undergone during the war. There was a reason for the resentment entertained by many officers and men which had nothing to do with the discussions at the peace conference or the failure to recognize Italy's rights. Mixed up with the patriotic resentment was another factor: the resentment of officers and men who heard insults hurled at them in the streets—'You're the ones who wanted the war, it's you who are responsible . . .' Thus an internal problem had developed; it was now a question not merely of the peace conference's discussions, of Italians and Yugoslavs, Wilson, Clemenceau, and Lloyd George, but also of the attitude of a part of the Italian people towards the war and those who had fought in it, an attitude due largely to the internal changes which the war had brought with it.

I POVERTY AND ECONOMIC RUIN OF THE MIDDLE CLASSES

The most important of these changes were in the social sphere. What effect had the war had on Italy's social structure? The conduct of the war had called into question the Government's whole economic and fiscal policy. In studying the history of modern Italy it should be borne in mind that this was the first great trial of military strength which the country had experienced. Italy was still a very young State: only four years before her entry into the war, in 1911, the fiftieth anniversary of the constitution of the Kingdom of Italy had been celebrated in Rome and Turin. Fifty years is a short time for a country to develop traditions. The great States of Western Europe, France and Britain, could look back to centuries of national military tradition and participation in large-scale wars. But in Italy for the first time a population of over 36 million found itself plunged into a four-year-long struggle which was not only bloody but also financially ruinous.

Italy is far less wealthy than the other Great Powers, notwithstanding the great advances achieved since the unification. The average diet of an Italian in 1914 corresponded to about 3,200 calories a day, more than a fifth below that of an Englishman. The average income *per capita* in 1911–13 was 549 for the United States, 481 for Britain, 351 for France, 301 for Germany, and only 158 for Italy.[1]

But Italy nevertheless consumed more than she produced: between 1909 and 1913 the excess of imports over exports averaged 1,250 million lire. To put it another way, on a total volume of foreign trade amounting in value to about $5\frac{1}{2}$ milliard lire, Italy had a deficit of $1\frac{1}{4}$ milliard. How was this gap to be filled? The answer was, largely by income from tourism and emigrants' remittances: for in those years the number of emigrants leaving Italy was sometimes as high as 873,000 in a year, with an annual average of 650,000 over the years 1909–13, and their savings from earnings abroad went back to their families at home.

One of the reasons why the veteran statesman Giolitti disapproved of the Salandra–Sonnino Cabinet's policy in embarking on war in 1915 was because the Italian Government was known to cherish the illusion that it would be a short war. Giolitti, on the

---

[1] Reckoned in international units (I U) according to Colin Clark's method: cf. F. Coppola d'Anna, *Popolazione, reddito e finanze pubbliche dell'Italia dal 1860 ad oggi*, Rome, 1946, p. 67.

contrary, believed that the war would be long and difficult to sustain, especially on the financial side.

From the economic and financial standpoint, a long-term situation should have been envisaged and an organized plan prepared to meet it. But the Italian Government's financial policy provided for no such plan. This point has been clearly brought out by Luigi Einaudi in his book, *La condotta economica e gli effetti sociali della guerra italiana* (The economic conduct and social effects of the war in Italy), published in 1933. In fiscal and financial policy, as in foreign policy, the mistake was made of believing that the war would end quickly. This did not happen, and the Government found itself increasingly under the pressing necessity of finding the means to meet the Treasury's needs by loans or by taxation which, given the system of taxation adopted in Italy, fell very unevenly upon the taxpayer. Budget expenditure rose from 2,501 million lire in 1913–14 (the last normal year) to 10,550 million in 1915–16; 17,315 million in 1916–17; 25,334 million in 1917–18; and 30,857 million in 1918–19. In those same years the deficit rose by stages from 214 million to 23,345 million. Note circulation, which amounted to 2,007 million at 30 June 1914, reached 20,000 million at the end of December 1920. The public debt rose from 14,089 million lire in 1910 to 95,017 million in 1920.

The consequences of all this were extremely serious. The hardest hit were those classes of the population which hitherto had formed the real backbone, in the political sense, of the Italian State—the small and medium *bourgeoisie* (those engaged in the liberal professions, in trade and industry, and owners of property) and the small landowners who were in the habit of farming-out their estates.

The burden of taxation hit these groups with ever-increasing force. The same was true of property owners living on rents. Rents of land and house-property were blocked, as we shall see later; incomes therefore remained unchanged, or altered only slightly, whereas costs rapidly increased. These are phenomena with which we today are only too familiar, but at that time they were completely novel and unexpected. There was also the plight of those who had subscribed to the public debt or to 'victory' loans during the war. Einaudi has calculated that between 1916 and 1918 some 30 per cent of the national income went to the Treasury in the form of loans. The rapid devaluation of the lira between 1919 and 1920 (in the second half of 1920 it was worth only one-fifth of its 1914 value) spelt impoverishment for many and downright ruin for some.

On the other hand, in contrast to those who saw their economic situation steadily worsening day by day, there were others who experienced just the opposite: as always in war, the industrialists were getting enormous orders and coining money. Especially in trade, including the black market (though it never reached anything like the scale of the Second World War), huge fortunes were made from one day to the next. Thus while some were faced with economic ruin, others found themselves suddenly wealthy: in short, a 'new rich' society was arising while the old well-to-do *bourgeoisie* collapsed.

In this situation the end of the war was eagerly awaited since it was expected to bring back tranquillity, especially from the financial point of view. This is a fact worth mentioning, for it seems to me to give, better than any other comment, the measure of the mental climate of the times. In the first months of 1919 Italy's trade was so greatly reduced that even retail trade was affected. Consumers refused to buy in the hope that prices would fall. This seems to me typically indicative of the prevailing psychological attitude of much of the country: the hope that once the war was over the happy days of the past would return.

During the Second World War illusions of this kind were no longer cherished; nobody believed that with the coming of peace prices would revert to their pre-war level, or even that they would be stabilized at their wartime maximum. The experience of the First World War had immunized us against such illusions. Peace did not bring serenity in foreign affairs, nor financial tranquillity for most of that *bourgeoisie* which had hitherto constituted the foundation of Italian political life. On the contrary, the cost of living rose steadily. With the end of the war, exchange control, established in July 1918 by agreement with the United States, Britain, and France, also came to an end, on 25 March 1919, and the lira at once collapsed. In June 1914 the dollar was worth 5 lire, 18 cents; in December 1919 it had risen to 13·07 lire; in April 1920 to 22·94; and in December 1920 to 28·57 lire. This meant a rise in the cost of living, since Italy had to import wheat, coal, and oil. She was especially short of wheat. Before 1914 Italy used to produce on an average 50 million quintals a year (the maximum yield per hectare was 12·3 quintals in 1913) and she had to import some 14 million quintals; but during the war production fell to a minimum of 38 million quintals (the lowest yield per hectare was 8·4 quintals, in 1920). In 1920 the total cereal harvest (wheat, maize, rice, etc.) was 18 million quintals below the average of 1909–14. If Italians had not been able to look abroad for supplies they would have starved, for they are a people whose basic diet consists of cereals and especially wheat.

Such were the anxieties preoccupying the Italian Prime Minister, Nitti, in 1919, and therein lies the explanation of his desire to put an end to the exacerbated discussions of foreign policy: if the United States were to stop sending supplies to Italy, what would happen next?

To make matters worse, in July 1919 the populace in the towns, large and small, began to assail the warehouses where supplies were stored. To counter these disorders the authorities imposed a compulsory 50 per cent reduction in prices; this merely had the effect of temporarily arresting the rising curve. The weekly expenditure of a typical Milanese working-class family at this time was 120·05 lire in June 1919; 109·24 in July; and 108·07 in August, rising however in November to 118·53; to 124·67 in January 1920; and 189·76 in December 1920. In relation to 1914, the rise in the cost of living for a working-class family in the first half of 1921 could be estimated at 560 per cent. The situation of middle-class families was even worse. Salaries of office workers, or at any rate of the civil servants who constitute a considerable part of the Italian lower middle classes, failed to follow the rising curve of prices; owners of house-property and landowners in receipt of rents fixed in cash found themselves saddled with leases blocked by a law which permitted only a ludicrously small increase of rent. On the other hand taxes went up. State taxation has already been mentioned, but to get a correct idea of the situation in 1919–21 communal taxation must also be taken into account. For the communes were at grips with serious financial problems and were pushing up their taxes and supertaxes.

Finally, the plight of the large number of reserve officers must not be forgotten. These men, who had played a prominent part in the war, often suffering for it in their own persons, now had to return to civilian life—for in the summer of 1919 Nitti began to reduce the army cadres, with the laudable aim of bringing down military expenditure and assisting the recovery of the State Budget. But civilian life was extremely expensive for these young men who, once out of uniform, found themselves without jobs and often superceded by others who had not fought but had merely stayed at home looking after their own affairs. These young men, too, came from the middle classes.

II THE PEASANTS AND THE STRUGGLE FOR LAND

Italy was at that time a predominantly agricultural country. This is indeed still the case, but it was much more so then. In 1914, 55 per cent of the population lived by agriculture (the figure for 1862 was 75 per cent), whereas the percentage in France was 43, in Germany 35, and in Britain 12. Those employed in industry represented 28 per cent of the total population, as against 32 per cent in France, 40 per cent in Germany, and 44 per cent in Britain. Trade accounted for 8 per cent of the population in Italy (France 14, Germany 12, and Britain 23 per cent).

These figures illustrate a fundamental fact: that although Italy's industrial development between 1861 and 1914 was considerable the country still remained largely agricultural in character.

But what does it amount to, this agriculture on which the major part of the population lives? First and foremost, it is necessary to dispel the widely believed legend of the richness of the Italian land. Certainly Italy is a fascinating land because of its natural beauty and its picturesque countryside, but it is not a rich land. Only 20 per cent of the national territory is fertile plain, consisting of good land where farming can produce high yields and high profits; 40 per cent of the country is hilly and the remaining 40 per cent mountainous. These percentages alone suffice to give an idea of Italy's agricultural poverty.

But that is not the whole story. Many of the mountainsides and hills are deforested, especially in Central and Southern Italy, and even in the Western Alps the same phenomenon is beginning to appear, especially as a result of the unsystematic cutting down of trees during the two world wars. This has had serious consequences on the flow of rivers and on humidity, and therefore on the productive capacity of the land itself. Moreover, these are lands which have been tilled for centuries. The soil has been overworked and its productive value is on the downgrade.

These are facts to be taken into account and remembered for

they provide the reasons for the immense toil that man must bring to the cultivation of such soil. Italy is not a land which by the grace of God and without further trouble can provide nourishment for its people. On the contrary, except for certain regions—the Po Valley, the immediate surroundings of Naples, Apulia, some valleys at the mouths of rivers in Southern Italy, the plain of Palermo, and the plain of Catania—Italy is a land that exacts relentless, unremitting toil from him who would cultivate it.

Given these facts, what is the structure of property-holding? In 1914, 55 per cent of the population lived by the land, and there were five million landowners. But what did they own? Nine-tenths of them possessed not even as much as a hectare, or, taken together, only three million hectares out of a total twenty-two million. This meant that the mass of the peasant population possessed plots too small to permit of a livelihood. Consequently they were forced either to rent land from the medium or large landowners, or to work as labourers on their estates.

Another phenomenon deserves attention because it is typically Italian: in France, for instance, it exists only on a much smaller scale. This is the problem of the *braccianti*, the agricultural labourers, whose only asset is their manual strength; and this problem is a really serious one. It concerns the large mass of the peasantry living, in particular, in the districts round Bologna, Ferrara, Cremona, and Mantua, and in the Piedmontese provinces of Vercelli and Novara, that is to say, in regions of intensive cultivation where, however, for reasons of production (e.g. rice growing around Vercelli, etc.), the land is not divided up among many owners. These peasants can obtain a living only because the large and medium landowners need hands to cultivate their land. The consequence is that at every crisis in farming or in agricultural prices the landowners try to reduce either the labourer's wages or the number of labourers employed. Thus there is the constant risk, today become a reality, of large-scale rural unemployment. There are today (i.e. in 1948) two million unemployed in Italy; and of those two million a considerable number are agricultural labourers who find themselves at the mercy of the landowners and the economic situation. Even when there is no particular state of crisis, the labourer's life is extremely hard: he can be sure of regular work for only a part of the year, according to the season, and wages, especially in Southern Italy—and this is still true today—only permit of a wretched existence. There is a very great difference in wage levels, and thus in standard of living, between the North and the South of Italy: the Calabrian peasant, for example, still lives in quite primitive conditions.

These countless small farmers and labourers cherish but a single dream—a dream intensified by the war, for it was the peasants who formed the backbone of the army and paid for victory in their own persons: the dream of land for the peasants. The Italian peasant is hungry for land. It can safely be said that his ideal is simply to possess a piece of land of his own, large enough to make a living from it. Among all the problems raised by the war—and it must never be forgotten that this was the first time the Italian people had fought a large-scale war within the framework of the unified state—one of the most acute was, what recompense should be given to these ex-servicemen once peace came.

Thus even during the war the cry of 'Land for the peasants' was heard. In 1917 the matter began to be taken up by the press; in August of that year, at a meeting in Rome of representatives of the General Labour Confederation and other organizations, a demand was raised for the waste lands to be requisitioned on behalf of those who were prepared to till them. A member of Parliament, Ciccotti, put forward a draft law for improving the condition of the peasants. Even official propaganda, especially after Caporetto, did not hesitate to make promises, if only vague ones; the future, officially, was painted in rosy colours.

The war ended, and the demobilized peasants returned home in a state of fevered anticipation prepared to accept miracles. The next stage was easily predictable. In July and August 1919 hordes of peasants, with the red flag in front and the bands playing, sometimes even with the church-bells ringing, occupied the waste lands belonging to the big owners, and in some cases the cultivated land as well, around the capital itself. (The same phenomenon, incidentally, was repeated in Calabria in October 1949 and in parts of the Po Valley early in 1950.)

Notice that this was not merely the manifestation of a particular political point of view: it was not only the Reds who marched to occupy the land. There were among the marchers, naturally, peasants who were organized in the General Labour Confederation and labourers belonging to the Red unions. But in the agrarian movement which shook Italy in 1919–20 there was also what has been described as 'White Bolshevism', in other words those

Catholics who, in the agrarian sphere, proposed solutions not so very different from those of the Communists. The head of this movement was Guido Miglioli, a deputy belonging to the Catholic Partito Popolare. In November 1920, no longer in the surroundings of Rome or in the South where much of the land was still uncultivated or badly farmed, but in the neighbourhood of Cremona, at Soresina, right in the middle of the Po Valley, in one of the best farmed and richest parts of Italy, peasants under Miglioli's leadership occupied the land with the slogan: 'Let the land be run by the farmers themselves through a collective organization' (i.e. a farm council).

There was, however, an important difference between the 'Reds' and the 'Whites'. The Whites—the Catholic groups—aimed at creating agricultural undertakings run by farm councils, which meant that profits from the undertaking would be shared between all the farmers associated in it. The Reds, on the other hand, especially those in the North, had a quite different programme. Their slogan was: 'Work for the peasants': agricultural unemployment must be abolished, and to that end the landowners must employ all hands available on the labour market regardless of whether or not they were economically essential. The Socialist Reds were concerned first and foremost with the labourers, the *braccianti*, and they justifiably reproached the 'Soresina system' for creating an 'aristocracy' of co-operative farmers at the expense of the labourers.

But, whatever the differences, the movement for occupation of the land was now under way, embracing the country from the Centre to the South and reaching up into the Po Valley.

III THE RISE OF THE INDUSTRIAL PROLETARIAT

As has already been mentioned, industry in Italy was still a long way behind the stage of development achieved in France or Britain. At the time of which we are speaking, the traditional handicrafts and small-scale industry still predominated: in 1911, out of 243,926 factories or concerns, 160,496 employed no more than five persons including the owner. Nevertheless there were already in existence large industrial centres with a big working-class population; these were mainly in the North of Italy, in particular Turin with the Fiat works, Genoa with the Ansaldo concern, and Milan and its surroundings—the three towns forming the so-called 'industrial triangle'.

The war naturally provided a stimulus for industry and progress. Consequently by 1919 the working-class masses already represented a strong body. It is interesting to note in this connection that up to 1880 most Italian politicians had denied that a 'red peril' could ever arise in Italy. After the Paris Commune, throughout Western and Central Europe fears had been entertained of a 'red explosion' and of what the International might mean in terms of a danger to society. At that time and in the years that followed the majority of Italian statesmen, and in particular Crispi, always categorical in his affirmations, continued to repeat that Italy would never experience a threat from Socialism since there were no working-class masses there. But now, on the contrary, big industrial concerns had developed in Italy, bringing their problems in their wake.

The working-class masses, most of them specialized workers (for example the Fiat employees in Turin), became, so to speak, the armoured divisions first of the Socialist and then of the Communist movement. Groups of workers began to be formed, fully conscious of their own strength. In Turin they found political leaders such as Antonio Gramsci, editor of the paper *Ordine Nuovo*, who carried on the struggle in much more determined fashion than the old leaders of the Italian Socialist Party.

Thus a working-class *élite* developed which carried a considerable body of opinion with it. In 1920, the General Confederation of Labour, in the hands of the Socialists, had a membership of over two million, a third of them peasants and the rest chiefly industrial workers.

For the workers, and especially for the *élite* in the big industrial towns, the watchword was Russia. At that time, in 1918–19, little was known about the precise development of the situation in Russia. Nevertheless among the workers there was constant talk of Lenin, of factory councils and the abolition of capitalism, and the word spread. One day—it was 21 January 1919—at a Socialist meeting, the man who can be reckoned the 'father of Italian Socialism' and who because of his lofty personality had come to be its leader, Filippo Turati, was explaining: 'We must prepare the way for the coming of a Socialist society, but, at the same time, we must work for the gradual transformation of society.' A voice interrupted him: 'It takes too long!' Turati said, 'If you know a shorter way, tell me.' And many voices shouted in reply: 'Russia Russia, long live Lenin!'

These few words exchanged between Turati and his anonymous militant Socialist heckler seem to me sufficiently to reveal the state of mind of the working-class masses. They knew little about Russia, but the idea of the victorious revolution in that country fired their imagination. They therefore began to raise such problems as factory councils, workers' control in factory management, socialization of the land and the subsoil, and so on. In the meantime they succeeded in obtaining some important concessions: an eight-hour day (in 1919), wage increases, etc. I referred earlier to the disastrous economic effects of the war on the middle classes. As far as the working classes were concerned, it must be admitted that after a certain point the wage curve followed the price curve pretty closely; the increase in the cost of food and of living as a whole was compensated, for the workers in the big cities, by a progressive rise in wages, obtained, naturally, by means of strikes and by the constant pressure and efforts of the General Labour Confederation.

Thus there was gradually taking shape among the working classes a desire for political revolution; and among them this desire was—as indeed was natural—much clearer, more precise, and more definite in character than among the peasant masses. Italy, in fact, was assailed from two sides: on the one hand by the working classes, with the peasants' demands for land and the industrial workers' claims for improvement in status, and on the other by the middle classes, and especially the petty *bourgeoisie*, with all their grievances, anxieties, and fears for the future.

It is also important to note that these groups of ex-servicemen (especially students and young university men who had become officers during the war), deeply patriotic and already disturbed at the disputes over the Adriatic question, often found themselves in opposition to the workers in the towns, who adopted an openly critical attitude not only towards the war itself and the leaders who instigated and directed it, but also towards those who fought in it.

This attitude of the workers was in any case a great mistake. It was one of the tragedies of Italian Socialism before 1922 that this rift between patriotism and class was allowed to grow up. In this respect Socialism in Italy developed much more slowly than in France: the French Socialists were more ready to accept the responsibilities of government and thus succeeded in overcoming more quickly the division that had arisen in the second half of the nineteenth century between the 'patrie' of the middle classes and the 'International' of the workers. That did not happen with Italian Socialism. True, such men as Turati, Treves, Modigliani, and Prampolini, the most eminent personalities in the Socialist Party, loved their country; they loved it with all their hearts, possibly more deeply than certain truculent nationalists who made a great deal of noise about it. But the political action of the Socialist Party—and that was what counted—remained anchored to doctrinal positions which paralysed it. It would have been necessary to win over the sentiments and interests of the petty *bourgeoisie* (for whom their country represented something sacred) if Socialism was ever to become a force capable of dominating the post-war crisis politically and taking the place of the old governing classes in the country.

In Socialist propaganda, the *patria* was still what it had been for the nineteenth-century internationalists: a *bourgeois* concept, the *patria* of a social class against whom Socialism was bound to fight.

Another important consideration was the fear of losing the confidence of the working classes, the fundamental source of support of the Socialist Party, who had been stirred up against the war; and, moreover, there were the consequences of the war itself. Opinions rooted in people's minds by thirty years of propaganda cannot lightly be eradicated; and it was just here that the slower development of Italian Socialism made itself felt.

The profound upheaval effected by the war in Italian life impinged upon every sphere of interest and sentiment. The interests of all were hit, from the petty *bourgeois* who fell upon evil days economically to the big landowner who feared the coming of an Italian form of Bolshevism and viewed with horror the land occupations, strikes, and workers' agitations. And sentiments were offended: first and foremost, the love of country, both abroad and at home. As for the masses, they were waiting for something new to happen, after all the talk of peace and greater social justice, and all the appeals to the people promising them a better future.

Faced with so complex and confused a situation, what were the Government and the parties to do?

3 THE PARTIES AND THE GOVERNMENT

WE MUST NOW TURN TO EXAMINE the political problem itself. What were the main political parties in Italy at this time, and what attitude did they adopt in relation to the confused situation that has just been described?

I POLITICS IN ITALY UP TO THE FIRST WORLD WAR

Up to 1914 it is doubtful whether, except for the Socialist Party, political parties as we understand them today really existed in Italy. Until that time Italian political and parliamentary history had developed without the present rigid party structure, according to which the conduct of deputies in relation to the various problems is fixed in advance by the party leadership. Today political life has become rigid, and the party leadership decides on the direction to be taken. The deputies and senators vote, at any rate on important questions, according to the decisions taken by their parties' leaders. Freedom of personal choice is strictly limited. Nothing of this existed before 1914. Only the Socialist Party, with its own particular clearly defined features, was already a rigid-structured 'party' in the strict sense. Another group with a distinctive character of its own was the small collection of Republican deputies; the difference between them and the great mass of the Liberals lay in their attitude towards the monarchy. The Republicans, as their name implies, maintained their non-acceptance of the monarchical form of régime in Italy. They were the pure descendants of Mazzini, looking askance at the Quirinal and refusing to set foot in it; but even they agreed during the war to form part of the government.

Another group which began to make its appearance in parliamentary life was that of the Nationalists. Their numbers were insignificant—they had only three deputies after the elections of 26 October 1913—but they had a definite and somewhat disquieting programme, which bid fair to influence the mental outlook of the country's youth a good deal more cogently than might have been expected from their small representation in Parliament.

In addition, there were numerous party labels. In the 1913 elections, the last before the war, Liberals, Democrats, and Radicals also took part. But these were not rigid parties. The differences in programme were much less marked than they would be today; often it was a case of a group formed around some prominent personality who thus gave it its character—for example, the friends of Giolitti or of Salandra. But above all there was no compact organization capable of functioning permanently as well as during the pre-election period—nothing resembling the kind of organization which accounts for the strength of the parties today and for their ascendancy, as 'parties', over the men elected to represent them.

Finally, and this was a decisive factor, the elections were carried out under the system of single-member constituencies, which meant that greater significance was attached to the personality of the deputy and his personal clique than to the party itself.

Such were the conditions of Italian political life before the first war; and because of these conditions it can fairly be said that in pre-1914 Italy the parties had virtually no policy—policy lay with Parliament and the parliamentarians.

These conditions also explain the policy of Giolitti, Italy's most outstanding statesman between 1910 and 1914. His policy—which incidentally continued the traditional line of Depretis and of Cavour himself—was directed towards the formation of a parliamentary majority of the centre which would make it possible to govern by dissolving, so to speak, the theoretical programmatic differences in the crucible of parliamentary practice.

Giolitti's tactics failed where the Socialist Party was concerned. As far back as 1903 he had offered the Socialist leader Turati a place in the Government: his great idea was in fact to 'absorb' Socialism, to blunt the edge of its revolutionary tenets and transform it bit by bit into a party of law and order. Turati refused, and the official Socialist Party remained in opposition (though the Reformist Socialists did not; they became detached from the main party in 1912 and two of their members, Bissolati and Bonomi, participated in the wartime government). Turati, Treves, and the other Socialist leaders respected Giolitti as a person, but it was another matter to take part in a *bourgeois* government.

II CHANGES IN ITALIAN POLITICAL LIFE: THE ELECTIONS OF 1919

But in January 1919 a second real political party appeared on the scene, one whose aim was to be truly a party and not just a collection of deputies. This was the Partito Pololare, that is to say, the Catholic Party, whose successor today is the Christian Democrat Party. Its animating force was a Sicilian priest, Don Luigi Sturzo, a man deserving of great respect. What did the new party stand for? In certain ways its advent represented a fact of great importance, indeed the most notable event in Italian history in the twentieth century, especially by comparison with the century before: it signified the official return of the Catholics in force into Italian political life. It is difficult for anyone who is not an Italian to appreciate what this meant. We need only recall that after the formation of the Kingdom of Italy the watchword for Catholics was: 'No collaboration with the new régime.' They could neither vote nor stand for Parliament.

In point of fact it cannot be said that all Catholics abstained from voting. But in practice the ban had meant that up to the end of the nineteenth century Italian Catholicism was officially divorced from the life of the State. Here too Giolitti had tried to blunt the edge of the ban; he had even succeeded in concluding agreements with the Catholics (the Gentiloni Pact of 1913), and twenty-nine Catholic deputies were elected in 1913 (there were 3 in 1904, 16 in 1909). During the war the most important of them, Filippo Meda, had agreed to take part in the Government. That a publicly avowed Catholic should assume the office of a Minister of the Kingdom of Italy, in Rome, the capital still not recognized by the Pope, was a significant fact in itself. But it was not until 1919, with the constitution of the Partito Popolare, that the Catholics emerged into Italian political life as a compact organized mass with a well-defined programme of their own.

In the elections of 1919 they succeeded in sending 100 deputies to the Chamber. The official Socialist Party had 156. This meant that the régime of the old ministerial majorities typical of the Giolittian era was finished for ever. Henceforth it was no longer possible for a Prime Minister to form a Cabinet without the support of either the Popolari or the Socialists. These two parties were the strongest groupings in the Chamber, together representing a majority (256 deputies out of a total of 508). The old groups, the Liberals, Radicals, etc., disappeared.

The Partito Popolare was a 'rigid' party which did not permit of the personal agreements typical of the old-style Parliament. The approval of the party secretary, Don Sturzo, had to be obtained. This annoyed Giolitti, who could not bear Don Sturzo or the fact that anyone who was not even a deputy or senator should attempt to have a say in matters of State. Giolitti could not concede that Don Sturzo, a mere party secretary with no parliamentary mandate, should come and discuss with him, the Prime Minister, political questions which, in his view, were purely the concern of Parliament and its members. Giolitti, in fact, had ceased to grasp the terms of the political and parliamentary struggle on its new basis.

The change in the electoral system effected in 1919 was also partly responsible for the revolution in the old parliamentary régime. Proportional representation was introduced, and this had the effect of both reducing the importance of a candidate's personality (and the old parties were still the richest in men of personal prestige) and increasing the importance of the party, the organization.

A rapid glance at some statistics will demonstrate this truth. If voting in 1913 had been by the proportional method, the official Socialist Party would have had 89 deputies instead of the 52 it obtained by the single-constituency method; the Liberals, on the other hand, would have had 242 instead of 270, and the Radicals 60 instead of 73.

Thus the political struggle now became a genuinely inter-party affair; and the strongest parties, in 1919–20, were the two 'mass' parties, the official Socialists and the Popolari. Their strength increased thanks to the support of organizations which, while not political in the strict sense, were closely associated with politics: the trade union and social organizations. (It should be noted that the specifically Catholic organization, Catholic Action, did not at this time openly support the Partito Popolare; in this its policy differed from the line it took in relation to the Christian Democrats in 1948).

We must now consider the Socialist Party. The Socialists had advanced greatly since before the war. In 1919, as has been said, they had 156 deputies as compared with only 52 in 1913. In the 1919 elections they obtained 1,834,792 votes as against 883,409 in 1913. That was a remarkable achievement considering that the Socialist Party had opposed the war; in 1917 it declared that the conflict had lasted long enough and that Italian soldiers should not spend another winter in the trenches. For this the party was accused of having sabotaged the war. I do not propose here to go into the details of this accusation, which was largely false. Italy had sustained some military defeats, notably at Caporetto; but they are not to be explained, as some have maintained, by Socialist propaganda, but by the difficult strategic position in which the Italian army was placed. The mistakes made were military and attributable much more to the High Command than to party propaganda. And these mistakes in turn were due to two causes: the excessive length of the front, and the survival of old prejudices among the army leaders, and in particular their obsession about the importance of every inch of ground gained—a commander felt that he was failing in his duty if he did not advance a hundred yards, even at the risk of landing his troops in a completely untenable position.

Leaving aside these secondary aspects, suffice it to say that at that time the Socialist Party was, in the eyes of the people, the party that had opposed the war. And now, when the war had been won, this 'anti-war' party more than doubled its pre-war vote and nearly trebled its representation in Parliament.

Moreover, it is not only the political elections that are important in the life of a country: municipal elections count for something too. And in 1920 the Socialists achieved a majority in 2,022 communes, or in 24 per cent of the total number.

Thus at the end of 1920 the Socialists controlled over 2,000 communes, 156 deputies, 36 provincial councils, and 3,000 party sections, while the CGIL, the trade union organization, also under their control, had 2,150,000 members. They were, in fact, to all appearances, an extremely powerful force.

The Popolari, as we have seen, had 100 deputies. In the local elections of 1920 they won control of 1,613 communes, or around

13 per cent of the total. They had 22 daily papers and 93 weeklies. They controlled some of the big banks such as the Banco di Roma, and a number of small local country banks in which the clergy had for decades pursued an interest and which, in such regions as Piedmont, gave them a remarkable hold on the population. They also controlled many local agricultural co-operatives: in 1921, in the Po Valley alone there were 311 such Catholic co-operatives, as against 236 in Socialist and Republican hands. To compete with the CGIL, they created the *Confederazione italiana dei lavoratori*, the Italian Workers' Confederation, allied to the Partito Popolare, which in 1920 had a membership of 1,161,238; of these, 944,812 were farmers, which meant that in the countryside the Catholics—the 'Whites'—were stronger than the Socialists, the 'Reds', who had only 750,000 members. For this reason the Socialists failed to win over the rural masses as they had done with the urban workers.

Thus the old parliamentary groups found themselves in a position where they could not govern without previous agreement with either the Popolari or the Socialists.

At this point the tragedy of Italian Socialism begins to take shape. It developed for two reasons. First, as we have seen the idea was allowed to grow up—partly with justification because of the attitude of some militant Socialist leaders—that the party was 'anti-national'. This cost it the votes of the majority of the small *bourgeoisie*. Secondly, Italian Socialism, as visualized by its old leaders, did not want a violent revolution. But at the same time it was torn by a serious internal crisis which paralysed its political action. The prevalent revolutionary fever, exacerbated by what was known and rumoured about Russia, made its strongest impact, as was to be expected, on the party of Turati, Treves, and Modigliani. The talk was less of Marx than of Lenin. The extreme Left, which in 1921 was to split off to found the Communist Party, wanted to go all out for a decisive and fundamental struggle against the *bourgeoisie* and display a revolutionary will such as Russia had shown to conquer the State. Such men as Turati were very far from accepting these ideas; they inclined to reformism, not to revolution. Between these two extremes was the revolutionary speechifying, the vehement if sporadic agitation of a considerable part of the party which aimed to attract to itself the masses enticed by the image of Russia. The result was continuous strikes and disorders, which served merely to irritate their opponents without making any real impression on them.

That is not the way to make a real revolution; but, equally, it is not the way to get into the Government. The Socialists could not make up their minds either to conquer power by force or to share it with the *bourgeoisie*. Among the party leaders and in articles in *Avanti!* the same slogan was repeated time and again: 'We must be ourselves!'—we must remain faithful to our great principles, the proletariat, the struggle against the *bourgeoisie*. But often these were only words, with no definite plan of action behind them.

On the other hand there were the Popolari. Theirs was a party that already followed the rules of the same system that we know today: the secretariat kept the direction of the party firmly in its hands and decided on the political line to be adopted. The party secretary was an extremely capable man, but he was to shoulder a heavy responsibility when, in February 1922, he opposed Giolitti's return to power. (This brought about the advent to power of Facta, an honest provincial lawyer without the qualities necessary to lead a Government. He was brought in because the parties vetoed other more eminent candidates.) The Partito Popolare, too, like the Socialists, though numerically strong was also divided within itself. It included sincere democrats such as Sturzo, but also 'conservatives' who regarded the new party merely as a means to defend their own positions. There was in fact a bit of everything, from Miglioli, who organized the occupations of land in the Po Valley, to the old-fashioned Catholic conservatives. A party, in short, that was anything but homogeneous; and its political action showed it.

III THE POLITICAL CRISIS: ITS CAUSES AND MANIFESTATIONS

To sum up: with the Socialists in opposition and the Popolari proving difficult allies, the burden of government weighed heavily on the men of the old political groups who still retained the reins of power in their hands. Italian political life was taking on a quite new direction, and the old remedies no longer sufficed. Nevertheless Giolitti, faithful to past methods, dissolved the Chamber and in May 1921 played the great card of calling a General Election, in the hope of breaking the power of the two chief disturbing elements, the Socialist Party and the Popolari, and restoring a Chamber with a majority, on the old lines. It was a mistake. The Socialists lost ground, their representation falling to 123, but at the same time 15 Communist deputies were elected, now representing a party that had detached itself from Socialism. Moreover the Popolari increased their poll, winning 108 deputies instead of 100. In the 'national blocs' favoured by Giolitti, the Fascists now made their appearance: they gained thirty-five seats in the new Chamber of Deputies, the first Fascist group to sit there. But the composition of the Chamber as a whole did not permit of the type of parliamentary manoeuvring at which Giolitti was such an adept and which had for years formed the basis of his tactics. The veteran statesman had to retire for the time being.

Between 1919 and 1922 there were five different Governments. Even when no actual crisis arose, the position of the Government was constantly precarious for lack of a solid majority.

All this was taking place in a country which was already profoundly disturbed by the state of confusion and uncertainty described in the two earlier chapters, and which had to face serious difficulties in foreign policy. The Prime Minister, Nitti, resolutely opposed the occupation of Fiume by D'Annunzio. Giolitti settled the Adriatic problems in 1920, and in November of that year he and his Foreign Minister, Count Sforza, signed the Treaty of Rapallo—a treaty embodying an agreement which could well have been reached long before but for the errors of the policy of Sonnino and the no less serious mistakes of Yugoslavia. Had it been signed two years earlier, the Treaty of Rapallo might have changed many things not only in the history of Italy but also in the whole post-war political history of Danubian Europe.

Now, however, with the agreement signed, Giolitti as head of the Government had to find a solution for the Fiume question. He therefore ordered D'Annunzio to abandon Fiume, telling him that unless he withdrew Italian troops would be ordered to enter the town. This in fact was what happened in the so-called 'Bloody Christmas' of 1920.

On the international plane, the question was settled. But Giolitti's unavoidable action against D'Annunzio provoked fresh outbursts of nationalistic fervour in which the Fascists now joined.

Meanwhile at home strike followed strike in rapid succession. In the first half of 1920 there were probably more strikes in Italy than anywhere else in Europe. The most serious one was in September 1920, following the high-handed action of some Milanese industrialists (it is worth noting that the first provocation came not from the workers but from the industrialist side): a recently published document of the Ministry of Labour gave rise to the suspicion that industrialists had tried to persuade the Government to use force against the workers. The workers replied by occupying the factories in North Italy, and especially in Turin.

This occupation of the factories was the culminating point in the post-war crisis. Was the next stage to be revolution? It is interesting to observe how at this decisive moment a real will for revolution was lacking, at any rate among the great majority of the people. At a meeting of the National Council of the General Confederation of Labour on 10 and 11 September, the representative of the Socialist Party Directorate rose and, appealing to the revolutionary drive of the working-class movement, called on the Directorate of the Socialist Party, as a political party, to assume the leadership of the movement as a whole and give it a revolutionary character. The CGL gave a negative reply; it considered that this was not the time to risk revolution, both for fear of failure and also for fear of causing famine in a country so dependent as Italy on imports of wheat and raw materials from abroad.

As a matter of fact, at the very moment when the crisis reached its highest point of danger it was already beginning to decline. Giolitti had completely grasped the situation. He did nothing: he was staying in the country at the time, and he never budged. Only when he had to meet Millerand to discuss with him the solution of the Adriatic problem and prepare the ground for what was to be, two months later, the Treaty of Rapallo, did he leave to keep the appointment. When Millerand saw him arrive he said, 'I was sure you would put off our talks.' 'Why?' answered Giolitti. 'Because of the situation in Italy? That's nothing to worry about.' And the Prime Minister, the man responsible for public order, tranquilly prepared to discuss the agenda with the French Minister.

But Giolitti himself affords us a very clear explanation of the situation as he saw it. He was a past-master in the art of police technique. He had always kept the Ministry of Home Affairs in his own hands, and had had the opportunity to display his great ability during the pre-1914 strike periods. The first General Strike in Italy was in 1904, when Giolitti was Prime Minister. He telegraphed to the Prefects telling them that there were no serious economic causes for the strike and they should therefore keep calm and not worry. His technique lay in disposing the police at a few main strategic points chosen to ensure the maintenance, whatever happened, of the public services. Apart from that, he just let matters ride. He said to the strikers: 'You can parade and shout in the streets to your hearts' content: the post offices, the telephone service, the station, the Prefecture, and the Bank of Italy are all in my hands.' He did just the same during the occupation of the factories in 1920: 'If I use the police and the troops to occupy the factories,' he said, 'who will there be to guard the really vital places for me?'

This technique, astute as it undoubtedly was, was moreover only one aspect of a much wider political vision: 'I wanted the workers to make the experiment for themselves so that they would realize that it is pure imagination to think you can make a factory run without capital, technicians, or bank credits. They'll try it, they'll find out it doesn't work, and that will cure them of their dangerous illusions.'

This estimate of the situation proved perfectly correct. The workers, even those of Turin whom I described earlier as the armoured divisions of the extreme Left, had to abandon the factories of their own free will leaving no dead, no martyrs for the cause. They realized that it was not possible to carry out their plan. And that fact was decisive.

From that point onwards the crisis waned. The danger of a revolution had developed during 1919–20 with the pillaging of the shops in 1919 and the occupation of the factories in 1920. That was the culminating point. After that, disillusionment corroded the workers' will and weakened their enthusiasm.

Clear-sighted Italians now felt that the moment for revolution was definitely past. From another very important angle, too, the crisis-curve had reached its highest point. The financial situation, till then wellnigh desperate, began to improve, especially after Soleri, Giolitti's Minister for Supplies, brought before Parliament in February 1921 the law abolishing the bread subsidy. This was an act of great courage. Hitherto people had been paying a good deal less than the economic price for their bread, and the Government had made up the difference between the cost price and the price of sale to the public. Given the rapid devaluation of the lira and the rise in exchange values (for Italy had to pay in dollars for the wheat she imported), this meant a burden on the Budget of some 500 million lire a month.

If this situation had continued the State would have gone bankrupt. The law of 27 February 1921 made it possible to readjust the Budget. There was of course a deficit for some time; but the Budget was saved on the day when Giolitti and Soleri decided to end the bread subsidy.

Thus alike from the purely political and the financial points of view, seen in retrospect, the historian can affirm that between the end of the summer and the beginning of the autumn of 1920 Italy's crisis had reached its culmination; after that the obvious next task was to embark on readjustment. On the other hand, while it is true that historians today are in a position to demonstrate this fact, it is equally clear that it could not be perceived at once by the masses, who certainly did not consist of historians judging the situation from a distance of twenty or thirty years, or indeed of persons of any great perspicacity. This was why, at the very moment when the real danger was waning, anxiety and fear of revolution steadily increased among a large part of the *bourgeoisie*. We all know how it happens that when we have just escaped some physical danger we suddenly feel terrified on looking back at the difficulties we have evaded. Fear can also be retrospective.

Thus, on the one hand, there was widespread apprehension and uncertainty as a result of the constant strikes and unrest, with no immediate prospect of the longed-for day when peace would return; while on the other hand those who felt their interests to be threatened in various ways were beginning to combine together. The General Confederation of Industry had already emerged in 1919 as a counterblast to the General Confederation of Labour: one block of interests was lining up against the other. Faced with the workers' demands and the land occupations, those whose interests were threatened closed their ranks and moved over to the counter-offensive. This happened particularly among the landowners of the Po Valley.

And towards the end of 1920 came a sudden and unexpected upsurge of the movement known as Fascism.

PART TWO

FASCISM

1 THE RISE OF FASCISM

IT WAS NOT UNTIL THE END of 1920 that Fascism became a front-rank political power. Founded in Milan on 23 March 1919, it was not at that time a party but merely a movement. Later on, Mussolini himself was to write, in the article on Fascism in the *Enciclopedia italiana* (1932): '. . . I had no specific doctrinal plan in mind. My doctrine . . . had been a doctrine of action. Fascism . . . was born of a need for action, and it itself was action.' Such doctrinaire elements as he could not dispense with were arrived at by Mussolini almost haphazard; he was a nationalist, but not even that always, at least in the early days. For example, unlike the nationalists, he approved of the Treaty of Rapallo with Yugoslavia (12 November 1920), whereby Italy renounced Dalmatia, except for the town of Zara, as well as the islands of Lagosta and Pelagosa, and Fiume, which became a Free State. (The Treaty was to be followed later by the Treaty of Rome, of 27 January 1924, signed by Mussolini, on the basis of which Fiume was annexed to Italy.)

I MUSSOLINI AND THE BEGINNING OF FASCISM

The Nationalist Party and Fascism, though 'associated' during 1920–22, remained separate until 1923. After Mussolini's advent to power and the fusion of the two parties, it was the Nationalists who transmitted their doctrine to Fascism. But in 1919 matters had not yet reached that point; Mussolini's newspaper, the *Popolo d'Italia*, proclaimed itself the 'serviceman's and producer's' paper. But exactly who were the producers? This was by no means clear. Mussolini, it must be remembered, had been a Socialist up to 1914 and had held considerable influence in the party from

1912 to 1914—it was he who had caused the expulsion of Bissolati, Bonomi, etc. from the party at the Reggio Emilia Congress of 1912—and was editor of its paper *Avanti!*; in October 1914 he was himself expelled from the party because of his attitude in favour of Italy's entry into the war against Austria and Germany. In Mussolini the man, the influence of Georges Sorel and his doctrine of 'violence' is strongly discernible. Above all, he felt a constant need for action (in this respect his remarks in the *Enciclopedia* article are completely true to type); and action meant opening up a road for himself, his own personal road. His almost physical need of struggle permeated his whole conduct as head of the Government; his strength lay in large part in his undeniable ability to rouse the masses by means of an oratory which was always polemical and violent, often vulgar, but never obscure or colourless. Principles did not interest him; doctrines were for him just a tactical expedient to be used according to the particular people and circumstances concerned: for these he undoubtedly had an exceptional flair, at any rate throughout the period up to 1936.

Such was the leader. Around him, in the early days, we find groups of ex-servicemen who were moved, as I said earlier, by a feeling of revolt against everything which, whether abroad or at home, seemed in their eyes to humiliate the fatherland. (Subsequently, many of these men were to withdraw from Fascism when they realized that it was on the way to becoming a dictatorship and was exploiting for its own ends such phrases and concepts as the 'fatherland', 'victory betrayed', etc.; indeed in 1925 the Ex-Servicemen's Association even asked the King to intervene against Fascism.)

Side by side with people of this kind there were also others with quite different motives. Some were actuated more or less solely by the desire for action and adventure: the climate of the war, in which many of them had fought with great bravery, still weighed upon them making a peaceful and ordered civilian life insupportable. This is a phenomenon typical of post-war periods and their psychological upheavals. Others again, such as Roberto Farinacci, had played no part as combatants in the war; they had stayed quietly at home, although they talked a lot about victory, national greatness, and the dead of the Carso and the Grappa; among them the motive of adventure and the urge to make their own way were particularly strong. In general, all these different groups reflected the psychology of their leader. Drawn from among their ranks were those who later became known as the 'ras' of Fascism: these were leaders who had succeeded in creating around themselves a local, personal force which they exploited as a base from which to exercise strong influence on party decisions, as did, for example, Farinacci in Cremona, Balbo in Ferrara, etc. Behind them were the ever-increasing numbers of the 'action squad' men who took part in punitive expeditions against the Socialists: a heterogeneous mass including, side by side with genuine enthusiasts convinced of the need for their action, others who simply wanted to take part in an adventure and who could be described as 'professionals' in violence. The numbers of these last, not surprisingly, were constantly on the increase.

The first clash between Fascists and Socialists occurred in Milan towards the middle of April 1919. Those taking part in it were mainly ex-service students of the Milan Polytechnic who clashed with strikers in the streets and then sacked the headquarters of the Socialist daily, *Avanti!*.

The Fascists were at first concentrated in just a few towns, gaining ground gradually between 1919 and 1920. It was not until after the occupation of the factories at the end of 1920 that Fascism really developed and became widespread; it then recruited within a short period some 300,000 members and established 2,000 sections, doing particularly well in country districts. Up till then Fascism had been largely an urban movement, but now in some respects its centre of gravity altered. One of its main strongholds developed in the region between Bologna and Ferrara, where lived such leaders as Balbo and Grandi, among the movement's most resolute men of action. Balbo was one of the main organizers of Fascism on the military side, while Grandi, later to become a minister and an ambassador, was for the time being a trade union agitator. It was he, in particular, who rightly judged the significance of trade union and labour problems at this time: up till then the overall trade union organizations were either Socialist (the General Confederation of Labour) or Catholic (the Italian Workers' Confederation), but now Fascist trade unions also began to emerge.

The country between Bologna and Ferrara has always been a stronghold of the Left. It should be remembered that the wage increases which the trade unions had succeeded in obtaining from the landowners had had the effect not only of improving conditions among the peasants but also of encouraging production, since the landowners had found themselves forced to adopt more modern methods, with a corresponding increase of production.

But side by side with this progress on the social side, deplorable acts of violence were also taking place. The regions chiefly affected were those of Emilia and Romagna, but Tuscany too soon came into the picture. These are regions where the spirit of faction often proves stronger than any party loyalty: this is an old story in Italy's history. Violent passions are aroused and often gain the upper hand: we have seen to what lengths the Reds went, and now the Blackshirts too embarked on ever-increasing violence. This reached such a pitch that in 1921 Mussolini felt it necessary to check it, and in the summer of that year a peace pact was agreed to on both sides. But the Balbos and Grandis refused to recognize it, and in November the pact was denounced by the Fascists. The truth was that the big agrarian landowners had now taken a hand. Behind the attempts of the Fascists and their friends to form trade unions were the ranks of the landowners, eager to avenge the occupation of their lands and determined to put an end once and for all to the cry of 'Land for the peasants'. With the advent of the Fascist trade unions, which compelled agricultural labourers to obey their orders, wages went down—in other words, the trade unions when drawing up contracts in effect favoured the cause of the landowners at the expense of the peasants.

Thus agrarian reaction set in, perhaps even more intense and purblind than that of the industrialists. But the latter, for their part, by no means remained supine in the new situation but reacted too. They supported Fascism. If the landowners would have nothing to do with 'land for the peasants' or with labour taxes, the industrialists for their part refused to accept the idea of workers' control of the factories. The support given to Fascism by the industrialists, especially in the way of finance, is beyond dispute. But the landowners showed themselves even more reactionary. The landowner mentality, especially when faced with the question of increasing wages, is generally found to be much narrower than that of the industrialist.

In any case, the fact remains that at the very moment when the danger of revolution was averted and it at least seemed possible that the balance of the Budget might be restored, Fascism began to advance with great strides.

II CAUSES OF THE FASCIST SUCCESS

What were the causes of this rapid advance which six months earlier had seemed unthinkable? I described just now the various interests which were involved in the political struggle and induced Fascism to take action: the industrialists, the big landowners, especially in the region between Bologna and Ferrara, where Grandi and Balbo were active. That region constituted what might henceforth be called the 'agrarian' centre of Fascism. It lies on the borders of Tuscany; and between the end of 1920 and the beginning of 1921 Tuscan Fascism lent its support to the already strong Fascist organization in Emilia-Romagna, thus producing an experienced combat group which at a certain point adopted an attitude of opposition even towards Mussolini himself.

But the interests working in favour of Fascism are by no means the whole story: they played an important part, but there were other factors as well. We must now consider, in particular, the situation of the small *bourgeoisie*—clerks, small tradespeople, and professional men.

The Fascists also included some workers among their numbers. At the Rome congress of 1921 there were 310,000 registered party members. A sort of census carried out over about half that number showed 22,418 industrial workers and 36,847 peasants. Nevertheless the percentage of Fascist workers was very low in relation to the total numbers of the working classes. What is important, moreover, is not so much the number of those registered in a party as the attitude of the countless non-registered towards the various political trends. This is particularly true of the *bourgeoisie*, always—and especially so at that time—somewhat unwilling to accept party discipline, but nevertheless prepared to give the support of their vote: this is what is known as public opinion, in the long run a formidably important source of support. Now among the working classes the prevalent opinions and ideals were Socialist or Communist, sometimes Catholic, but always anti-Fascist; and the small percentage of workers adhering to Fascism in no way altered the general orientation of the working masses.

What was the attitude of the lesser *bourgeoisie*? It will be recalled that Fascism had found its earliest adherents among this class, in the ex-officers and students who had followed Mussolini largely because of wounded national pride—wounded because of the long-drawn-out delays of the peace conference and the discussions on the eastern frontiers, or because a part of the population had failed to recognize the sacrifices made in the war. Fascism had found its first recruits among such people. But it was soon to find others. What did the small *bourgeoisie* really want? They too, feared revolution above everything else. As I said earlier, the occupation of the factories in September 1920 and its failure made it clear to any intelligent observer that the hopes of a revolution in Italy had now vanished. But, I added, the perspicacious observer is rare: the great mass of the small and medium *bourgeoisie* had remained strongly under the impression of those events, which appeared to them not as a climax prefacing a decline but rather as the first act in a tragedy destined to end in total revolution. Viewed in this light Giolitti's tactics—his policy of letting the workers have their head and not shooting them but allowing them to occupy the factories so that they could discover for themselves their own inability to run them—may have been wise from a political point of view, but they were destined to produce highly negative effects on *bourgeois* mentalities and feelings. Clerks and professional men asked themselves how the State was reacting towards this serious situation: the State which, according to all the time-honoured principles, had the duty to ensure the protection of the life and property of its citizens. But what did the State do? It appeared impotent; if the Government took no action against the workers, it must be because it lacked the strength to act. Thus the prudence which was an element of strength in Giolitti's action was transformed in the mind of the masses into an element of weakness: for them the important fact was the State's failure to intervene.

After September 1920, although revolutionary fervour was now on the decline, strikes continued and there were also other manifestations of disorder, unrest, and violence on the part of the Reds. People asked themselves how it would all end. They complained of the number of working days lost and the inconveniences of the strikes, often called, it must be confessed, for trivial or unjustifiable reasons. (I have already spoken of the mistakes made by the Socialists, of their revolutionary hankerings and how, though unable to reach the point of revolution themselves, they refused to share power with the *bourgeoisie*. The same mistake can be seen with the workers: they administered too many pinpricks which irritated their opponents without influencing them.) The clerk or lawyer who had to go to his office and found all the buses and trams off asked himself why the State did not intervene to put an end to this perpetual state of disorder.

Thus a general state of fear, discontent, and disorder prevailed. And in addition to all this there was another strong feeling among the educated *bourgeoisie*, people who read D'Annunzio and recalled the 'patriotic' poet Carducci and looked upon the Risorgimento and the unification of Italy as the outstanding achievement of their forefathers: this was the feeling of patriotism. Who, they asked, were these masses who inveighed against the tricolour and the fatherland, who even said the 'patria' did not exist? It was their patriotic sentiment that was wounded.

All these considerations explain how it was that Fascism obtained fresh followers among the *bourgeoisie*. Fascism is a highly complex phenomenon which cannot be explained by any rigid formula. There is certainly an element of 'class struggle' in it; but there are also other elements which cannot be reduced to pure and simple terms of class struggle. Above all, Fascism cannot be explained simply as an emanation of big industry and landownership. Even after the March on Rome, when it had the government of the country in its hands, and throughout its subsequent evolution up to the Second World War, even then Fascism could not be characterized solely on a basis of class considerations. That it defended certain class interests is obvious, and some of its earliest decrees show it. Giolitti had made compulsory (by a law of 24 September 1920) the registration of shares in the holder's name. The aim of this measure was fiscal, and the result was to hit the wealthy man's income. By another law, also of 24 September 1920, Giolitti, with the same aim of countering the Budget deficit by imposing taxes on the well-to-do classes, had established death duties so heavy as to amount to total confiscation in the case of large inheritances and distant heirs. On 10 November 1922, thirteen days after the March on Rome, the Fascist Government abolished the compulsory registration of shares in the holder's name, a measure which had met with considerable opposition ever since Giolitti introduced it; and on 20 August 1923 another law abolished the law on inheritance. Thus the decisions of Giolitti's Government were annulled, and the taxes on inheritance were not only reduced but in the case of direct heirs (sons, wives, brothers, etc.) were completely suppressed. These measures were obviously intended to pacify certain sections of society—it is superfluous to point out which.

But there was more to Fascism than this. Some of its manifestations can only be explained by what I call a super-emphasis on the idea of the *bourgeoisie*, or rather the small *bourgeoisie*, from a spiritual and sentimental as well as an economic angle. The *bourgeoisie* was no longer thought of merely as a social class or an economic phenomenon but was regarded also as representing, so to speak, a state of mind. Consider, for instance, one of the epoch-making events of the régime, the conclusion of the Lateran Pacts with the Holy See on 11 February 1929. These agreements were received with enthusiasm by a large part of the Italian population: at last peace had been made with the Church. It is true that in 1929 the Roman Question was no longer what it was in 1882; there was no danger that the Pope might leave Rome, as Leo XIII had more than once threatened to do; the question had, in fact, with time become much less acute. The fact that a prominent Catholic such as Meda had taken part in the Italian Government during the war was in itself an indication of considerable progress. After 23 March 1920, the date of Benedict XV's Encyclical *Pacem Dei munus*, Catholic Heads of State could visit the King in the Quirinal, a thing hitherto not permitted by the Vatican. But the knowledge that the Church was not yet formally reconciled with the royal government and continued to maintain reserve on matters of principle left a feeling of discomfort in the minds of the Italian *bourgeoisie*. These were for the most part Catholics whom the anti-clerical propaganda of the years between 1860 and 1914 had affected only superficially even when it touched them at all. They loved their country, united Italy, and its capital Rome; but they were believers in their faith. An Italy at peace with the Papacy would guarantee for ever their spiritual quiet and interior tranquillity. Why is it that the image of Pius IX in 1847, the 'Italian' Pius IX, has always traditionally been so popular and survived to appear in all the school text-books? The reason is because for a short time it seemed that he might realize this dream.

Mussolini, naturally, had another and more immediate aim: the Concordat was signed in February 1929, and in March elections were due to take place. But the mere tactical aims of the moment do not suffice to explain the attitude adopted by the Fascist régime in reviving and putting into effect Orlando's earlier attempts of 1919 at conciliation, while at the same time making concessions to the Church which could never have been contemplated by a

Liberal Government. Mussolini, who, at least up to 1935-6, showed an undeniable flair for what would appeal to the masses, fastened on to this deeply rooted sentiment in the Italian *bourgeois* mind. This characteristic of Fascism also shows itself in other forms: it can be seen, in particular, in relation to the patriotic lesser *bourgeoisie* who wanted to see the country respected and liked the idea of enjoying a certain prestige in the world, and who, therefore, could be influenced by nationalistic press campaigns and speeches. Nevertheless this *bourgeoisie*, devoted as it was to peace, order and respectability, would never go beyond certain limits.

This explains how it was that in the last years of Fascism a breach developed between the régime and the *bourgeois* masses. It began even before the war; and in this connection a single fact will suffice to explain a great many things. The racial laws enacted against the Jews in 1938 took the nation completely unawares. There was a profound difference here between the Fascist and the Nazi régimes, between Italy and Germany. The laws were indeed applied in Italy, but most of the population did their best to help the Jews under persecution. The violent passion of anti-semitism was something unknown in Italy that went against the grain. This time no one followed Mussolini's lead.

Thus it is clear that in the rise of Fascism a complex variety of interests and passions played their part. They included some clearly defined class interests on the part of the big landowners, who hoped to break the resistance of the farm workers, and on the part of the industrialists. But such interests were also intermingled with simple considerations of passion and sentiment: wounded patriotism, the fear of revolution after September 1920, the dread of disorder and anarchy—all of them motives that were no less strongly felt by those who would have had little to lose by a change of social structure.

III DEEPER REASONS FOR FASCISM'S RISE TO POWER

Such, in brief, were the causes behind the hold obtained by Fascism between the end of 1920 and the beginning of 1921.

How are we to interpret the events of the years leading up to the March on Rome of 28 October 1922, and Fascism's advent to power? What did its supporters want? Was it dictatorship? A big industrialist has said: 'We did not want dictatorship; all we wanted was simply that Mussolini, when he took over the government, should bring back order and tranquillity to the country. After that, we would have gone back to the old system.'

That may well be true. But there is also another and more important factor. Very few of the leading politicians realized that they were on the threshold of a highly dangerous venture into which Italy was to be drawn for twenty years, culminating in catastrophe. The example of Giolitti is typical. No one can doubt that Giolitti was wholly and profoundly liberal at heart. When he perceived that Fascism was taking a very different course from that envisaged, he adopted a highly dignified attitude. He never left the Chamber of Deputies, and on some occasions he confronted Mussolini practically alone. Four months before his death, in March 1928, on the occasion of the vote on the new electoral law which in effect put an end to the *Statuto* (it introduced the single list of candidates, drawn up by the Fascist Grand Council), the veteran Piedmontese statesman, then aged eighty-six, rose to declare his formal opposition to this draft law, which represented the definite break of the Fascist régime with the old order based on the *Statuto* of 1848. His words were aimed beyond Mussolini, at the King. In fact, Giolitti, once he had realized his error, failed neither in courage nor in dignity. But in the early stages he too had been mistaken. What was it that he hoped for? There has recently been published a letter of his, dated 1 January 1923, to his journalist friend Luigi Ambrosini, in which he said: 'You are astonished that a "Fifth Estate" should arise with such extraordinary speed; but this is really one of the most common phenomena in history. After violent agitations (and what could be more violent than the last war?) there comes a wave of youthful Saint-Justs, Napoleons, Hoches, and thousands of unknowns. But the really significant people make themselves felt and remain in the forefront, the others disappear, and then the world resumes its normal rhythm.' Here is the explanation of his attitude. Giolitti believed that he could do the same with Fascism as he had partly succeeded in doing with the Socialists before the war: breaking their revolutionary impetus.

The whole of Giolitti's post-1919 policy is but a repetition of his earlier political methods. In this connection a speech he made in the Chamber on 2 February 1921 is indicative. In it he recalled the line he had adopted after he became Prime Minister at the beginning of the century, when strikes were looked upon as something monstrous: 'In 1904 there was a strike movement which I viewed with distrust. It was the first General Strike of a political character. I remember very well that I telegraphed to the prefects saying: "This strike does not arise from any vital cause or deep-rooted feeling among the masses; therefore, don't worry—it will only last a few days."' This harking back of the eighty-year-old statesman to his way of dealing with an earlier crisis shows clearly how his mind was working twenty years after. He believed that he could still overcome the present difficulties by the same methods as in the past—that Fascism could be lulled, canalized, and absorbed. He argued roughly like this: 'I'll give them two or three ministries, but the Ministry of the Interior I'll keep in my own hands; in that way I shall control the police, and the prefects will have to obey me. After a time the revolutionary impetus of the movement will be spent and the crisis will be resolved.'

In short, the country was faced with a profound crisis which the old political leaders were incapable of understanding or appreciating in its essential terms: they were therefore incapable of dominating it. In May 1921 Giolitti even helped the Fascists to enter the Chamber as deputies. He believed that he could make use of them against the Socialists or the Partito Popolare—against, in other words, the two parties who were making it impossible for him to govern according to the old methods. Indeed, in the letter to Ambrosini just quoted, Giolitti goes on to say: 'Political and above all parliamentary affairs could not continue in this way without bringing the country to ruin. That wretched electoral law (i.e. the law introducing proportional representation, which worked in favour of well-organized parties and reduced the scope for the old Giolittian tactics of manoeuvring with individuals) had split the Chamber in such a way as to make it impossible to have a strong Government with a definite programme. The point had been reached when an intriguing little priest (i.e. Don Sturzo) with no superior qualities dominated the whole Italian political scene.' These words were written after the March on Rome. And Giolitti was certainly not an isolated case; there were scores of others among the old Liberals who thought the same.

Thus the policy was, in case of need, to make use of Fascism, for its potentially subversive qualities were still discounted.

Fascism was measured and evaluated according to the same antiquated criteria that had been used in estimating parties and political forces in the past. And indeed, viewed from this angle, it seemed unlikely that Fascism, even after its successes of 1921, could come to power unaided. It was a minority, a considerable one it is true, but still a minority; and a minority—it must be remembered—it was to remain, even at the time of the March on Rome. I spoke earlier of the adherents to Fascism among the small *bourgeoisie*, but this class was a long way from joining Fascism *en bloc*. Some university students certainly became Fascists, but in 1922 and even after most of them still remained firmly anchored to the idea of liberty and hostile to Fascism, violence and armed struggle. In the elections of May 1921, even after the advances made in the winter of 1920-1, Fascist deputies numbered only 35 out of a total of 535. Even in the elections of 1924, carried out after Fascism had come to power and in a climate of violence, the Fascist list fell considerably short of obtaining 'plebiscitary' adherence; it registered 4,635,488 votes, or 64·9 per cent out of a total of 7,165,502 voters—and by that time the Fascist régime was already an accomplished fact.

Thus in 1921-2 anyone evaluating Fascism on the basis of the old formulae of political and parliamentary struggle could still believe in the possibility of blandishing it, making use of it, and giving it the role of a subordinate assistant to be dispensed with later on.

But it was just here that the basic error in evaluation lay. Fascism was not a political force of the old stamp. Its leaders—granting that it had any—had nothing in common with the men who had guided politics hitherto. Legality did not concern them; liberty, the preservation of Parliament, all the old principles of the liberal State were foreign to them. They might talk about them for simple reasons of opportunism or tactics, but in reality they cared not a jot for them. At the beginning, the movement amounted merely to action without any definite objective; but as it gradually developed and gained strength and weight in the country's life, its leaders began to aim at something more than action for its own sake. The conquest of the State, the March on Rome? These would come later, as the final goal; but already the desire could be detected to occupy a place in the forefront of public life, a place not transient but permanent. This was a far cry from the simple reaction against 'anti-patriotism'—the longing to conquer power had entered in. As early as 1921 some leaders, mindful of D'Annunzio's expedition to Fiume, were thinking of a 'march on Rome'. Always, and in any case, the belief was that 'force' would succeed in gaining the upper hand—and, if need be, armed force.

The Fascist party (transformed from 'movement' to 'party' at the Rome Congress of November 1921) represented, from the point of view of organization and technique, something new by comparison with the traditional parties. It possessed a military organization whose moving spirits, in the early stages, were Balbo, De Vecchi, and De Bono, an Italian Army General who had gone over to Fascism. The feeling for military and revolutionary technique can be clearly discerned from the importance attached to securing the control of the main railway junctions (Bologna, Verona, Alessandria), a measure which was to prove its value in October 1922.

To sum up, Fascism, alike from the standpoint of principles and of organization, represented a novelty which could not be absorbed into the liberal and constitutional system. Failure to perceive this dangerous novelty in time was the cardinal mistake of the majority of those who till then had been at the head of Italian political life. In this lies the main cause of what happened in October 1922: the conquest of power by Fascism required no real revolution, no basic overthrow: in fact, when the news of the March on Rome reached the capital, the King refused to sign the proclamation of a state of siege and decided to entrust the task of forming a new Government first to Salandra and then, immediately after, to Mussolini. When the Blackshirts reached the capital their victory was already an accomplished fact; their entry was a parade, not a battle. The King was by no means the only person responsible. According to the *Memoirs* of Soleri[1], Minister of War in 1922, it would seem that the Prime Minister himself, Facta, advised the King not to sign the decree proposed by the Cabinet proclaiming a state of siege, on the ground that it would have provoked the intervention of the army against the Fascists. Facta had started negotiations with one of the Blackshirt leaders, Michele Bianchi, with a view to arranging the entry of the Fascists into his Government; and perhaps he hoped to the last that he would succeed, thus avoiding bloodshed and chaos and 'absorbing' the Fascists. Once again the same mistake . . . Giolitti, too,

[1] Einaudi, 1949.

had embarked on negotiations with Mussolini, through the prefect of Milan. The plan was the same: to form a Government with the inclusion of the Fascists (Mussolini had demanded five ministries) and so to canalize the movement and bring it on to the legal and parliamentary plane of liberal practice.

Mussolini was quite ready to negotiate, for he did not want to exclude a parliamentary solution in the old style if that seemed necessary. He was the kind of man who would never slam any door against himself. But, at the same time, he was a man full of doubts and uncertainties. During these first years, at least, he was not always the one who made the daring gestures. The 'duri', the toughs of those days who believed in fighting to the limit, were Farinacci, Balbo, Grandi, and the like. In the summer and autumn of 1924, after the murder of the Socialist deputy Matteotti, when Italian public opinion woke up with a start and even the Fascists themselves were in a state of alarm, the party's man with the iron fist was Farinacci. Besides, Mussolini had the gift of recovering from his crises at the right moment and regaining the upper hand.

After all, he would argue, negotiations served only to lull his adversaries into a sense of security. It would never be his real line to accept normal parliamentary tactics. Moreover, side by side with Mussolini were Fascists who would never hear of anything of the kind, and who had always in mind that example which I mentioned earlier: D'Annunzio's expedition to Fiume. And that was a serious matter, not only because D'Annunzio's followers provided the first instance of insubordination in the Italian army, but also because Fascist leaders such as Balbo looked on the expedition as a sort of dress rehearsal for what was to come.

The Government lacked resolution and daring. The impression of weakness which it gave, and which, as I said earlier, alarmed the small and medium *bourgeoisie*, corresponded only too nearly to reality. Now it was from among the *bourgeoisie* that the prefects, senior police officials and generals came, and Fascism undoubtedly aroused a certain sympathy among these high officials, who preferred to shut their eyes when they should have decided to act. There was also some sympathy for it in the army; for example, the name of General Giardino, one of the big army leaders in the 1915-18 war, was spoken of in that connection.

Yet another source of indulgence towards Fascism was to be found in the House of Savoy, if not actually in the person of the King himself, in a possibly even more dangerous figure, the Duke of Aosta, who enjoyed great popularity. So much so, in fact, that Victor Emmanuel III felt some apprehension about his cousin's ambitions towards the Crown. Fascism did not hide its hand here: it argued something like this: 'If the King doesn't want to help us, we shall get on very well with the monarchy without him: we'll turn out Victor Emmanuel III from the Quirinal and instal the Duke of Aosta in his place.'

Finally, there was the Queen Mother, Queen Margherita. The Queen Mother had had in the course of her life the great good fortune to encounter a poet of the stature of Carducci who extolled her grace and beauty. This is one of those cases when it is possible to gauge what an effect the words of a great poet and writer can have in transfiguring a personality by presenting it under guises that conceal the true reality. Beneath a very attractive outward appearance—for she possessed the art of pleasing, and knew it—the Queen was a woman of iron will and, from the political point of view (the only one that need concern us here), completely reactionary. Now the Queen Mother, too, cherished a great sympathy for Fascism.

Taking all these elements together, it is easy to understand why the old liberal state was on the verge of collapsing to make way for a dictatorship in which, nevertheless, many people could not yet believe.

2 THE FASCIST RÉGIME

FASCISM HAD NOW COME TO POWER. How did it manage to keep that power for twenty years?

I THE ESTABLISHMENT OF THE DICTATORSHIP AND ITS INSTITUTIONS

Let us first examine the legal and technical forms which the Fascist régime adopted in its organization—forms which represented a complete break with the parliamentary régime in Italy from 1861 to 1922. The establishment of the organization falls into two distinct periods: from November 1922 to January 1925, and from 3 January 1925 onwards.

During the first period, apart from the politically decisive fact of the official and legalized formation of a party army, the militia, to which we shall revert later, there were no revolutionary changes of substance. In the first place, Mussolini, who up to September 1922 had made no secret of his preference for a republic, in a speech at Udine on 20 September 1922 accepted the monarchy. (The monarchy, for its part, had a number of its own adherents among the leading Fascists, such as, for example, De Vecchi, as well as all the nationalists.) Thus the institution which stood at the base of Italian life did not alter, and in fact remained unchanged to the last. In addition, during this period Mussolini still accepted the collaboration in the Government of the Liberals and the Popolari. He excluded the Partito Popolare's representatives from the Cabinet in April 1923, but the Liberals continued to participate in the Government till the end of 1924.

Formally, therefore, in this first period it is still possible to speak of co-operation between Fascism and some representatives of other parties. (I say 'some representatives' because Mussolini had by now practically decided not to enter into agreements with the parties as such. When would-be collaborators from the Partito Popolare attempted to continue acting as party members, Mussolini simply turned them out of the Government.) But it was a type of co-operation the exact reverse of what Giolitti and some of the old political leaders had had in mind; it was not the old parties that were 'incorporating' Fascism, but Fascism which formally accepted for a little longer the collaboration of the non-Fascists. Meanwhile, throughout the country violent methods continued to be used against the Socialists, Communists, and Popolari, in short against anything that was not Fascist. The local Fascist leaders, the 'ras', acquired a predominant position, and the party asserted itself *vis-à-vis* the Government's representatives (the prefects, etc.). The substance of things was rapidly changing while the form was so far affected only in part.

To begin with, Mussolini obtained a vote of confidence in his Government from the Chamber of Deputies, with 306 votes in favour and 116 against, and at the same time he was accorded full powers. Formally, therefore, he acted on the basis of a mandate from Parliament; but at the same time he set about preparing for a Chamber of Deputies that would follow his own wishes. Under an electoral law of 18 November 1923 the list heading the poll was to obtain two-thirds of the seats in the Chamber. Thus Fascism would need to secure only a relative—not even an absolute—majority to gain control of the Chamber. Effective means existed to obtain that majority by obstructing adverse propaganda and making it very difficult for voters to carry out their electoral duty. In this way, in the elections of 6 April 1924 the Fascist, or 'national', list got 64·9 per cent of the votes and obtained 374 seats in Parliament.

The electoral law of 1923 lasted only four years and was then replaced by a new law of 1928, of a very different stamp. It provided for only a single list, for which candidates were to be nominated by the trade unions and other organizations; they were to put forward 800 names, i.e. twice as many names as the number to be elected, from among which the Fascist Grand Council would choose half (400) and would submit those names to the electorate for its approval. With the advent of this law Italy formally moved right away not only from the parliamentary system but also, as Giolitti observed, from the constitutional system itself. The electoral system was abandoned in favour of the plebiscitary method; in short dictatorship was an established fact. The law of 1928 marked the beginning of Fascism's second period. Between the laws of 1923 and 1928 lay the formal breach with the old system which took place in 1925.

The second half of 1924 was a period of crisis. On 30 May 1924 the Socialist deputy Matteotti pronounced a violent speech in the Chamber against the Government in which he denounced the abuses perpetrated during the elections of the previous April. Some days after he was set upon by Fascists in the middle of Rome, and his corpse was only found several weeks later. It was immediately obvious that responsibility for the crime lay very high up, indeed in the entourage of Mussolini himself. The Ministry of the Interior and the police were suspected of being involved. The murder of Matteotti aroused strong reactions. It marked the end of their illusions for those who had believed it possible, while remaining faithful to the ideal of liberty, to enter into agreements with Fascism, even after the March on Rome, in the hope of canalizing it and preventing it from going beyond certain limits. The episode caused a crisis even among many of the Fascists, whether from fear of public opinion or because the murder, though far from being the first of its kind, suddenly shed a sinister light on the whole political scene: Fascism now had power in its hands, but was it using that power to maintain order, as it had promised, or itself to create disorder?

Above all, the most significant effect was the revival of the Opposition, led by Turati, Treves, Modigliani, and in particular by the Liberal Amendola. On 27 June 1924 the Opposition deputies decided to take no further part in the work of Parliament until the authority of law should be restored and the party militia abolished. This withdrawal became known as the 'Aventine secession'.

The Opposition viewed the problem as one of morality: Fascism must be morally isolated and its fall must be brought about by means of a moral revolt of the nation. In this way the complete breach between the two worlds, the worlds of freedom and of Fascism, would be created and made plain for all to see.

But from the political point of view the secession was undoubtedly a mistake. To bring down Mussolini and Fascism called for energetic, forceful, and decisive action producing a clean break: this was essential, if for no other reason, in order to draw in the monarchy, towards which all eyes were turned, and persuade it to intervene. But nothing of the kind happened. The King delayed and made no move; he was blind and deaf, he declared, and the Chamber and Senate should be his eyes and ears. The Opposition mounted a campaign in the press. The main newspapers, especially the Milan *Corriere della Sera* under its editor Senator Albertini, one of the Opposition leaders, the Turin *Stampa*, etc., all attacked Fascism. But Fascism withstood the onslaught. The provincial leaders, and in particular Farinacci, reacted violently, reorganized their squads, and moved over to the counter attack. Violence began afresh. The method was always the same: reliance on force against public opinion; and force always won.

On 3 January 1925 Mussolini made a speech in the Chamber which marked the end of the first period, which I shall call 'the transition period of Fascism', and the true dictatorship began. In this speech he declared, among other things: 'Article 47 of the Statute states: "The Chamber of Deputies has the right to accuse the King's ministers and to bring them before the High Court of Justice." I formally ask you whether there is in this Chamber or outside it anyone who wants to make use of Article 47. . . . Well then, I declare here in the sight of this Assembly and in the sight of all the Italian people that I and I alone assume the political, moral, and historical responsibility for everything that has happened.'

This meant the massive come-back of Fascism. And, this time, it meant also the abandonment of the tactics of collaboration with the non-Fascists: all power now passed into the hands of Fascism. The next stage was to be the introduction of typically Fascist laws: for the dictatorship had now reached the stage when it no longer feared to proclaim itself on a formal plane.

The law of 24 December 1925 is a fundamental one because it concerns the powers of the Head of Government. Many of its articles are significant. Article 2 says: 'The Head of Government . . . is appointed and dismissed by the King and is responsible to the King for the general political line adopted by the Government. . . . The Ministers . . . are appointed and dismissed by the King on the proposal of the Head of Government. . . . They are responsible to the King and the Head of Government.' Article 3 states: 'The Head of Government . . . directs and co-ordinates the work of the ministers.' All this was new. The Statute did not

c

envisage the existence of a Head of Government as distinct from the Cabinet.

On the basis of the Statute of King Charles Albert, of 1848, which was still in force in the Kingdom, the King appointed and dismissed his ministers (Art. 65), who were 'responsible' (Art. 67) to Parliament; around the principle of the responsibility of ministers to the Chamber there had been created in Italy, as in many other countries, a parliamentary as well as a purely constitutional system. Now, however, the Head of Government ceased to be responsible to Parliament; the Chamber of Deputies could demonstrate its confidence or non-confidence, but the Head of Government remained in office. The King alone had power to dismiss him.

Article 6 of the new law was quite explicit: no question could be placed on the agenda for Parliament without the previous approval of the Head of Government. This meant the end of parliamentary discussion as an essential basis of the life of a government: all political debate could thus be avoided.

The law on the Fascist Grand Council, of 9 December 1928 (later to be completed by another law of 14 December 1929), put the finishing touches to the law of 1925. The Council was to keep always at hand a list of names to be presented to the Crown for the posts of Head of Government and Ministers. In this way the nomination passed from Parliament to the Fascist Party; the Head of Government was at the same time head of the party; his responsibility towards the King was nominal, and was effective only in relation to the party. Thus it was necessary for the party to be dissolved and the Grand Council to oppose Mussolini, before the King could take the decision to intervene. Thus we arrive at a Party-State.

The law on the press effected the transformation of the main organs of the Italian press; the *Stampa* of Turin and the *Corriere della Sera* of Milan passed into the hands of the Fascists.

As to the powers of the Fascist Grand Council, its opinion became obligatory on all questions of a constitutional character. For the rest, it could express an opinion, at the request of the Head of Government, on any political, economic, or social question of a national character. Among the constitutional questions falling within the Grand Council's sphere of competence were those of the succession to the throne and the attributes and prerogatives of the Crown. This signified a sort of warning to the monarchy, an open and definite limitation of its powers, and a way of saying in effect in the highest quarter: 'Be careful—we are monarchists, but only in so far as it suits us.' In reality, the task of the Grand Council consisted merely of approving what had already been decided. True, there was some quite lively discussion at the time of the racial laws. Balbo, who was certainly not lacking in courage, fought to prevent the approval of the decrees. But the only time that the Grand Council played a part of real significance was on the night of 24/25 July 1943, at the moment of Fascism's greatest crisis, when by an overwhelming majority it appealed to the Crown against Mussolini.

Thus these laws created the formal premises for the authority of the Head of Government, including as they did laws of repression against the press and laws against the old parties (for example, on 9 November 1926 the Chamber proclaimed that the Aventinian secessionists should cease to be Deputies). In addition, on 25 November 1926 a tribunal 'for the defence of the State' was set up to adjudicate on so-called political crimes. This tribunal was later to operate with great severity. Even in relatively unimportant cases, it gave heavy sentences to those accused of plotting against the sovereignty of the State, in other words, the anti-Fascists.

We now come to the most typical emanation of the dictatorship, the 'Voluntary Militia for National Safety' (MVSN), established on 13 January 1923 at the first meeting of the Grand Council. Its origins lie in the action squads, the Blackshirts of the period before Fascism came to power. After the March on Rome the problem arose of how these men were to be used. Mussolini obviously had no intention of abandoning this instrument, which formed the real basis of his power. So he created the 'militia'. The Blackshirts swore an oath of loyalty to the King, but they still remained under the orders of the Head of Government, and their task was to preserve and defend 'the rights of the revolution'. We have here one of the most typical signs of the difference between nineteenth- and twentieth-century dictatorships; the same thing, in fact, happened in Germany, where side by side with the *Wehrmacht* the SS developed. There was nothing new about the laws restricting freedom of the press, nor was it any novelty to condemn political opponents to exile. The real novelty lies in the fact that while nineteenth-century dictatorships appealed to the regular army and carried out their *coups d'état* with its support, those of the twentieth century, whether Fascist or Nazi, secured power thanks to a military organization of their own, specially prepared for the purpose, and destined to remain in existence side by side with the regular army.

This fact had serious consequences from the political point of view. This was already apparent at the time of Fascism's advent to power, when the military organization of the Blackshirts provided Fascism with an 'assault force' in a way quite unknown among the old political parties. We find the same thing after the advent to power: the existence of an organized military force which was loyal to the Fascist leader (for the oath of loyalty to the King was only a screen and deceived no one) made it possible for Mussolini to remain at his post in June 1924, at a moment when any normal Government would have had to resign precipitately, and enabled him to challenge the 'moral forces of public opinion'. The militia also continued to represent a guarantee for the régime after 1925. Even when Mussolini sought to win 'assent' for his actions in the most obvious way, as when in 1932-3 he packed the Fascist Party with the greatest number of members in order to effect its identification with the nation, even then the militia—in other words, an armed force—continued to be his constant support.

Thus public opinion was overborne. Among the anti-Fascists, some were killed or died as a result of Fascist attacks, like Amendola, the head of the Liberal opposition, or young Piero Gobetti of Turin, who from the first had gathered together opponents of Fascism around his paper, *La rivoluzione liberale*. Others such as Turati, Treves, and Modigliani were forced to go into exile after 1925; so were the historian Salvemini, a professor of Florence University, and the former Prime Minister Nitti, Don Sturzo, and Count Sforza, former Minister of Foreign Affairs. Giolitti died in 1928. Of those who stayed on in Italy, a good number were put in prison. The Communist Party was more successful than any other in maintaining clandestine activities; but action had to be carried on in secret, and there was a heavy personal price to pay whenever anyone fell into the hands of the tribunal for the defence of the State. The Communist leader Gramsci was put in prison and eventually left it only to die. Rosselli fell in France, stabbed to death at the hands of hired Fascist assassins.

In the Chamber of Deputies, Giolitti and the other Liberals who had not joined the Aventine secession adopted a more rigid attitude and moved over into complete opposition. The Congress of Leghorn, in the autumn of 1924, was the landmark for this move of the Liberal Party into unequivocal opposition to Fascism. Even a right-wing Liberal such as Salandra, hitherto inclined towards collaboration, now joined the anti-Fascist Liberals. The Liberal Party as such therefore ranked among the opponents of Fascism, but many of its members, including some deputies, left the party to join the Fascists.

After the plebiscitary elections of 1929 there was no longer any place for opposition voices. In the Senate, a meagre group of Senators—Croce, Ruffini, Albertini, Bergamini, and a few others—continued openly to oppose Fascism. Benedetto Croce's review, *La Critica*, managed to continue to express its views publicly, the outward cultural form (it was a review dealing with philosophy, history, and literature) masking the political substance. In this way Croce became the standard-bearer of the ideals of freedom and anti-Fascism.

The rest is silence.

II CONSOLIDATION OF THE RÉGIME

Having said all this, it must also be added that coercion alone does not suffice to explain the Fascist phenomenon. Violence was undoubtedly the origin of Fascism's success and its consolidation. I have explained how that came about, and there is no need to repeat it. But I have also described how, from the very beginning, there were people who were prepared to fall in with the régime. It was by now established and consolidated, and all the forecasts made about it, even as late as 1925, had proved wrong. It thus acquired, so to speak, the persuasive power of a permanent institution. People got used to it, and the force of habit is strong; it leads them to accept what they cannot destroy.

Meanwhile abroad, it is as well to remember, voices were being raised, and sometimes quite important and authoritative ones, in praise of Fascism. These certainly did not come from Left-wing circles—least of all in France; but they included a good many European conservatives. It would be possible to compile a large volume of the collected expressions of approval of Fascism, especially from the English-speaking world; order now reigned in Italy, the trains ran on time, and all those tiresome strikes had stopped. There was praise, even adulation, for Fascism, which in the eyes of certain foreign circles appeared harmful and worthy of condemnation only when it posed some problem of foreign policy, as it did in 1935 and after. Up till then, Fascism was regarded as a very good thing for Italy.

As time went on this praise made an impression on many of the Italians themselves. Those who cared for their country's prestige were strengthened in their Fascist convictions, or at least driven to stop arguing about an accomplished fact. Italy's situation *vis-à-vis* foreign countries seemed to have improved: in aviation, she was distinguishing herself through the great transatlantic and other flights organized by Balbo; she appeared strong militarily, and her official prestige had undoubtedly increased (incidentally, this explains how Fascism found ardent followers among some of the Italian emigrant colonies abroad, for instance in Argentina).

At home, too, the régime had some considerable successes to its credit. I have already mentioned, in speaking of the Lateran Pacts of 11 February 1929, that they were an important card in Mussolini's game. But other considerations come into it too.

Attitude of the Catholic Church. On 14 February 1929, Pope Pius XI, speaking to students of the Catholic University in Milan on the Lateran agreements, affirmed: 'We have also been nobly and abundantly supported from the other side. And perhaps there was need for a man such as Providence has caused us to encounter. . . .' The man of Providence was Mussolini.

As a matter of fact, the clergy did not favour the March on Rome. But once it had happened, the Church quickly adapted itself. The Catholics accepted Mussolini's Government at once. Indeed at the very beginning Don Sturzo himself reacted in a way not unlike Giolitti in being prepared to try collaboration. But only a few days after the Turin congress of the Partito Popolare (12/13 April 1923) Mussolini turned out the Popolari from his Government.

And what happened when Mussolini's newspaper, the *Popolo d'Italia,* demanded the expulsion of Don Sturzo from the party? The Church quite openly took up a position against him. The Popolari who wanted to continue resistance were left without support. Don Sturzo himself ended by going into exile and spent more than twenty years abroad, latterly in the United States, returning to Italy only after the Liberation. The Partito Popolare included, as I said, a right and a left wing which differed considerably from each other. I have made mention earlier of Miglioli, who represented the extreme left; at the other extreme were the old conservatives, big landowners and members of the aristocracy who after the March on Rome had declared their readiness to collaborate with the Government, and preferred to abandon Don Sturzo rather than Mussolini. Until the last years of the régime, up to about 1938, it certainly cannot be said that the Church opposed Fascism. True, there were difficulties from time to time; for instance, some months after the signature of the Lateran Pacts, Mussolini in one of his sudden wild pronouncements went so far as to say in the Chamber on 14 May 1929: 'Within the State, the Church is not sovereign nor even free.' Worse still: 'This [Christian] religion was born in Palestine but became Catholic in Rome. If it had stayed in Palestine, it would very likely have remained one of the many sects that flourished in those perfervid surroundings, like the Essenes or the Therapeuts, and would probably have died out leaving no trace.' Which was tantamount to saying that Christianity owed its universal power to the fact of having been transplanted to Rome.

In 1931 the problem of Catholic Action produced a serious crisis. On the Fascist side it was stated that 'the education and instruction of youth can be entrusted only to the State'. The Holy See, for its part, wanted at all costs to preserve Catholic Action, which under the pontificate of Pius XI had taken on a vigour and impulse unknown in the days of Benedict XV. But here too a compromise was reached. Among other things, the Church agreed not to entrust the highest posts in Catholic Action to men who were known to be anti-Fascists.

All this represented a considerable achievement for the régime: it had won prestige abroad, as many eminent personalities confirmed; and at home it had reached agreement with the Church.

The Corporative System. At this point a new development occurred which aroused both interest and hopes. I refer to the manifestation which became known as the 'corporative system'.

What was this corporative system? From 1926 onwards Fascism began to concern itself with the question of collective labour relations. The term 'corporative' appeared officially for the first time in a decree of 1 July 1926. On 21 April 1927 the Labour Charter came into being. (Fascism went in for striking phrases like this, designed to appeal to the imagination; thus we shall find Mussolini speaking of the 'battle of the lira', the 'battle for wheat', and so on; for the time being, it was the 'Labour Charter'.) This Charter consisted of thirty articles which were to provide the framework of the corporative State. They proclaimed: 'Work ... is a social duty. In virtue of this, and this alone, it is protected by the State. All production forms a single whole from the national point of view; its aims are unitary and comprise the wellbeing of individual citizens and the development of national power' (Art. 2). We note at once the bringing together of the two terms: 'the wellbeing of individual citizens' and 'the development of national power'. Economic life must depend on the State; it is no longer to be left to liberal individualism or to be the result of purely individual efforts. And for what end? For the greatness and power of the nation. Mussolini was to repeat this again. He reiterated that the existence of the corporations, as directive organs of the nation's economic life, was indispensable. On 5 February 1934 the law on the corporations was proclaimed. On 10 November Mussolini spoke as follows to the twenty-two corporations which had just been set up: 'What is the aim? At home, to establish an organization which will gradually and inflexibly reduce the distance between the greatest and the least or non-existent possibilities in life. This is what I call a higher "social justice" ... In relation to the outer world, the object of the corporation is to increase constantly the global power of the nation to further the ends of its expansion in the world.' On the one hand social peace, on the other the nation's power and expansion (in other words, a national or rather nationalistic aim) —these two ideas are constantly associated alike in 1927 and in 1934.

At that time we were in the midst of the economic crisis, and Mussolini declared: 'This is a crisis of the system as a whole, not a crisis within the system.' When he said these words the crisis had already reached its peak: the worst year was, in fact, 1932, and he was speaking in 1934. But in 1934, if the crisis was getting no worse, it was still going on. Let us try to clarify the sentence: 'The crisis in which we and the whole world are living is not a crisis within the system: it is a crisis of the system as a whole.' That meant that it was not a case of a crisis that could be cured, even by exceptional methods, so long as the principles of liberal economy were adhered to. On the contrary, it was a crisis of the system itself. It was therefore necessary to create a new economic system, disciplined and organized with a view to the collective benefit. The sphere of economy must henceforth fall within the world of the State. The time of *laissez-faire* was at an end.

From the point of view of the economic system, the following observations may be made. During the First World War an economic system had been created in Italy designed to meet wartime needs and largely controlled from above. The Government had to organize and direct the Commissions for the collection and distribution of supplies. Reasons of State imposed State control of the economy. Such control fostered the view that the State should provide against all difficulties: it was its job to look after everyone, from the workers and peasants to the big industrialists.

After the war, from 1919 onwards a reaction against this system set in. Everywhere people were saying: 'Let us alone, we've had enough of restrictions. The State ought to stop interfering in our affairs . . .' (unless it was a question of an industry or a bank having to meet a deficit . . . in which case the State was sharply reminded of its 'duty'). Fascism signified a return to control. But this time it meant not a temporary or limited return, dictated by military needs, but a definite and permanent economic policy. It meant autarky.

This, at any rate, was how Mussolini saw it. He created twenty-two corporations which together embraced all the different branches of the whole economy. The National Council of Corporations became the supreme arbiter of the country's economic life.

By 1939 Italy had advanced so far along this road that, as had already been foreshadowed in 1936, the corporations replaced the old system of political representation. A law of 19 January 1939 abolished the Chamber of Deputies; the new Chamber was called the Chamber of Fasces and Corporations, and it, together with the Senate which was still appointed by the King, was to collaborate with the Government in drawing up laws. It was all perfectly simple. There was no likelihood of the slightest opposition. The Chamber of Deputies no longer had the task of discussing the Government's policy; it merely had to 'collaborate'.

This meant a quite new electoral system; and the country was already on the threshold of war. The Chamber was to consist of the members of the Fascist Grand Council and the National Council of Corporations; consequently any member of the latter body automatically belonged also to the Chamber of Fasces. Thus, by the time the war began, even from a formal point of view the old organization of legislative power had completely vanished in Italy.

The corporative system nevertheless achieved for a time a reputation to be reckoned with. Between 1931 and 1935, that is to say up to the Abyssinian war, it was the centre of real interest. Many young people and university students believed they saw in it a way of circumventing and overcoming the absolute dictatorship. Groups consisting chiefly of such young people who chafed against the idea of a permanent personal dictatorship came to feel at a certain point that thanks to the evolution of the corporative system there might be a possibility of emerging from the grip of the dictatorship and advancing in a new direction. During this period the corporative system was the one topic that could be discussed in Italy with some degree of freedom. A congress on the subject held in Ferrara gave rise to a quite lively debate. The two themes stressed both in the corporative laws and in Mussolini's speeches, those of 'social justice' and 'expansion in the world', lent themselves to two different interpretations. Was the new system to be used as an instrument in the struggle for a nationalist policy, or was it really to be the means of producing a radical transformation in the structure of Italian society—to realize, in fact, that social justice that was so much talked about? Thus out of the discussions on the corporative system there soon emerged a definite leftward trend championing ideas of social reform. Fascists were to be found who proclaimed the necessity for a 'war on capitalism'. One result of this was to awaken fresh interest in Fascism, especially among young people. Might it not, they urged, after all contain possibilities of development which would enable them to overcome the purely dictatorial phase?

The corporative system also attracted attention abroad. Economists discussed its efficacy and significance, asking what it really meant: was it all just words, or was it something new which deserved to be studied and might open up new prospects in political and social organization?

The corporative system took shape and came to completion in a period in which life in Italy, as in other countries, was disturbed by an economic crisis. The great crisis of 1929 had immediate repercussions in Italy as in the rest of the world; between 1930 and 1934 the crisis of prices, salaries, and wages hit a poor country such as Italy very seriously. Prices collapsed. In agriculture, they had stood at 413·4 in 1930 and fell to 297·9 in 1934. Wheat prices, reckoned at 100 in 1928, fell to 79·7 in 1931 and 66·8 in 1934; but they rose again in 1935 and 1936, reaching 88·6 in the latter year. On the other hand wine, another important product in Italy's economy, remained in a state of crisis: on the basis of 1928 = 100, the price index in 1936 was 35·6. At the same time, wages were falling even more sharply: taking the same basis of 1928 = 100, by 1934 they were down to 71·8 (according, that is, to the official statistics, but the actual facts were even worse; between 1926 and 1934 agricultural workers could be reckoned to have lost the major part of their earnings). In 1933 there were 336,000 unemployed in agriculture alone.

The crisis also hit landowners, who were the more vulnerable because they were perennially burdened with debts to the banks. In the period before 1929, at a time of rising prices, many of them had borrowed in order to carry out improvements on their properties. Thus the crisis in prices and incomes was particularly serious for them.

In industry, the worst period of depression was around 1932. The available data on the subject are very vague. There are two sets of figures, those compiled by the Ministry of Corporations and those of the General Confederation of Industry. All we can do here is to point out the differences between them. The Confederation of Industry's figures for industrial production, taking 1929 = 100, are 72·4 in 1932, and 81 in 1935, at the beginning of the Abyssinian war. (The Ministry's figures, on the other hand, are 1928 = 100, 1932 = 73, 1935 = 102·4.) The textile industry, a basic feature of Italy's economic life, was the worst hit: while the average figure for industrial production in 1932 was 72·4, that for textiles was 67·4. Prices of manufactured goods fell from 440 in 1930 to 317·2 in 1934. In 1932, out of 2,939 industrial concerns with a capital of over a million lire, 1,216 showed a deficit. There was also a considerable decline in industrial wages between 1926 and 1934.

There were, of course, some good sides to the question. Wheat production undeniably increased: in the period 1931–5 it reached a yearly average of around 73 million quintals, with a maximum harvest, in the exceptionally good year of 1933, of 81 million quintals, representing an average yield of 16 quintals per hectare. Consumption needs were thus almost, if not quite (except in 1933), satisfied by national production. This meant a considerable reduction in Italy's purchases on foreign markets.

But despite all this, Italy's economy found itself involved in a very serious crisis: just how serious it was can be deduced from the increase in unemployment (officially reaching 961,000 unemployed in 1934, of whom 750,000, or 21 per cent of all workers, were in industry and trade) and from the statistics given above, even allowing for their variations.

The prevailing atmosphere of crisis no doubt accounts for the lively tone of the discussions of this period. What was to be done? Should the economy come completely under the control of the State, or not? And if not, what was the point of organizing it according to the corporative system? Did that system represent the future form of the State, which would eventually allow the phase of dictatorship to be surmounted, or was it only a propaganda move, a tactical weapon like so many others, created to delude public opinion? And, above all, of the two objectives proclaimed, social justice and national power, which was the true one, the real end in view?

So we come to the Abyssinian venture. That venture inaugurated a new period, the last period of Fascism. It signified a completely new turn in every respect in Mussolini's dictatorship. Up till then it must be admitted that Fascism, despite the economic crisis, seemed and indeed was soundly established. The years between 1929 and 1934 were the time when the régime achieved the greatest general support. I have briefly indicated the reasons for this support, differing widely in kind but all tending towards the same result.

There seemed to be no way out. The determined anti-Fascists were either in prison, or carrying on the struggle underground constantly harassed by the police, or condemned to restricting their activities to the cultural sphere. For the rest of the populace, the sole reaction was indifference or resignation.

III THE ABYSSINIAN WAR AND ITS CONSEQUENCES FOR THE RÉGIME

Reasons for Italy's Entry into the Abyssinian War. The Abyssinian war marked a profound change in the situation. The newspapers, in attempting to explain it, declared that it was a vital necessity for Italy, given her superabundant population. That problem undoubtedly existed: excess of population in relation to the country's productive capacity was a very real problem, then as now, and it was certainly not Fascism that created it. The rising birth-rate had by 1936 brought the population to nearly 43 million. Emigration to the United States and Latin America had been much reduced after the introduction of restrictions on entry by the United States in 1921. The pre-war average of 600,000 emigrants a year fell to 70,000 in the years 1931–40. Large-scale public works of land reclamation were undertaken, such as the draining of the Pontine marshes, and this meant not only an increase of production but also a means of establishing a number of peasant families on the land. Indeed, in the plains near Rome the population rose in a few years from some hundreds to 60,000. But such measures were totally inadequate to meet the need for employment.

Nevertheless, this was not the main reason which led Mussolini to embark on the Abyssinian campaign; nor was it the need to divert attention from the serious economic situation, though that probably influenced him to a minor extent. But the political motive was the main one in Mussolini's mind—the motive of Italy's power and national prestige. I have already referred to Mussolini's indifference in 1919–22 to principles and programmes. But once he had achieved power and got what he wanted, as time went on he became increasingly sensitive to the doctrinaire influence of nationalism. Sometimes sudden flashes of recollection of his Socialist past would rise up in him, and then for a brief period he would talk about social justice. But his real concern now was nationalism. More and more his eyes turned to the outer world and his mind to Italy's power and prestige, which was bound up with his own personal power and prestige. This is the inevitable law of dictatorships: success abroad is made to compensate for the loss of liberty at home.

In September 1935 the decision was already taken. War broke out on 3 October. I do not propose to consider the Abyssinian question from the international angle, for that would involve reconstructing the whole history of European politics and the relations between the Great Powers in 1935–6. What is important here are the internal repercussions of the war on the Fascist régime and the state of mind of the Italians. At first, when the Abyssinian question seemed to boil down to a simple matter of colonial expansion, the attitude of most people in Italy was one of indifference and even hostility. It was a great mistake on the part of the British to make popular a war which would otherwise have been anything but that. This result was brought about through the threat of the British fleet in the Mediterranean in September 1935—a threat which was in fact mere bluff, for the fleet was not in a state to risk an encounter. But the British move played into Mussolini's hands at home in bringing about a change in public opinion, which lost sight of Abyssinia and believed that Italy herself was actually threatened by Britain.

The proclamation of the Empire in May 1936 introduced changes of grave consequence. Those who had entertained hopes of the corporative State, of social peace and justice, now said: 'Obviously, it was all just words and bluff. The real aim is clearly conquest... and a policy of that kind is all to the advantage of the industrialists.' It was quite true that immediately after the outbreak of war the industrial situation suddenly improved. In 1931 the net profit of share companies in relation to invested capital was 0·08 per cent; in 1932, the peak year of the crisis, it was − 1·38, rising in 1933 to 2·18 and in 1934 to 4·10 per cent. But it was in 1935–6 that profits began to increase really noticeably. In 1935 they rose to 5·74 and in 1936 to 7·28 per cent. This meant that industry, and in particular the war industries, was reaping immediate benefit from the war.

Nevertheless, it seems to me difficult to maintain that the war was decided on because of pressure from the industrialists. Obviously they derived advantages from it; but it is going too far to suggest that it was their hope of these gains that caused the war. Its origin, it must be stressed, was political.

In any case, if there had ever been any prospect of social reform, it had now vanished. The hopes centring round the corporative State were quickly dispersed, and all illusions crumbled.

Intervention in Spain and alignment with Germany. Italy's intervention in the Spanish civil war followed hard on the heels of the Abyssinian war, and from 1935 onwards the country's industry was working for military ends. The rising power of the big industrial groups acted as a brake on any genuine attempt at establishing greater social justice. Autarky assumed an increasingly political and military character; and the corporative State came more and more to resemble a State preparing for war. Germany, which was beginning to exercise an influence on Fascism and especially on Mussolini, was there to provide an example. The aim was to create a great State able to burst its bonds abroad in the same way that the Fascist Party had in the past shown itself able to break up the structure of the old ruling classes.

Illusions about corporativism fell to the ground. The ideal of 'social justice' gave way to that of 'Italy's expansion and world power'. Other illusions, too, were destined to disappear.

Many people, even among those in responsible positions, were convinced that it was necessary to embark on the venture in Abyssinia, where Italy would find work to do for many years to come, investing in the country and developing it and thereby solving her own economic difficulties. In the eyes of some (as can be seen from Ambassador Guariglia's *Memoirs*)[1], the acquisition of Abyssinia, in whatever form it came about, would in time facilitate an Italian understanding with Britain and France with a view to averting a European war. Such hopes proved illusory, just as did the hopes of Giolitti and others in 1922 when they believed they could neutralize Mussolini by giving him a Cabinet post. As we have seen, at that time things went just the other way. So they did now. It may be that Mussolini had by this time lost all sense of proportion. He undoubtedly had some remarkable qualities, especially in his approach to the masses and in his choice of men; and he was not without flair. But after the Abyssinian affair he lost control of himself. The application of sanctions, for instance, had a completely negative effect on him: he convinced himself that Italy had really won her case against fifty-two countries and was in a position to undertake even more difficult trials of strength. This idea recurs frequently in his public speeches.

What was even worse, however, was that the Abyssinian affair threw him into the arms of Hitler's Germany. In 1934-5, faced with Hitler's threat against Austria, his policy had undergone a sudden volte-face resulting in the Rome agreements between Italy and France, of 7 January 1935, and the Stresa agreements between Italy, France, and Britain, of 11-14 April 1935. In June 1934 Hitler came to the Veneto to visit Mussolini. But when the Vienna *putsch* broke out and Chancellor Dollfuss was murdered on 25 July 1934, Mussolini at once sent two divisions of Alpini to the Austrian frontier as a warning to Hitler that if a single German soldier went into Austria Italy would send in her army. Mussolini telegraphed to the Government in Vienna that Italy was determined to defend Austrian independence, which he then

[1] *Ricordi*, by Raffaele Guariglia (Rome, ESI, 1950).

believed to be vital for Italy's interests. (Incidentally, the Italian Government had made a great mistake in supporting Dollfuss, who in February 1934 had caused Socialists to be shot down in Vienna; it would, in fact, have been to the interest of Italy, if not of Fascism, to see a strong Socialist Party in Austria which could have opposed Hitlerism. But ideological arguments had proved stronger than the interests of the country itself.)

Thus between July 1934 and April 1935 an agreement began to develop between Britain, France, and Italy, based on the fundamental question of Austrian independence. For Italy, in particular, this was a problem of vital importance: we have seen what efforts Crispi made to avoid direct contact between Germany and Italy.

These were the lines on which Italian policy was running up to 1936. But in that year a radical change took place. During the Abyssinian war Hitler had been taken up with his own affairs; his troops had reoccupied the Rhineland and he had done nothing whatever to help Italy. Mussolini, on the other hand, felt angered and resentful about sanctions; such motives weighed strongly with him, and led him to embark on a policy of *rapprochement* with Germany which found its expression in the Rome-Berlin Axis of October 1936—for there was as yet no talk of an alliance, merely of an 'axis'.

Then came the war in Spain. But what, it may be asked, had war in Spain to do with Italy? She was embarking on a policy of adventures. . . . Even in Italy, where public discussion was taboo, people began to perceive the truth of what Carlo Rosselli was writing in Paris just at that time: 'Beware! A European conflict is developing. We have reached the moment when the two opposed worlds, the world of freedom and the world of authoritarianism, are about to find themselves face to face.' A great many people began to react against a foreign policy which seemed from day to day to become more fraught with danger.

The *rapprochement* with Germany, favoured by events in Spain, gave rise to anxiety and apprehension. Even in the Fascist Party there were two views on the subject: while some believed that because of their common ideology the two countries should go forward together, others were beginning to be seriously perturbed about Hitler's aims and to ask where this policy of collaboration with Germany was taking Italy.

In March 1938 came Hitler's occupation of Vienna and Austria. This time Mussolini did nothing. His speech in the Senate justifying Italy's passivity was perhaps the most disappointing he had ever made. You could sense the man's embarrassment at his inability to provide the Senate with an explanation of his conduct. Though he was a dictator to whom everything was permitted, he seemed profoundly disconcerted. This passive attitude on Mussolini's part provoked immediate and definite repercussions. The unquestionable prestige which he had enjoyed abroad crumbled, and the balance that had hitherto governed, at least formally, the relations between Italy and Germany was shattered: henceforward Fascism was dragged in the wake of Nazism.

The Racial Laws. Italy was a country that had never known racial persecution; but in September-October 1938 the racial question came up. In the past, a Jew, Luzzatti, had become Prime Minister, and another Jew, Artom, had been one of Cavour's collaborators and later a Senator. Mussolini himself in 1934–5 had publicly proclaimed his opposition to any idea of racial superiority. Now everything was changed: the Government began to proclaim racial laws and organize persecution of the Jews. Public opinion revolted. Opposition showed itself not only in the help given to the Jews by the great majority of citizens but in protests from the Catholic Church as well—for at this point the Holy See and the bishops took up a definite stand in saying that they could not countenance persecution of this kind. The racial laws provided a sure indication that Fascist Italy was now being dragged on by Hitler's Germany, where the struggle between the Catholic Church and the State had been going on incessantly since 1933; and they thus provoked—as the historian A. C. Jemolo has pointed out—the great breach between Church and State, between Catholic opinion and the Fascist régime.

The Catholic Church issued warnings pointing out that it was impossible for Catholic doctrine to accept a distinction between superior and inferior races. The steps being taken in the name of an alleged racial difference came up against the very foundations of the Church. It was common knowledge that the Pope was greatly disturbed. The tenth anniversary of the Lateran Pacts was due in February 1939, and everyone in Rome expected that His Holiness would this time take an open stand against the totalitarian system. Thus people looked forward anxiously to the anniversary date of 11 February 1939; but Pope Pius XI died on the morning of 10 February and the words he might have pronounced were never heard. Nevertheless, even if the message awaited with such trepidation never came, the fact remains that the Bishops and the Holy See did go over into opposition against the régime. In the year of the Concordat, and again in 1931, there had been conflicts between the Fascist régime and the Church; but these were only temporary disturbances, soon to be overcome. During the Abyssinian war the clergy had supported the Government's action, and at the time of Italy's intervention in Spain they had blessed the legionaries on their way to fight on the side of Catholic Franco against the 'godless Spanish Reds'. Now the understanding was broken, and in very definite fashion.

Thus on all sides the breach between the people and the régime was becoming more definite.

This breach was further aggravated by the 'Pact of Steel'. Mussolini himself recognized this, on 19 March 1939. It was only a few days after Hitler's occupation of Bohemia. The Munich agreements of 1938 had already become a dead letter. Count Ciano, then Minister of Foreign Affairs, received the news quite without preparation. Mussolini fell into a fit of depression for some days; it was a severe blow for him. Ciano, who had now had second thoughts about his earlier Germanophile enthusiasm, tried to profit by this set-back to get the idea of a German alliance shelved for good. He summed up as follows a conversation he had with Mussolini on 19 March: 'Long talk with the Duce. He has thought a lot about what we said in the last few days, and he agrees about the impossibility of now presenting the Italians with an alliance with Germany. The very stones would rise up.' This comment was made at a time of depression on Mussolini's part, and it was not long before letters from Ribbentrop caused him to revert to his original line of conduct. But the words had been spoken and remained: the very stones would rise up.

Thus we arrive at the 'Pact of Steel', announced in Milan on 7 May and signed in Berlin on 22 May 1939. It would be interesting to follow out the history of this pact in detail, for it embodies all the characteristics of Mussolini's policy and personality. For instance, the Minister for Foreign Affairs received the order by telephone to announce the pact while he was still in Milan. The meeting between Ciano and Ribbentrop was not in fact originally meant to take place in Milan but in a more secluded spot, Como. But on 5 May Mussolini read in the French press that there had been anti-German demonstrations in Milan. He was furious, and immediately decided that the meeting should take place in that city. He throve on controversy, and could be influenced by resentment and rancour even in dealing with major problems.

From the very beginning the pact was based on a misapprehension, or rather, to be precise, on a German lie. Ribbentrop had assured Ciano in Milan that the difficulties with Poland were not really very serious and concerned questions that could easily be settled: Germany, in fact, meant no harm to Poland. Hitler intended to proceed on the lines of trying to reach an agreement, and he wanted an extra-territorial corridor which would link East Prussia with Germany. True, he could not renounce Danzig; but the difficulties should not prove insurmountable. When Ciano arrived in Berlin on 22 May to sign the pact he was given assurances of peace for at least three years.

But Ciano had barely left Berlin when a secret meeting took place there, on 23 May, between Hitler, Goering, and the German high military authorities. At this meeting it was plainly stated that the Danzig question was not the true cause of dispute: Germany's real aim was an extension of her *Lebensraum* towards the east; in other words, Danzig must be the pretext for war. And Hitler added: 'Our decision is to attack Poland at the first opportunity.' The truth was not revealed to Ciano until the Salzburg conversations in August.

But however that may be, Mussolini had by now flung himself headlong into the venture which was to bring catastrophe for Italy. It was the outcome of that last phase of Fascism which opened in 1936–7 and heralded the definite breach between the régime and the country.

I have already stated, and it is worth repeating at this point, that adherence to Fascism, or at least acceptance of it, had reached its limits among a great part of the population. It is true that in some circles Fascism still commanded that enthusiastic, blind, and unqualified support which dated from the earliest days of 1919–20. But these circles represented only a small minority.

The others, those who from 1926 to 1934 had, if not accepted, at least concurred in the régime, would follow it up to a certain point but no farther. Such people represented the majority of registered party members—and the party had done everything it could to increase their numbers; for instance, from 1933 no one could get into a civil service job unless he was a party member; from that point of view Fascist tactics were quite different from those of the Nazis. The adherence of many people to the party was probably quite sincere, but it was not so deep-rooted as to represent a faith that would countenance the overstepping of certain limits. Those limits were overstepped in 1938 and 1939. Mussolini himself realized it. Sometimes he became threatening and seemed to want to revive his revolutionary attitudes of 1911–12. He was exasperated by the pity shown to persecuted Jews, and irritated by the love of peace he perceived among the people. At such times he could be heard to say: 'Those petty *bourgeois* are no good. At present I have questions of foreign policy to settle; but later on I shall have to have a reckoning with them.'

Thus Italy was dragged into the Second World War and so into disaster. The circumstances of war only served to widen the profound abyss that had opened up between the country and Mussolini. Military preparations were mere bluff: the soldiers did their duty well, but they were badly equipped (the Greek venture alone, in the autumn of 1940, gave sufficient proof of this). People began to ask: 'Where is all the military power we've heard so much about? Where are Mussolini's famous eight million bayonets? It's just another bluff; the corporative state was bluff, and so is all this talk of military preparedness.'

By 1939 Fascism no longer had the country behind it: the prestige of leader and régime alike had crumbled. It was ready to fall to pieces, like a machine whose springs are broken.

PART THREE

ITALY TODAY

1 THE WAR AND THE COLLAPSE OF THE FASCIST RÉGIME: THE RESISTANCE MOVEMENT

ONE TYPICAL FACT will suffice to indicate the extent of the breach between the Italian *bourgeoisie* and Fascism: in the war of 1940–3 the phenomenon of wartime volunteers, characteristic of so many other stages in Italy's history, was notably absent. (There were, of course, individual exceptions, but they never assumed any great proportions or took on the character of a collective movement.) Fighting by volunteers or irregulars is a typical phenomenon of Italy's history, and it accounts for the substantial difference between the development of unity in Italy and in Germany. German unity developed around a monarchy, a state, and a regular army. Bismarck and King Wilhelm I took the initiative and kept it throughout in their own hands. No initiative could be taken outside of the Government or without the knowledge of Bismarck in political matters, or of Moltke in military affairs. In Italy, on the contrary, the initiative came from two sources: on the one hand, the Sardinian Government took the decision in 1859 to bring the Piedmontese army into the struggle in Lombardy side by side with France against Austria; but, on the other hand, there was at the same time non-governmental action carried out by the irregular forces under Garibaldi. And in 1860 it was the volunteers led by Garibaldi who by their landing in Sicily brought about the collapse of the Kingdom of the Two Sicilies and thus enabled Cavour to reunite the North and South and finally to achieve the proclamation of Victor Emmanuel II as King of Italy.

The tradition of voluntary service, which goes back to the earliest origins of Italy's history, was fully maintained in the First World War. The *bourgeoisie* furnished a large number of the wartime volunteers who marched against the enemy in May 1915 and often paid the price with their lives.

But in the last war it was quite different, and there were no more volunteers. Troops and officers did their duty and fought with honour and, badly armed and equipped though they were, they inscribed many pages of heroism in the country's history. But where was the national enthusiasm of May 1915, December 1917, or June 1918? Where was that outburst of national feeling which after Caporetto, in November-December 1917, made it possible to put up a resistance against the enemy in conditions of the greatest difficulty on the Piave or the Grappa?

It was in this atmosphere that the war developed and the problems of Italy's immediate future began to arise.

I THE POLITICAL FRAMEWORK OF THE STRUGGLE AGAINST FASCISM

What were the anti-Fascists doing all this time?

The Communists. The Communist Party maintained its organization throughout the clandestine period. It suffered much, and many of its followers were put in prison, but its underground organization, which was almost of a military character, continued to function. Consequently the Communist Party was the best prepared of all the parties for future eventualities.

The Catholics. The Partito Popolare existed for only a few years, but the men who founded it, who led the party in the electoral campaigns of 1919 and 1921 and took part in all the struggles in Parliament, were still there, and kept in touch with each other. In Rome there was De Gasperi, the future Prime Minister under the Italian Republic; and in the capital and in every town there were others who had in common their experience of political struggle. In particular, while the Catholics lacked the clandestine organization of the Communists, they made up for it by having behind them the organization of Catholic Action. Benedict XV had allowed Catholic Action to decline, but under Pius XI it had revived, and had been a cause of violent dispute between Mussolini and the Holy See; since then it had expanded steadily and become a powerful force. Catholic Action had links with the clergy and exerted a moral and therefore political influence extending throughout Italy from top to toe; and this meant that the Catholics were quickly able to reorganize themselves in a political party. Thus Christian Democracy, the name of the new party which became the successor of the Partito Popolare, possessed a solid basis in the country.

The Socialists. The Socialists could also pride themselves on that great source of strength which resides, alike for a political party or for a nation, in tradition—a tradition, in their case, some half-century old. They were far less well organized than the Communists, indeed they had to reconstitute the party in 1942–3; and they lacked the enormous resources which the Catholics possessed in the Catholic Action organization and the moral influence of the clergy. Nevertheless they had behind them this tradition going back to the nineteenth century; and they still commanded the allegiance of a considerable part of the working classes. In the first elections held under free conditions after the war, the municipal elections of 7 April 1946, the Socialists won a victory over the Christian Democrats and Communists in the main centre of Italy's industry, trade, and finance, Milan—thus providing a clear proof of the continuity of Italian Socialism which, having survived the dictatorship, seemed to have taken on a new lease of life in 1945.

The Liberals. The Liberals were a smaller group. Their organization was always weaker than that of the mass parties described above. But they had among them some outstanding figures of great moral significance, first and foremost among them Benedetto Croce, the philosopher and historian, who, as I mentioned earlier, carried on the struggle for liberty in his review *La Critica* throughout the Fascist period. All anti-Fascists looked up to him as a standard-bearer of freedom.

Thus Croce came to represent a focal point for the Liberals. Among these were former Ministers such as Marcello Soleri, War Minister in 1922 before Fascism came to power; Luigi Einaudi, the famous economist; Alessandro Casati; and others. These were men who had an approach to the King, and this was an important factor, for the immediate problem was how to extricate the country from its tragic situation. The solution, it seemed, must lie with the King, for he alone could take action and call upon the army, without whose support nothing could be done. For this reason the most eminent members of the Liberal Party began at this time to approach the King and ask for audiences with him.

Such was the overall picture presented by the political parties. We must now consider briefly the general lines of their outlook and action; in so doing we shall, incidentally, arrive at a better understanding of the new factor on the political horizon, the Action Party.

What was the attitude of these parties towards the fundamental question of Italy's future? Let us take the Liberals first. Croce's views on this subject were quite clear. He had consistently maintained that Fascism was merely a parenthesis in Italy's history, a sickness that had attacked a body which remained in substance sound. Once the parenthesis was closed, the country would merely have to resume its advance on the same lines that had characterized the history of liberal Italy—in short, to return to the Italy of pre-1922. Certain questions would undoubtedly have to be discussed, for instance, the position of the King himself. It might be thought necessary for Victor Emmanuel III to abdicate, as being too greatly compromised with Fascism; but about the continuity of the country's institutions and its liberal tradition no doubts could be entertained. The Christian Democrats, too, were no revolutionaries. With them the demarcation line, the basis of their whole standpoint, was naturally governed by the question of religion. They aimed at a state in which Catholicism would be able to play the role from which it had been excluded since 1870. This was the central point: the Catholic forces, whose organization and political action were of such importance in the development of modern Italy, were prepared to accept, now that the Lateran Pacts had settled the Roman Question once and for all, the institutions fashioned for Italy by liberal nineteenth-century thought and the liberal parties. But, as a counterpart to this, the Italian State, which before 1914 had existed outside the influence of the Church and indeed had often, between 1870 and 1900, been opposed to Catholic political action, should now assume a largely Catholic character.

All this clearly meant that among the Catholics there was no tendency towards revolution. Both with the Liberals and the Christian Democrats, the aim was merely to overthrow Fascism and restore Italy's freedom, without destroying the old structure of the pre-Fascist State.

At the other extreme were the Communists. They, naturally, desired the overthrow of Fascism, but they also intended to proceed as quickly as possible to a complete reorganization of the country's social and political structure. With them there was no question of reverting to the Italian State as it was before 1922;

their aim was rather to work, in accordance with their programme, towards a total revolution. Circumstances might retard or accelerate the revolution; tactics might vary according to contingent necessities (and in fact, as we shall see, they proved highly elastic); but the final aim was perfectly clear. The Communists, there could be no doubt, wanted a revolution after the model of Lenin's and Stalin's Russia.

Among the Socialists there were oscillations of view which were to influence profoundly the history of post-war Italian Socialism and produce an eventual split within the movement. On the one hand some among them, while not accepting the Communist programme in its entirety, still preached the class struggle and maintained above all else the need for a united working class and for 'unity of action'; these Socialists made common cause with the Communists. On the other hand others, while demanding vast social reforms, boggled at the idea of total revolution, and in any case did not wish to unite themselves with the Communists because they wanted to maintain complete political independence for the Socialist Party.

Side by side with these parties whose aims were pretty clearly defined, there appeared on the scene in 1942 the Action Party.

The Action Party. This was a highly complex political group alike in its doctrines and its aspirations. It brought together men who had earlier belonged to the 'Giustizia e Libertà' (Justice and Liberty) movement, founded in 1929, which had been one of the most active anti-Fascist groups operating clandestinely in Italy and abroad among the emigrants. Its theoretician and head was Carlo Rosselli, who after his escape with two friends from internment in the Lipari Islands had established himself in France. Rosselli's ideas, expounded in his *Socialismo Liberale*, envisaged the birth of a Socialism on a new basis, a Socialism which would reject the Marxist view of inevitability, the 'necessity' of class struggle and ultimate revolution, and which, while firmly maintaining the need for reform of the social structure, would nevertheless accept the need for liberty—in other words, for the exercise of man's free will in contradistinction to Marxist fatalism.

Substantially similar to Rosselli's movement was the 'Liberal Socialism' of Aldo Capitini and Guido Calogero. This movement had succeeded in forming some active anti-Fascist centres, especially in Central Italy, from 1936–7 onwards—in other words, at the time when, as I mentioned earlier, a new spirit was beginning to stir, especially among young people and students (among whom Liberal Socialism had a considerable following), and when the Fascist régime was moving rapidly towards the policy that was to bring about the country's ruin and isolation. Some other adherents to the Action Party were more closely in sympathy with the ideas of Piero Gobetti of Turin, who between 1922 and 1925 had maintained the necessity of a 'liberal revolution'. According to Gobetti, Liberalism needed to recruit new blood from among the intellectual *élite* who both believed in liberal ideas and could carry with them the popular masses (he had a great admiration for the workers of Turin), thus transforming the working-class struggle into a present-day liberal struggle. So the Action Party included within it this group whose aim was to bring about a 'liberal revolution' and break up the old traditional political cadres against which Gobetti had directed his diatribes. Finally, other members of the party were associated in a more general way with liberal and democratic ideas and experience.

On the whole, the Action Party can be said to have combined within itself the various clandestine democratic anti-Fascist movements which continued to exist after 1925 or were formed subsequently. It was, in fact, the gathering-point of clandestine democracy. I referred earlier to the continuity of action of the Communist Party during the clandestine period; but there was also a continuous and resolute clandestine activity on the part of the democratic groups, and this activity, which suffered severe repression, now found expression in the new party. It is worth noting that while the clandestine activity of the extreme Left remained firmly linked to and emanated from the Communist Party, that of the democrats, on the contrary, became detached from the old parties and took the form of 'movements' or 'groups', only later establishing itself as a party. This is a fact of some significance, showing the desire of the consistent democrats to transcend the old pre-1919 political formations and their aims and methods. The Action Party, which to a certain extent was the fruit of this clandestine democracy, was to give proof of its avowed intention, shared by all its trends, to advance along new lines.

In its capacity as a product of clandestine democracy in general, the Action Party assumed considerable importance politically and played a foremost part in affairs in the years 1943–5. But the very fact of its origins also meant that there were within it differing ideological views, and this circumstance eventually operated against it. From the very beginning there were two main trends at work within the party: a socialist trend headed by Lussu, who had been a close collaborator of Rosselli's ever since the formation of the 'Giustizia e Libertà' movement, and a liberal-democratic one represented by La Malfa, who was among the party's founders. Other opposition trends already began to emerge clearly at the Cosenza congress of August 1944. The Action Party found a following among the intellectual and professional *élite*, but it was never able to influence the masses or compete with the big parties in that field, nor did it succeed in creating any wide basis of support among the small and medium *bourgeoisie*. For that reason this party, which played so outstanding a part in the Resistance, was destined to disappear altogether in 1947.

One essential point in the party's programme was, however, common to all its trends: this was the need for a fundamental change in the whole life of the State, beginning with the institutional framework, i.e. the monarchy. The Action Party was always uncompromisingly anti-monarchist: on this question of principle it showed itself even more completely intransigent than the other parties of the Left, and tenaciously carried on the struggle right up to the last moment of final success. This insistence on the need for a basic change in the whole set-up of the State represents the politically revolutionary aspect of the party's activity and caused it to ally itself with the Left-wing parties (the Socialists and Communists) in the Committees of National Liberation and to adopt a definitely different standpoint from that of the Liberals and the Christian Democrats. At the same time all this went on side by side with the other internal divergences which arose between those whose aim was to establish a new socialism and those who, mistrustful of ideologies and sceptical as to the feasibility of such a 'new socialist' doctrine, wanted to create a political formation capable of becoming a Government party and carrying out a precise and definite line of policy. These latter sought a 'third way', midway between liberalism and Marxist socialism, and looked to find it in the political rather than the ideological sphere, believing that such a course would confer on any party that could pursue it a pre-eminent position in public life.

I have talked at some length about the Action Party not only because it was a new party, whereas the other parties' programmes are familiar, but also because it is a typically Italian phenomenon that has no equivalent elsewhere.

Such was the political framework of the anti-Fascist struggle. It remains to make one fundamental observation: the struggle, first against Fascism and then against the Germans, brought together all the anti-Fascist forces, from the Liberals and Catholics to the Communists. The Catholics had always opposed Communism. At the time of the Spanish civil war the Italian clergy, shaken by the reported persecution of the clergy in Spain, did not conceal their sympathies for Franco's cause. But now the demands of a struggle that proved daily more and more terrible led to a reconciliation, and from 1942 onwards brought together representatives of the Liberals, the Christian Democrats, and the Communist Party within the committees of the anti-Fascist parties and later in the Committees of National Liberation. True, this did not mean that all mistrust had disappeared or that each man no longer tried to find out what his neighbour was up to; but at least it meant that on the plane of the fight against Fascism collaboration was possible.

II THE FALL OF FASCISM: THE POLITICAL SITUATION IN A DIVIDED ITALY

I have tried above to analyse the make-up and ideas of the political parties which emerged into the light of day on the morrow of 25 July 1943 and which formed the basis for the ensuing political struggle and, after the armistice of 8 September 1943, the organization of the Committees of National Liberation and the Resistance.

My aim in this brief analysis of present-day Italy is to explain how the internal aspects of the political situation developed. I shall therefore confine myself to mentioning only such events as serve to illustrate that theme. Having said this, it must be added that the crisis which brought about the downfall of the Fascist régime was not, nor indeed could it be, purely a direct result of the action of the political forces which I have described.

First of all, it must be borne in mind that the parties had been suppressed one after the other by the Public Security law of 6 November 1926, leaving the Fascist Party alone in existence, and consequently after that they could only carry on their activities underground. The Communist Party had succeeded better than the others in maintaining its own organization in these conditions. The other parties were only now beginning to revive their organization or even to create it for the first time. Thus they were obviously as yet unprepared for revolutionary action or revolt.

But above all it must be remembered—and this is a point I have stressed earlier—that Fascism was also an organized military force, whose fall could only be brought about with the aid of a similar force, namely the army—and the army could not move without orders from the King. The country was at war, and any change in the situation could only come from above. The sole feasible direct action that could be taken was the strikes among the working masses, and these had a definitely political character, as for example those of 5 March 1943, organized by the Communists, which began in Turin and spread throughout North Italy. In addition it was possible to exercise some influence on public opinion by means of the underground press which was becoming increasingly widely diffused.

The pressure of public opinion was bound to have some influence on the King. True, he always maintained silence in his meetings with those who came to make representations to him about the seriousness of the situation and the impossibility of allowing it to continue; and his own reserved character always left his interlocutors in doubt as to his intentions. Nevertheless he could not but realize that this time, after twenty-one years, he would have to intervene. Even the most loyal monarchists made it quite clear by their letters and appeals that unless he did so it would mean the end of the monarchy.

Thus public opinion was making itself felt. Moreover, from the spring of 1943 onwards the anti-Fascists themselves were bringing pressure to bear on court circles and even on the King himself. The main contact was through Bonomi, a Prime Minister of pre-Fascist days who was now a leader of the opposition and was destined to become Chairman of the Central Committee of National Liberation and eventually, after the liberation of Rome, Prime Minister. Long-drawn-out secret preparations preceded the coup of 25 July 1943, and all this time the anti-Fascist leaders were trying to urge the King into action.

By this time it was not just a question of the influence of public opinion in general but also of positive pressure on the part of the anti-Fascists, accompanied by a clear and definite programme.

But the decision still had to come from the King: this was what the Liberals wanted, and also the Catholics (who counted as well on support from the Vatican) and in general all those who had hitherto been opposed to any revolutionary solution. Even the Communists, from their different standpoint, were prepared to support a *coup d'état* brought about by the monarchy.

The military situation grew daily worse: the Allies landed in Sicily on 10 July; bombing from the air became increasingly intensive, disrupting transport and the life of the country in general. As I said earlier, the situation in 1943 was very different from that of 1917. After Caporetto, the whole nation rose against the enemy and carried the struggle through to victory. But now the nation, completely detached from the régime which had dragged it into this catastrophe, reacted in a quite different way. Its one idea was to put an end to the war. A small group of army officers, headed by the Chief of the General Staff General Ambrosio, had already prepared a plan to arrest Mussolini. The King had made his decision, and the plan was to be put into action on 26 July. But events moved even faster: on 25 July 1943 the King, taking advantage of a motion approved by the Grand Council on the night of the 24th/25th authorizing an appeal to the Crown, dismissed Mussolini, had him arrested, and entrusted the government to Marshal Badoglio. Thus the collapse came suddenly and, to the general astonishment, everything was carried out in perfect calm. Mussolini fell without attempting the slightest resistance. The King himself described the scene to the new Foreign Minister, Guariglia. 'Mussolini came to see me,' he said, 'on the afternoon of 25 July. Normally he never bothered himself about legal questions, but now he tried to convince me by a whole series of legal arguments that the Grand Council's motion had no legal significance.'

The total and immediate collapse of the Fascist régime, effected without any reaction from the Fascists and amid general popular enthusiasm, afforded decisive proof that the breach between the régime and the people had for long been an accomplished fact. But on the morrow of Mussolini's downfall as a result of the monarchy's intervention, problems began to arise. I shall confine myself here to discussing those concerned with domestic policy.

The King and Marshal Badoglio undoubtedly found themselves faced with an exceptionally difficult situation. Even before 25 July the Germans had occupied important positions in the very heart of the country (for example around Lake Bolsena, within easy marching distance of Rome). They now aimed to effect the military occupation of Italy and overthrow the new Government, and with this end in view they hastily increased their forces (which consisted of 16 German divisions, 7 of them motorized or armoured, and 13 Italian, only 2 of which were motorized or armoured, the remainder being disposed outside the peninsula). This direct German threat seriously hampered the action of the Badoglio Government.

At the same time differences between the new Government and the parties began to appear. The plan to overthrow Fascism which Bonomi had himself expounded to the King on 2 June 1943 comprised: (*a*) in the first stage, a military Ministry, followed immediately by a political Ministry; or, alternatively, from the very beginning, a Ministry headed by a military man but composed of politicians; (*b*) the immediate denunciation of the German alliance on the ground that it was an alliance between the Fascist and Nazi régimes (cf. in this connection the preamble to the Pact of Steel) which with the fall of the Fascist régime ceased to be binding. There was to be a complete *coup d'état*, definitely and plainly anti-Fascist in character, and an appeal by the Crown to the anti-Fascist parties and the people. Finally, an uncompromisingly anti-German standpoint should be adopted.

The King carried out the *coup d'état*, but his intentions and plans did not coincide with those of the parties. He would not hear of a decisive and immediate 'counter-revolution'; he wanted instead to solve the problem by stages, bit by bit. The Badoglio Ministry should therefore, in his view, be a Ministry of technicians and high officials. The same was true of the question of relations with Germany. The aim of destroying Fascism had indeed been achieved, but it was also a fact that the spirit of the *coup d'état* of 25 July as carried out by the King, his military collaborators, and his civilian adviser (Count Acquarone, Minister of the Royal House) by no means corresponded to that which inspired the parties' plan.

In consequence disagreement arose between Marshal Badoglio —or, rather, the King—and the parties, which combined to form a national committee and insisted after 25 July on a Government of national unity and an immediate break with Germany at all costs. On 13 August the parties approved a motion dissociating themselves completely from any responsibility for the Government's actions.

But among the parties, too, united though they were on essential questions, different trends began to appear. Some already maintained the need for a more decisively revolutionary programme and one more avowedly hostile to the monarchy, which they wanted to abolish. Others, on the other hand, were prepared to support the monarchy and even to advocate its continuance on the ground that through the *coup d'état* it had acquired merit in the eyes of the people. Finally, we must not forget the Communists, who, while reserving to themselves complete freedom of action in the future when the war should be ended, were prepared to postpone any discussion of the institutional question until the end of hostilities and to collaborate for the time being with the monarchy on condition that it accepted an alliance with the people—in other words, the line of conduct proposed by the parties. It should be noted that the Communists were much less intransigent than the other Left-wing parties, especially the Action Party; they showed themselves more moderate on questions of principle and more ready to work within the existing situation as they found it. We shall have cause to refer to this again later.

These internal difficulties and divergences of opinion so far revealed were to continue after 8 September 1943. On that day the armistice was announced, though it had in fact been signed on the 3rd. I do not propose here to go into the rights and wrongs of the armistice or the mistakes unquestionably made by the Italian Govenment or, no less, by the Allies. Such a discussion would take me too far from my immediate subject. I will therefore leave aside the preliminary negotiations and refer merely to the conclusion of the armistice on 3 September 1943 and its proclamation on the radio on the 8th by the commander of the Allied troops in the Mediterranean, General Eisenhower. The announcement took the Italian Government by surprise.

It must be recognized that the Allies had no confidence in the Rome Government's proposals. In this they were wrong, and they failed to grasp the real situation in Italy; but the fact of their mistrust remains. On the night of 7/8 September the American representative General Taylor arrived in Rome and during discussions with the Italian military leaders asked them: 'Do you want us to send a parachute division to Rome? What is the military situation there?' The Italian High Command replied that such a military operation would be absolutely impossible: the airports were either in German hands or under German threat and the parachute division would be destroyed. The Italian

Command asked the Allied High Command to agree to a discussion of some military questions. The following morning the American General left by plane with an Italian General to explain the military situation to General Eisenhower. But the proposed discussions would have meant delaying for some days the proclamation of the armistice. The Allied Command preferred instead to announce it at once.

There was also another great source of misunderstanding which affected the whole war in Italy, and which I will clear up without more ado. The Italian military authorities wanted the Allied landings to be made to the north of Rome; they thought that the Allies would now seriously concentrate their efforts on the Italian theatre of war. But for the Allied High Command, on the contrary, Italy was only a secondary theatre. The plan for the landings in Northern France had been fixed and the French campaign decided on. The campaign in Italy was intended to serve merely to keep a certain number of German troops occupied. Hitler would thus be forced to maintain some divisions in Italy which might otherwise have been used on the French or Russian fronts. It was a diversionary campaign and nothing more.

From this time onwards the forces employed by the Allies in Italy were no longer of any great significance; and when in 1944 divisions were needed in France and later in Greece, they were taken from General Alexander's army in Italy, thus still further reducing the possibility of action on that front.

When the armistice was announced on the evening of 8 September 1943 there was widespread panic among the Italian leaders, who were completely taken by surprise. The King and Marshal Badoglio left Rome early on the 9th and crossed Italy to Pescara, proceeding thence to Brindisi, which became for some months the centre of the Italian State. That State, it is important to realize, continued to exist legally within the peninsula's territory, with its own legal Government and in its own legal form, i.e. that of a monarchy. In Rome, the Foreign Minister was not even informed of what was happening: only on the morning of the 9th did he learn that the royal family and the head of the Government had left the city.

The orders given by the Naval Ministry were such that the whole Italian Fleet was able to execute them perfectly. Despite German air attacks which caused the loss of the cruiser *Roma*, the Admiral's ship, the entire fleet succeeded in taking refuge in Malta, as had been agreed under the terms of the armistice, where it was welcomed with full naval honours. It at once embarked on operations side by side with the Allies. But in every other sphere complete confusion reigned: the result in the following days was the collapse of the whole organization of the Italian army from a military point of view.

Rome was at once surrounded by German divisions. It was here that the first action of the Italian Resistance took place: grenadiers and other divisions of the Italian army resisted as long as they could, and the regular forces were joined by civilians both from the working classes and the *bourgeoisie*. On 10 September near Porta San Paolo the first Resistance fighter fell; he was a school-teacher.

Thus we come to the Resistance. But before continuing our analysis of the political forces and their action, a fact must be mentioned in connection with the Resistance which proved to be of decisive importance for the whole recent history of Italy.

As a result of the events of 8 September and the following days, Italy found herself divided in two. The Allies landed in the Salerno plain. After some days of fierce fighting they managed to consolidate their position and marched on Naples. But Naples did not wait until they came: on 27 September the city rose of its own accord. When the Allied forces entered it at eleven o'clock on the morning of 1 October it was already free. The German garrison was forced to surrender to the Neapolitan patriots after a fierce and bloody struggle. This was a fine page in the history of Naples.

But apart from this episode, what happened elsewhere in the South of Italy? The Allies succeeded in advancing up to a line stretching from the Garigliano, north of Naples, to the Adriatic south of Pescara. Once arrived there they halted, and from November-December 1943 to May 1944 the military situation remained immobilized on what the Germans called the Gustav Line. South of this line was the Italian monarchy, the Kingdom of the South, as it became known. In the North there was the German occupation and the Government set up by Mussolini, who had been liberated on 12 September by German parachutists at Campo Imperatore in the Abruzzi where he had been taken under police escort. This was the Italian Social Republic, or the 'Republic of Salò', as it was called from the name of the village on Lake Garda where the Government was centred. This Government, which was kept alive by the Germans, included among its ranks the most ardent of the Fascists and others who refused to accept the armistice. Italy, in fact, was in a state of civil war.

What was the course of events between September 1943 and May-June 1944? The first Allied armoured cars entered Rome on the evening of 4 June. Almost nine months went by during which in Southern Italy, though under Allied control, the King's Government functioned. Thus Southern Italy was never in a position to experience at first hand the partisan war or the real Committees of National Liberation. We shall see later what political consequences this fact brought forth.

The Allied forces began to move again in May 1944. They marched on Rome, entered it, and advanced into Tuscany. Florence was liberated in August. They reached the Apennines, where they came up against the German defences in the Gothic Line. But again the Allied advance was checked and fighting continued throughout the winter of 1944–5. It was not until April 1945 that the last German resistance collapsed and the Allies reached the Po Valley.

Thus there were, so to speak, three Italys: Southern Italy, which was occupied at once by the Allies; Central Italy, which remained under German rule until the summer of 1944; and Northern Italy which up to April 1945 was the theatre of the struggle against the Germans and the Fascists of the Salò Republic.

This fact was of fundamental political importance. But it was not only the long-drawn-out nature of the fighting that mattered, though that proved an important factor and one which had grave consequences in terms of prolonged human suffering in the neighbourhood of the two fronts where fighting went on for months on end, bringing with it enormous destruction (for example at Cassino). The essential point was, however, that each of these three parts of Italy underwent a quite different experience politically. We must now consider what effect all this had on Italian politics after 1945.

III THE RESISTANCE: MILITARY ORGANIZATION AND POLITICAL ACTION

It is essential for an understanding of the political evolution of modern Italy to grasp this fact of Italy's division into three distinct zones.

The 'Kingdom of the South'. The zone to the south of the most advanced line reached by the Allied troops in November-December 1943 ran across the Apennines. The whole of Italy south of this line was liberated at the time of the armistice or immediately after.

The King's Government was first established in Brindisi; later, in 1944, it was transferred to Salerno. In February 1944 the Allied authorities restored to Italian administrative authority the whole of Southern Italy south of the provinces of Foggia and Naples except for the islands of Pantelleria and Lampedusa. Nevertheless in those regions that came officially under the administration of the Italian Government the Allies continued to exercise effective control.

Thus a legitimate Government did actually exist in Italy. On 16 November 1943 the King entrusted Marshal Badoglio with the task of forming a new Ministry (the second of its kind) in place of the earlier military Government which had been established on 1 October. The Italian administration accomplished wonders in a very difficult situation. Such was the so-called Kingdom of the South.

In the South there was no actual Resistance movement, nor was there the occasion for it. True, there too Committees of National Liberation were set up, but they were quite different from those in the other regions, for by the time they were formed the struggle in those parts was already over. The Committees in the North, on the other hand, continued the fight for two years; many of their members risked their lives and a good number lost them. The population of the North knew that in them they had in their midst a body of men dedicated to the arduous task of leading the struggle.

In other words, this meant that both from the political and the military points of view the Southern population inevitably remained outside the partisan war (the great days of Naples were, as I said, an exception which did not alter this general rule).

The struggle between the parties in the South followed easily predictable lines and was conducted in quite favourable conditions. The parties confined themselves to discussing what form the Government should take. Naturally, here too there were revolutionary and non-revolutionary trends. The parties involved were the Communists, the Socialists, the Action Party, the Liberals, and the Christian Democrats. Their attitude was not very different from that of their comrades in the North. But it was a party struggle, not a war of resistance. The parties had no intention of collaborating with the King's Government—with Badoglio—as long as the King refused to abdicate. Indeed at a certain point they even demanded not only the King's abdication but also the withdrawal of the Crown Prince Umberto and the transfer of the State's leadership to his little son, Victor Emmanuel, Prince of Naples, under a regency council. This solution was favoured by men such as Croce who were opposed to revolutionary methods and who hoped in this way to preserve the monarchy; but the Left-wing parties would have nothing to do with it.

On 28/29 January 1944 a big congress of the anti-Fascist parties took place in Bari at which demands were put forward for the immediate abdication of the King and the summoning of a Constituent Assembly, to be elected as soon as the war ended.

Meanwhile the Badoglio Government, composed exclusively of technicians, continued its labours. After 25 July the King had been unwilling to have a Government of politicians, and Badoglio had perforce to continue on the same lines with a Government of technicians and high officials, since he was unable to reach any agreement with the democratic parties who sought the King's abdication.

But events now took an unexpected turn. This surprise move came from the USSR. The Badoglio Government had not yet been formally recognized by the Allied Powers; the Allies were beginning to feel some confidence in it and were by now convinced of Badoglio's desire to adhere to the terms of the armistice; but there had so far been no formal recognition. Suddenly, on 13 March 1944, to everyone's astonishment the USSR formally recognized the Badoglio Government and proposed the resumption of diplomatic relations between herself and Italy. The British and Americans, taken by surprise, were not particularly pleased to find the Russians getting in ahead of them. They too had to recognize the Badoglio Government, after which a competition began as to which Power could offer the most.

The anti-Fascist parties were demanding a democratic Government, but hitherto the Allies had turned a deaf ear to their requests; their main concern was to shelve the big internal problems (and it is noticeable how from this time onwards certain attitudes began to develop in this respect which later were to become further accentuated in the North). The armistice had been signed by the Badoglio Government, which had to bear the responsibility for it; the King and his Prime Minister, Badoglio, were responsible *vis-à-vis* the Allies, who for their part did not want to run into any difficulties in relation to the Action Party, the Socialists, or the Communists.

But the Allies, taken by surprise by the USSR's diplomatic move, realized that they could not persist in this attitude. They grasped the fact that if they stuck to their original line of discouraging the anti-Fascists from taking a lead in politics public sympathy would inevitably veer towards the Soviets.

The parties, as I said, wanted a democratic Government. But they also took up a very definite line about it: they declared that as long as Victor Emmanuel remained on the throne they would not participate in the Government. At this point came the second surprise, and it too was closely related to the USSR's decision concerning the Royal Government. Togliatti, the new leader of the Italian Communist Party, announced that the question of the monarchy must be postponed until after the war and that a new Government with the support of the democratic parties should be formed at once. He agreed to collaborate with the monarchy and Marshal Badoglio: the present need, he said, was for a Government of national unity, while the question of the monarchy could be left in suspense for the time being. This pronouncement brought about a complete volte-face in the political situation.

The tactics of the Communist Party which thus again became apparent, as in July-August 1943 but now much more clearly and decisively, were very different from the romantic revolutionarism of the barricades of 1848 or of 1919. The party now adopted a highly flexible line in politics, avoiding as far as possible all doctrinaire attitudes or questions of principle and showing itself prepared, while maintaining its strategic aims, to adapt its tactics to circumstances.

Faced with this change of front, even the most ardently republican parties had to modify their line, and on 21 April 1944 the first post-Fascist political Government was formed, still headed by Marshal Badoglio but consisting of politicians instead of mere technicians, and known as the 'six-party Government'. For a sixth party, the Democracy of Labour Party, had in the meantime arisen to join the ranks of those already mentioned. It functioned no further north than Florence, and was not represented on the northern CNLs. In politics it lay midway between radical and reformist socialist, and its prestige was based chiefly on a few personalities with a certain following; it did not really stand for anything new in the way of ideas or political strength.

It was agreed that after the liberation of Rome the King should hand over power to his son Prince Umberto as Lieutenant-General of the Kingdom, and he made a pronouncement to this effect on 12 April 1944. This was a perfectly constitutional solution. It did not compel the King's abdication or his exclusion from affairs, and in this way a truce was ensured on the question of the monarchy. The future of the monarchy itself was to be referred to a referendum of the people once the war was over. Thus the crisis of opposition between the parties and the Government was ended. Togliatti's initiative had provided a way out of a seemingly hopeless situation.

Central Italy: From Rome to Florence. With the liberation of Rome by the Allies the second or central zone in Italy opened up. The first zone, as we have seen, had no experience of the Resistance because liberation came to it so quickly. In that Southern zone, itself a region where the small and medium *bourgeoisie* was strongly conservative and closely linked to the monarchy, the State continued to function in its old form from the very first weeks. The King was there, and orders were given in his name and by a regular Government. Officials resumed their normal activities, and the whole administrative network, that complicated machinery of the modern State, functioned if not perfectly at least adequately.

The difficulties encountered were tremendous, due to the very bad state of communications. Railway traffic had been largely disrupted by bombing; telegraph and telephone lines were destroyed. But nevertheless the administrative machine gradually began to get into its stride again.

The problems became even greater in the second zone, that between the Gustav and the Gothic Lines, and first and foremost in Rome itself. There, on the morrow of 9 September, a centre of military resistance was established in the city under the command of Colonel Montezemolo, who, in contact with the Southern Government and the High Command, organized and directed some partisan formations which were thus in direct touch with the regular army.

Also on 9 September, a central Committee of National Liberation (CNL) was established, consisting of representatives of the

D*

various parties, and in addition military formations were organized depending on the CNL's military committee. In the surroundings of the capital and the hills (the Castelli Romani) a number of guerrilla and sabotage actions were carried out. In Rome itself, on 23 March 1944, thirty-two Germans of the SS were killed in an action in Via Rasella; and in reprisals for this action 335 Italians were massacred, including Colonel Montezemolo himself. To the east, in the Abruzzi, partisan bands were active, among them those in the Maiella mountains, and the Resistance organization began to operate in that region.

In Rome, side by side with the CNL and partisan activities, there was also, as I said, a purely military organization dependent on the Badoglio Government. The Southern Government had no intention of allowing itself to be supplanted by the CNLs, and there was a good deal of opposition between them. When Rome was finally liberated, a representative of the Badoglio Government, General Bencivenga, was put in command of the city, and he was quite clear about not wanting to be under any control from the CNL.

But there was yet another force which came into the picture in Rome, and that was the Vatican. On the morrow of the city's liberation the people crowded into Piazza San Pietro to acclaim the Pope and express their gratitude to him. Pius XII was called the 'defensor urbis', and the Romans gave thanks to him because their city had been spared from damage in the fighting between the Allies and the Germans.

Indeed the Roman priests and clergy and the Vatican played a very important part during these months in obtaining food supplies for the people and helping them in all sorts of ways. Many political refugees from German persecution were given shelter in ancient churches and abbeys. The churches of San Paolo Without the Walls, San Giovanni in Laterano, and many monasteries became a last refuge for men pursued by the enemy. When I think of those days so close to us in time, I always recall what happened in the fifth century, when the German hordes came down upon the Roman Empire. In AD 410, for the first time after seven centuries, Rome was taken by storm and sacked by the Visigoths. The world's greatest city fell, and, as St. Augustine said, before its churches the fury of the barbarian invaders was checked; they did not dare to penetrate into places consecrated by Christ, and the population was saved. That episode of fifteen centuries ago was the origin of the power and political strength of the Roman Church. In presenting themselves as defenders of a populace abandoned by the Roman imperial authorities, the Popes laid the foundation during the fifth century of all the power and political influence of the Church of Rome.

During the German occupation too, the Church shone out over Rome in a way not so very different from the role it had played in the fifth century. Rome found itself from one day to the next without a Government; the monarchy had fled, and the Government too, and the people turned their eyes towards St. Peter's. One source of authority had collapsed, but in Rome, unique in this respect, there existed another, and one of immense scope and power. The result was that although the CNL had its committee and military organization in Rome, for the Roman population itself what the Papacy was doing day by day appeared of far greater importance. In other words, here too the resistance led by the CNL, and the activities of the various political parties, came up against formidable limits inherent in the situation as a whole.

Events followed a different course to the north of Rome, in Central Italy, in Tuscany and in Umbria. Take, for instance, Florence. As we have seen, in the South the regular Government still existed, and in Rome the power that most strongly influenced public opinion was undoubtedly the Vatican rather than the Committee of Liberation. But in Florence for the first time the picture altered. Not only was there open fighting between partisans and Germans in the heart of the city itself and in its streets, but also from the political point of view (which is what concerns us here, because it enables us to follow the evolution of the main factors of the general political situation) the parties were definitely in a position to develop their activities. For them it was not enough just to fight against the Germans and the Fascists of the Salò Republic. The struggle must be carried through to the end, and at the same time the foundations of Italy's political future must be laid, a future that could not be other than democratic, the fruit of a profound change in the country's institutional framework.

In August 1944 there was fierce fighting in Florence, with partisans attacking the German troops. There was, in fact, the same kind of popular 'insurrection' that had taken place in Naples and that failed to happen in Rome. The liberation of Florence was not due to the Allies alone. It afforded proof of the effectiveness of Italian action as well, and this was recognized in the appointment of an administration whose powers emanated from the CNL. It was argued that if before the Allied Military Government arrived the city's administration could be organized under a body appointed by the CNL, the CNL itself would acquire the status of representative of Italian democracy, and the legal basis of power would rest with it.

The outstanding factor in the whole story of these years is the profound difference in the course of events not only as between Central and Southern Italy but also as between Florence and Rome. In Florence the CNL was able to influence the situation in a way which would have been quite impossible in Rome. The position in Florence provided a foretaste of what was to happen in Northern Italy.

Northern Italy. Northern Italy is for the purpose of our analysis by far the most interesting zone. In the first place, armed resistance reached its full development there. This region of Italy was for more than eighteen months (September 1943 to April 1945) under German control, backed up by the Republican Fascists. Thus the struggle there surpassed in gravity, duration, and bitterness anything encountered even in Central Italy. There the Resistance reached its highest point both militarily and politically. My task here is to explain the political situation in Italy as it developed after 1945, and in order to do that I must concentrate on the political aspects of these last eighteen months of the war and must therefore refrain from describing in detail the bitter fighting which went on during all that time between the Italian partisan Resistance, supported by the population, and the Germans and Fascists. This may, however, be the right place to say something about the Italian Resistance in general.

In the period from 9 September 1943 to the end of April 1945, in the course of resistance against the Germans and the struggle for liberation 72,500 Italians were killed and 39,167 wounded (including, in both cases, civilians). Commissions appointed to study the partisan war have estimated the number of persons qualifying as partisans at something over 232,000, and the number of 'patriots'—i.e. active fighters throughout the Resistance period—at around 125,700. In the month of October 1944 between six and eight of the twenty-six German divisions deployed in Italy against the Allied armies were engaged in the struggle against the partisans.

In addition to the partisan action there was also, after the autumn of 1943, action by forces of the Italian regular army. The Badoglio Government declared war on Germany on 13 October and was then recognized by the Allies as a 'co-belligerent'; and after considerable difficulties it succeeded in securing the participation of troops of the Italian regular army (known as the Italian Corps of Liberation) in the fighting against the Germans. Their first encounter took place early in December 1943. After that, five Italian divisions fought side by side with the Allies right up to the end of the war, and it was certainly no fault of the Italians if the number was not greater. The fact was that the Allies did not want any 'excessive' effort on the part of the Italians, whether from the partisans or from the regular army.

The 'active participation in the war against Germany' by the Italian armed forces, whether regular or of the Resistance, was explicitly recognized by the Allies in the Preamble to the peace treaty. 'Active participation' included not only civilians shot in reprisals or because of help given to the partisans, but also the sacking and burning of many villages and small towns.

Finally, popular opinion also found other means of expression, such as strikes by the workers, and in particular the large-scale strike of 1 March 1944, when, at the height of the German occupation, the workers of Turin, Milan, and other towns abandoned work altogether for a week. This was the first time that anything of the kind had occurred in German-occupied Europe. These strikes, moreover, were definitely political in character, so much so indeed that the German authorities used all kinds of threats in their efforts to put an end to them.

To return to the armed resistance: side by side with the partisans (who were organized first in bands and later in divisions and brigades with a central general command) there were also the GAP (patriotic action groups) and the SAP (patriotic action squads). The GAP were created in November 1944, largely in the towns, as a result of Communist initiative, and they carried on sabotage activities etc.; the SAP developed during the summer of 1944, also at the prompting of the Communists, and were mainly defensive in aim (though not exclusively so, for they often moved over into the attack), protecting the population against requisitioning, the labour call-up, and so on.

As far as its social composition was concerned, the Resistance was not the monopoly of any one class. All social strata were represented in it, and in the maquis students, office workers, and professional men were to be found side by side with industrial workers and peasants. The first incomplete statistics about the partisans in Piedmont[1] show the following percentages: industrial workers, 31·51; middle classes, 29·83; peasants, 20·39; small craftsmen, 13·63; leisured classes, 5·69.

Obviously, in order to attach real meaning to these statistics it would be necessary to relate them to the social composition of the population as a whole. Their true significance can only be seen by comparing them with another set of figures, those concerning the working population in Piedmont, and there we find that 42·3 per cent was employed in agriculture, 36·5 per cent in industry. Moreover it would be necessary to establish precisely what was covered by the terms *bourgeoisie* (owners, technicians, office workers), industrial workers, and peasants. Without going into details, however, these statistics at least suffice to confirm the generally recognized fact that all social classes took part in the Resistance.

In the CNLs, which had their headquarters in the towns and carried on an arduous and highly dangerous activity constantly hunted by the police, representatives of the *bourgeoisie* and the workers sat side by side. On the day on which the military committee of the Turin CNL was arrested and brought before the judges, there appeared together in court a general[2], a workman, a university professor, and several lawyers, professional men, and officials. Most of them were shot.

It was, in fact, a true struggle of the people regardless of social distinctions. While the *bourgeoisie* continued in the maquis its tradition of volunteer service, recalling 1915–18 and, going even farther back, 1848–9, 1859, and 1860, for the industrial workers and craftsmen—who also had shared in this tradition during the Risorgimento struggles and the civil risings such as those of Milan (March 1848), but not after—and above all for the peasants, this kind of warfare in which service was given voluntarily, without conscription, was something new. This was a factor of great importance. It showed that the active and definite participation of the masses in political life and the life of the community as a whole was now an established fact, which it had never been during the years between the achievement of Italy's unity and the

[1] See R. Battaglia, *Storia della Resistenza italiana* (Turin, Einaudi, 1953).
[2] General Giuseppe Perotti, leader of the Turin CNL military committee.

First World War. This alone would suffice to explain why political life in Italy after 1945 was different from that of the pre-1914 period.

The political problems of the Resistance. Let us now consider the political aspect of the Resistance. That aspect was obvious, at any rate to a great extent, from its very beginnings. In the first place, there were some bands which wanted to remain, and did in fact remain, purely military. After 8 September many officers chose not to return home but instead took refuge with their men in the hills or mountains and prepared to take part in the country's defence. Not all of them managed to stick it out, but several bands developed and gradually became organized and resisted to the end. There were also the so-called 'autonomous' bands which had no particular political affiliation; several of them did extremely well.

Side by side with these 'autonomous' bands was another organization, the 'Franchi', headed by Edgardo Sogno, which was of a different kind and carried on different activities in the way of sabotage, etc., mainly in the large towns of Northern Italy.

Then there were some bands that were both political and military, and were connected with one or other of the parties. In these cases, side by side with the military commander of the band there was also a 'political commissar'.

The two parties which were the most active, producing the greatest military effort and remaining throughout in the forefront of the struggle, were the Communist Party and the Action Party. The Communist bands were known as the 'Garibaldi' brigades, while those of the Action Party were the 'Giustizia e Libertà' (GL) brigades. But there were also Christian Democrat and Socialist brigades (the latter known as Matteotti brigades). Many of them distinguished themselves in brilliant actions led by commanders of wide renown whose *noms de guerre* were familiar to all.

Numerically, the Garibaldi brigades were the strongest; they had more bands than any others in the maquis, followed by the autonomous brigades, the 'Giustizia e Libertà', etc. The relative strength of the various bands naturally varied from region to region: the highest percentage of Garibaldi bands was in Emilia and Liguria, while those of 'Giustizia e Libertà' were strongest in Piedmont. Here too we reach the same conclusion as when considering the Resistance from the social angle—namely, that it was a collective affair embracing all parties and anti-Fascist trends, and aiming at a common effort going beyond party divergences.

What, then, were the political aims which began to emerge in the course of the Resistance period?

As early as September 1943, the Communist Party launched an appeal to the people denouncing the failure of the old political classes which had directed the State in the past, and proclaiming the revolutionary function of the Committee of National Liberation.

At the end of March 1944, the political commissar of the Action Party partisans attached to the second sector of the province of Cuneo, the province where that party was strongest, sent out a circular to all its centres giving the following instructions. Leaders should:

(i) make the partisans understand clearly that they were soldiers of a *new, revolutionary* army, the Army of National Liberation, which was in no way to be identified with, or regarded as the successor of, the old royal army that had failed so miserably;

(ii) explain just what the CNL was, i.e. the only organization which after the flight of the King and his court and ministers had raised the banner of active resistance against the Nazis and Fascists and had promoted, inspired, sustained, and carried on that struggle. It was, in effect, *the true and authentic national government of invaded Italy*, and from it alone, and not from the Badoglio Government, could the partisan formations receive orders and directives;

(iii) illustrate the character, duties, and objectives of the Army of National Liberation, and in particular explain clearly that the soldiers of that army were not so much, or at least not solely, the champions of a generic patriotism aimed merely at 'evicting the foreign invader from the sacred soil of Italy', but were, rather, the armed vanguard of a movement for reconstruction, of a revolutionary process which concerned the country's whole political and social structure and which should make of Italy, humiliated and disgraced by the Fascist tyranny and its accomplices, a new free, democratic, and civilized nation.

The revolutionary note is clearly apparent in this manifesto. The same cannot of course be said of the Liberals or Christian Democrats: both of them were ready to carry on the military and political fight against the Germans and Fascists but they wanted no 'internal political' struggle. Their ideal, especially that of the Liberals, was to have purely military formations which had nothing to do with the parties: the partisans in the North should be just a projection of the Italian regular army. For this reason the autonomous political bands were eventually to end up by supporting, by and large, the Liberal and Christian Democrat programme.

The discussions which arose within the Northern CNL reflected these different attitudes. On the one hand were those who wanted to give the Resistance a politically revolutionary stamp and were not prepared to accept a pure and simple return to the old form of State (the debate started by the Action Party between November 1944 and February 1945 was typical in this connection). Their opponents, on the other hand, did not agree with this view but maintained that while they were fighting to regain freedom, from the political standpoint they were prepared to accept the structure of the old liberal State, with the requisite reforms. In short, they wanted to have nothing to do with any revolution sponsored by the CNL.

What was to be the outcome of these fundamentally different trends? In what circumstances could the revolutionary trend succeed? And what were the elements in the general situation which were soon to hamper such a development? In fact, through force of circumstances after 1944 the political revolutionary impetus suffered a distinct check. It became necessary at a certain point to negotiate with the Allies. Apart from other general considerations, the partisans needed arms and supplies, and their daring exploits in seizing arms from the Germans and Fascists could not provide for all the equipment they needed.

The bands grew larger. In the spring of 1944 there was a call-up for the Fascist Republican Army, and a good many young men who were eligible for it chose instead to flee to the mountains and join the partisans there. Thus the problem of equipment and supplies became more acute.

True, the Allies could drop supplies to them, but it was questionable whether they really wanted to do so in all cases irrespective of the partisans' political leanings, and Allied doubts on this score clearly increased as the war drew to an end.

Here, too, the difference in aim between the Italians and the Allies can be discerned. Contrary to the hopes cherished by the

Badoglio Government at the end of August and beginning of September 1943, the Allies attributed only a secondary importance to the Italian theatre of war. They did not want any large-scale support from the Italian regular army, and tended to confine its role to the fighting against the Germans. Similarly, in relation to the Resistance, they preferred that the partisan bands should not be too numerous and should restrict their activities to sabotage rather than undertaking any significant large-scale military action. The Allies, moreover, feared a politico-revolutionary movement. The events in Greece of early December 1944, involving clashes between ELAS (the Greek partisans) and British troops, increased the uneasiness of the Allied High Command, which had no intention of supplying arms to what might later become a revolutionary movement. At the beginning of April 1945 the military leader of the partisans, General Cadorna, was again called upon to assure Field-Marshal Alexander that in Italy 'no situation resembling that in Greece would arise'.

Thus when in December 1944 four delegates from the North Italian Liberation Committee (*Comitato di Liberazione Nazionale dell' Alta Italia*, or CLNAI) came to Rome, an agreement was signed between them and the Allied General Maitland Wilson. The text of this agreement, dated 7 December 1944, is very significant. It can be summarized as follows:

> 1. The Allied High Command desires that the closest military co-operation should be maintained between the elements carrying on activities within the Resistance movement. The CLNAI is charged with ensuring and maintaining such collaboration and also bringing together all the active elements of the Resistance movement, whether belonging to the anti-Fascist parties of the CLNAI or to other anti-Fascist organizations.

In other words, this meant that a partisan high command was to be set up, with at its head a general of the Italian regular army, General Cadorna. The General had been parachuted into Northern Italy in August; but discussions continued about the single command, and in particular about the relations between the military command and the CLNAI, in accordance with the standpoint adopted by the Allies.

At the moment of liberation the commander of the Freedom Volunteers' Corps (*Corpo dei Volontari della Libertà*, or CVL, the name given to the partisan bands as a whole) was in fact General Cadorna, son of the commander of the Italian forces in the First World War. Beside him as deputy-commanders of the CVL were Ferruccio Parri, of the Action Party, and Luigi Longo, a Communist.

Secondly, during the enemy occupation, the general command of the CVL was to follow all the instructions given by the Allied High Command. Among the Command's chief aims was that particular attention was to be given to safeguarding the economic resources in occupied territory from sabotage or destruction. During the past months the partisans had in fact been particularly careful to protect industrial installations, and the fact that the industrial plants in North Italy emerged from the war largely intact was due to their care—for it had been feared up to the last that the Germans would, for instance, blow up the main power plants.

Thirdly, the CVL commander should be an officer accepted by the Allied Command.

Fourthly, when the enemy retreated from occupied territory the CLNAI should make every effort to maintain law and order and continue to safeguard the country's economic resources until the Allied Military Government should be set up.

The Liberation Committee should undertake to recognize the Allied Military Government and hand over to it all the administrative and local government powers it had hitherto held.

At the time of the enemy's retreat, all the members of the CVL command would become directly subordinate to the commander of the Allied forces: they would be expected to carry out all orders received, including the order to hand over their arms and dissolve the partisan bands.

The text of the agreement was concise and the Allies' attitude perfectly clear: they wanted neither disorders nor any political revolutionary movement.

Another important episode in the conduct of the Allied Command occurred on 13 November 1944, when Field-Marshal Alexander issued instructions which were in effect a call for demobilization. The effect of this was disastrous: one wonders how, in fact, a partisan who had chosen the path of resistance could be expected to go quietly home for the winter and then come back again to the maquis. But the Allies' line of conduct remained perfectly clear and consistent: the Italian Resistance was not to acquire too much importance. From this point onwards the politico-revolutionary impetus of the Resistance inevitably began to weaken as a result of circumstances imposed by the situation as a whole.

Some weeks later, on 26 December 1944, the Prime Minister, Bonomi, signed an agreement in Rome with the North Italian Liberation Committee. This agreement stated:

> The Italian Government recognizes the CLNAI as the organ of the anti-Fascist parties in enemy-occupied territory. The Italian Government delegates the CLNAI to represent it in the struggle which the patriots have undertaken against the Fascists and Germans in the part of Italy not yet liberated. The CLNAI agrees to act to this end as Delegate of the Italian Government, which is recognized by the Allied Governments as the successor of the Government which signed the armistice and is the sole legitimate authority in that part of Italy which has been or will eventually be restored to the Italian Government by the Allied Military Government.

Thus the Committee was officially recognized by the Italian Government, which delegated certain powers to it, if only of a very general kind. The Committee consequently acquired a legal and official status *vis-à-vis* the Rome Government.

The agreements of 7 and 26 December 1944 set the official seal upon the North Italian Resistance organization. It marked a great success for it. Nevertheless both these agreements represented a compromise from the politico-revolutionary point of view.

The Committee was now in a position to proclaim itself to the people as the legal representative of the sole legitimate Government. But it was only a question of 'representing' the Government. Note the insistence in the agreement of 26 December on the fact that the Rome Government was the 'sole legitimate authority' in the part of Italy that had been or would eventually be restored etc. It is perfectly clear: much clearer than the formula concerning the delegation of powers, which was, in any case, confined to the period of the 'struggle'.

If these facts are related to the discussions within the CLNAI as to whether or not the Committee should seek to impose itself as an 'extraordinary secret Government', it is easy to understand how from the political standpoint its revolutionary impetus received a check.

COLLAPSE OF THE FASCIST RÉGIME

Thus the effect of the action of the Allies and the Rome Government was to put all the weight in one particular direction (and the Allies, obviously, carried a weight that could not be disregarded), while at the same time within the CLNAI itself the moderate parties, the Liberals and Christian Democrats, were operating in the same sense.

IV THE POLITICAL SITUATION AT THE TIME OF LIBERATION OF ALL ITALY

In April 1945, when liberation came, the revolutionary aspirations which had animated certain sections of the Resistance finally petered out.

By the time the Allies arrived the towns of Northern Italy were already free. The partisans had fulfilled their mission. Administration passed into the hands of the CNLs, which still consisted of representatives of the same five parties.

The organized strength of the parties also remained the same as hitherto, but there was as yet no knowing what strength they would command in the elections. For the time being, their only visible support came from their military strength, in other words from the partisan bands grouped around them. For instance, the Action Party, which was to have but small success in the elections, was strong militarily, and its 'Giustizia e Libertà' bands were among the best organized.

The parties therefore regarded themselves as equals and accepted the principle of parity; this meant that the various public offices to be filled were shared out between the five parties on that basis. For example, the first Prefect of Milan was an Action Party man, while the Mayor was a Socialist; in Turin there was a Socialist Prefect and a Communist Mayor. Thus the Allies found themselves faced with men who, in the name of the Liberation Committees, had at once taken over power. The Allies of course installed their own military administration, the Allied Military Government (AMG), which controlled public life.

Such was the situation immediately after Liberation. But what was the next step to be? The whole of Italy was free, but now there were not only the Allies but also the Bonomi Government to be reckoned with. After a year and a half of separation the

North was to be reunited with the Centre and South, but what would happen then? In the words of Nenni, the leader of the Socialist Party, 'A "wind from the North" is on the way, bringing with it changes and sweeping all opposition before it.' But obstacles were to arise to prevent that 'wind from the North' from blowing freely.

The revolutionary impetus no longer had any hope of fulfilment by April 1945. I have already mentioned the agreements of December 1944 between the CLNAI representatives, General Wilson, and the Bonomi Government: they demonstrate how, from the political point of view, from the moment they were signed moderation had won the day.

The Allies, it must be remembered, were still in Italy with their military forces. But that was not all. As soon as Northern Italy was reunited with the Centre and South, the moral and political consequences of the country's division into three parts, which I stressed earlier, became obvious. Southern Italy, apart from the Naples rising, had no first-hand knowledge of the Resistance. Rome, certainly, had some experience of it, but its period of detachment was brief, and its links with the Bonomi Government were always close and practically continuous. The liberation of Rome was effected with the entry of the Allied troops and not, as in Genoa, Turin, Milan, and elsewhere, with the arrival of partisan formations. Finally, in Rome, the whole picture was dominated by the Pope and the Vatican, representing a power far superior to that of the CNL, which had been unable to play any great part there.

Moreover by April 1945 the regular Government had been functioning again in Rome for nearly a year. Life in the capital had gradually reverted to normal. The State tradition and its organization and technical administration were resuming their former strength—which naturally was opposed to disturbances and upheavals.

For these reasons the 'men from the North' found a different climate in Rome from that of Milan or Turin.

What were the aims of these Committees of National Liberation which had sprouted like mushrooms everywhere? For in North Italy, side by side with the political committees, factory committees and others were also arising. This was alarming and, some thought, might even presage a return to the factory councils of the past. When the Liberal Party secretary, Leone Cattani, during the formation of the new Government in May 1945 launched a violent counter-attack in the dispute on the rival merits of Rome and Milan, he had behind him a considerable section of public opinion in those regions of Italy which had inevitably remained outside the Resistance struggle. People asked themselves just what these Liberation Committees amounted to. It was difficult for a population which had been divided for a year and a half to grasp what had been going on in the other part of the country. It was not merely a question of the outside power of the American Military Police; it was Italy itself that was divided through too widely differing experiences. If the climate in Rome was different from that of Milan or Turin, it was no one's fault but that of events themselves.

At this point a new movement made its unexpected appearance, the 'Uomo Qualunque' movement, definitely hostile to the policy of the CNL; it soon achieved great success. A journalist and writer, Guglielmo Giannini, launched a newspaper called *L'Uomo Qualunque* as the organ of this political movement, which made such remarkable progress that in the 1946 elections it secured thirty seats. It represented the reaction of the medium and small *bourgeoisie* from Rome southwards to the experiences and aspirations of the North. In the 1948 elections, however, the movement collapsed, being in fact little more than a gesture of protest: it expressed a particular reaction to a given situation and after a time had fulfilled its function. But in the meantime the movement was quite strong, especially in Rome, Naples, and Apulia, as can be seen from the above-mentioned thirty deputies which the 'Uomo Qualunque Front' achieved in the elections of 2 June 1946. Of the twenty deputies elected in individual constituencies (the other ten being in the 'national list'), only one came from the North (from the constituency of Milan-Pavia): the other nineteen were elected for Rome, Benevento-Campobasso, Naples-Caserta and Bari-Foggia (where the votes were highest, with four deputies for each constituency), Salerno, and in Calabria, Sicily, and Sardinia. In the municipal elections of the same year, 1946, the 'Uomo Qualunque' movement obtained the election of 30 of its candidates in the North, 68 in the Centre (including 58 in Rome and the adjoining provinces), 981 in the South, and 218 in Sicily and Sardinia.

Rome, for its part, had no real, effective experience of the CNLs. What happened there was quite unique. As I said earlier, the authority to which Rome looked was the Pope, not the Committees of Liberation. The influence of religious feeling is a constant factor to be reckoned with among the Italians.

To recapitulate, the main features of the situation were:

(i) The military strength of the Allies who controlled Italy. The Allied Military Administration in general favoured the moderate rather than the revolutionary elements. This was apparent in the South and Centre and later on in the North.

(ii) The definite difference in opinion and attitude between North Italy (plus some regions of the Centre) and the rest of the country from Rome southwards.

These factors alone would in general have sufficed to ensure the victory of the moderate parties in the CNL, the Liberals and Christian Democrats, and to bar the way to any 'revolutionary' effort towards far-reaching changes in the State itself. But yet another factor came into the picture.

(iii) This was the very great power represented in the modern State by bureaucracy and the administrative structure of the State. Its power was less obvious than that of the parties, but it had continuity and could therefore with time exercise perhaps a stronger influence than they could. The modern state signifies to a great extent the technical organization of public life, in other words, as I said, bureaucracy. Now a bureaucracy is by nature conservative; its strength lies in continuity, certainly not in drastic change. Individual Communists, Socialists, or Action Party members might work in it, but on the whole it is an organization tending towards continuity and conservatism. The technical power of the bureaucracy thus becomes a political power of great importance, even though this may not be very obvious.

Salvemini, in the analysis of Fascism given in his book, *Under the Axe of Fascism*[1], insists on the fact that even for Fascism the support of the higher bureaucracy was an element of the first importance. I myself pointed out earlier how one of the reasons which partly explain the acquiescence accorded to Fascism is to be sought in its seeming stability, which gave it the persuasive force of something likely to last. The State continued to function, indeed it had to be made to function, for professional pride was at stake. In the eyes of the official, the State always appears as an

[1] New York, 1936.

entity in itself, above political strife, an entity compounded of laws, regulations, and the continuity of administrative functions, and so to be preserved at all costs.

The same thing happened now. Italy had been devastated and pillaged; everything seemed paralysed; and the whole machinery of the State had to be set in motion again. This meant not only making the trains run but also imposing anew the application of laws and regulations and restoring to the various offices the functions which in many cases they had lost. The CNLs had taken over the powers of the Prefects, the police, etc.; now it was necessary to return to normal.

So a new 'third force' came into play, that of conservatism. By the time the North was liberated it had already largely regained its power of action in the Centre and the South.

Thus at the time of general liberation the initial revolutionary impetus was already shattered. Discussions between the CNLAI and the Rome politicians about the new Government lasted a month and a half. This long-drawn-out crisis reflected the difficulties of the situation.

Two leading politicians claimed on behalf of their respective parties the right to lead the Government: Nenni for the Socialists and De Gasperi for the Christian Democrats. The solution reached appeared to be a triumph for the Resistance, but in reality it was only a temporary compromise: Ferruccio Parri, one of the three leaders of the CVL and a member of the Action Party, was chosen as Prime Minister.

Parri's Government did not last long. He became Prime Minister in June but in November the Liberals launched an attack against him. They left the Government, and the Christian Democrat Ministers also resigned. The Communist and Socialist parties failed to support Parri. So on 10 December 1945 the Christian Democrat leader Alcide De Gasperi became Prime Minister.

On 1 January 1946 the Allied Military Government restored the administration of Northern Italy to the Italian Government. The Prefects and police officials appointed by the CNLs, who were not career civil servants, were invited to enter the regular administration, in other words to become State officials: if they refused, they would be replaced by career officials. Practically all the Prefects appointed by the CNLs did in fact refuse and went back to their normal occupations. Consequently career Prefects, i.e. representatives of the Government, returned to head the various Provinces, thereby bringing about the restoration of the traditional method of government and administration. The Government installed in these key posts its own trusted representatives in place of those of the CNL. The period of 'political' prefects was over.

Thus the bureaucracy, with its immense power as the representative of continuity and tradition and of the old State which had managed to remain in being, in the South almost without interruption, now regained strength and resumed control of the political situation and of public order. Once that had happened the revolutionary period could be said to be completely at an end.

Nevertheless one essential point in what we have called the 'revolutionary' programme of the Resistance was to be realized later on: this was the establishment of the Republic by means of the referendum held on 2 June 1946. With this the Resistance period came to a close.

Politically, it ended, by and large, with the success of what we may call the 'moderates', including in this term both the Liberals —who subsequently found no support among the great masses of the electorate—and the Christian Democrats, who, on the contrary, emerged victorious in the elections.

But one thing remained as the common heritage of the Resistance: the popular struggle for freedom, which still stands as an outstanding achievement in Italy's history.

2 THE POLITICAL PARTIES IN REPUBLICAN ITALY

WE HAVE ALREADY EXAMINED political developments up to the Liberation and shown how the revolutionary trends in Italian politics lost their impetus in 1944 and 1945. I have also tried to explain the facts and reasons leading up to this situation, which can be summed up in a few words: the old State regained strength, its organs were reconstituted, and its functions revived.

I THE FIRST ELECTIONS IN FREE ITALY

As we have seen, during the period of collaboration in the Resistance, and in the absence of any electoral basis, all the anti-Fascist parties considered themselves as equals, and entitled to equal shares in everything. The distribution of political offices at the end of April 1945 conformed to this principle.

The same method, inevitable until elections could be held, was also followed, at least in part, in the formation of the *Consulta* which held its first meeting in Rome on 25 September 1945, and in which a certain number of the members were appointed by each party. The *Consulta* was to collaborate with the Government in preparing the way for a Constituent Assembly, and was to be a consultative organ in the sphere of government legislation to work out the method of election to the Assembly.

The Municipal Elections of 1946. With the municipal elections of the spring of 1946 the whole picture changed. These were the first elections in which the Italian people had taken part for many years, for the Fascists had done away with municipal councils and elected mayors, substituting instead the office of *podestà* (also corresponding roughly to mayor), appointed from above.

During the Resistance period, municipal elections had already been held in spite of the war in some regions of North Italy occupied by the partisans, and this had a definite significance both morally and politically.

Thus the parties had now for the first time to appeal to popular vote, and their political strength was to be tested by the only valid yardstick, the vote itself.

The municipal elections were held only a few months before the political general election and the referendum of the following June, and they thus provided some valuable indications of how matters lay with respect to the relative strength of the parties and their geographical distribution. They did not take place at the same time throughout the country, being held partly in March-April, partly in November (chiefly in the big cities). Except for a few necessary details, we shall give only the overall results here; they provide a fairly consistent picture.

One preliminary observation must be made. Anyone consulting the statistics given in the official volume published by the Italian Central Statistical Institute, the *Annuario statistico italiano* 1944–8, will find himself faced with a problem. In general, he will notice that only a rather small number of municipal councillors are listed under the particular heading of 'Italian Socialist Party' or 'Italian Communist Party'. The fact is that the strength of the Left-wing parties cannot be estimated merely from the numbers appearing under those headings. In order to do so the so-called 'lists of mainly Left-wing trend' or 'Left-wing concentrations' must also be included.

These lists were by no means composed exclusively of Communists and Socialists. These 'popular blocs' or Left-wing lists also included members of the Action Party, Republicans, and so-called Independents, i.e. candidates who did not want to stand under the auspices of a specific party but who showed a definite inclination towards the Left.

It is true that municipal elections, being more closely linked to local situations, do not always show the same marked characteristics as political elections. But it is nevertheless obvious that the political weight of these Left-wing lists operated in favour of the two big specifically Left-wing parties, the Socialists (as yet undivided) and the Communists, which represented the main support of the blocs and whose members formed their structure. These were the parties who derived the greatest advantage from these electoral combinations. That is why, in making a political evaluation of the municipal elections, it is legitimate to reckon under the same heading the Left-wing trend lists and the official Socialist and Communist lists.

The Christian Democrats, on the other hand, fought the election alone, accepting no 'blocs' except in a few particular cases.

Let us take, for example, the case of Piedmont, where 4,018 Christian Democrat municipal councillors were elected, as against only 1,094 Socialists and 601 Communists elected as such on the official lists. From those figures alone it would appear that Christian Democracy in Piedmont obtained more than twice as many votes as the Communist and Socialist parties combined. But that would not in fact be true, for under the Left-wing lists I mentioned, which were also in opposition to the Christian Democrats, 5,166 councillors were elected, and these must be added in, to give a resulting total of 6,861 councillors of the Left.

It is not possible to give all the results here, and I will mention only those in a few especially typical areas.

Piedmont, as we have seen, had a Left-wing majority. The same was true of Lombardy, where 10,128 Christian Democrats were elected as against 11,137 of the Left (though there were only 469 'official' Communists and 1,074 Socialists).

In Trentino, a stronghold of Christian Democracy, the picture was completely different: there, 843 Christian Democrat councillors were elected as against 260 of the combined Left, thus achieving an overwhelming majority. In the Veneto, 6,575 Christian Democrats were elected as against 3,964 of the combined Left.

Thus the western region of North Italy tended towards the Left, though with a very considerable Christian Democrat minority, while the Christian Democrats were strongest in the east.

I have stressed these results, which were to be further confirmed in the political elections, because they provide a first indication of the parties' geographical distribution and so enable us to obtain a clear picture of their respective social and psychological bases in the various regions.

In Liguria the Left had a not very marked but still quite definite majority (1,677, as against 1,454 for the Christian Democrats). Then we come to the 'red areas'—Emilia-Romagna, Tuscany, Umbria, and the Marche.

If Trentino and the Veneto produced a clear majority for the Christian Democrats, Emilia provided an even more overwhelming one for the Left: there, 1,595 Christian Democrat councillors were elected as against 5,356 for all the Left-wing parties, official and otherwise. The results in Tuscany showed 1,383 Christian Democrats, 4,289 for the Left; in Umbria, 277 CD, 1,190 Left; the Marche, 1,361 CD, 2,306 Left. Taken together, the Marche, Umbria, Emilia, and Tuscany constituted the main stronghold of the Left.

Around Rome, the Left on the whole did slightly better than the Christian Democrats, with 2,286 councillors as against the CD's 1,992. In Rome itself the 'popular bloc' (i.e. Communists, Socialists, Action Party, etc.) obtained 186,599 votes against 102,352 for the Christian Democrat party, which reached only third place, for the 'Uomo Qualunque' party won second place with 105,741 votes. We shall see later on how these 1946 figures compare with those of 1948.

In the province of Naples, Christian Democracy won almost twice as many votes as the Left; it also obtained majorities in the Abruzzi and Sardinia. On the other hand in Apulia, Basilicata, Calabria, and Sicily the Left-wing parties did best.

To sum up: the Left-wing parties had a majority in the north-west of the country, the Christian Democrats in the north-east; in the Centre, the Left was slightly ahead; while in the South the two sides each obtained majorities in different regions.

In considering these results I have concentrated on the three mass parties because they form the basis of the political situation in Italy today. But in the South another factor must be taken into account. There, considerable success was achieved by lists which were neither Christian Democrat nor Communist or Socialist— for example by the 'Uomo Qualunque' party, which did quite well in the South whereas in the North it disappeared altogether. Thus in the South, unlike the North (where it was only in Piedmont that a high percentage of votes went to various lists of a local character) or, even more, the Centre, there existed lists of a national and not purely local character which were quite separate from, and even opposed to, the big parties and which derived from this fact the main basis of their success.

Moreover, corresponding to the Left-wing lists described above, there were also lists of the 'centre', based on the Liberals, and of the Right: in the North the Left-wing lists secured 25,341 councillors, those of the centre 1,341, and those of the Right only 74; the corresponding results in the central part of Italy were 8,764, 1,233, and 150; but in the South, on the other hand, the respective figures were 6,897, 4,396, and 1,709, and in the Islands 2,864, 1,541, and 500. Consequently out of 2,433 specifically Right-wing councillors, 2,209 were elected south of Rome. These figures confirm our earlier estimate as to the political orientation of the different regions of Italy.

Yet another point to consider is what happened in cases where the Communist and Socialist parties each presented separate lists, as distinct from the Left-wing 'bloc' lists. It is interesting to notice that when such cases arose in Piedmont and Lombardy—in other words, in the big industrial centres—the Socialists did better than the Communists. In Piedmont, Lombardy, Trentino, the Veneto, Umbria, Lazio, the Abruzzi, and in the South except for Apulia, Calabria, and Sardinia, separate lists signified a majority for the Socialists, while in Liguria, Emilia, Tuscany, and the Marche they produced a majority for the Communists. There were also two regions of the South where the Communist Party was stronger than the Socialist: these were Apulia and Calabria, and the same was true also of Sardinia.

In conclusion, reviewing the overall results of these municipal elections of 1946, one major fact emerges which is of great significance for the later evolution of political life in Italy, namely, that two of the original CNL parties, the Liberal Party and the Action Party, could not reckon on the electoral support of the masses. This is obvious from the results. The Liberal Party obtained its highest vote in the area round Naples, where it secured 962 councillors; but elsewhere it got very few—323 in Piedmont, 77 in Lombardy, 25 in the Veneto, 2 in Emilia. In the 5,596 communes with under 30,000 inhabitants, where elections were held in March-April, the Liberals obtained a majority in 95 communal councils. Even taking into account the 298 communes where the centre blocs had a majority, the percentage still remains very low.

The Action Party too had undergone its test, and had shown that it had no real following among the electorate. For in only seven of the 5,596 communes did it achieve a majority.

It was by now apparent that the main struggle would be between Christian Democracy, which obtained the majority in these elections, and the Communist and Socialist Left, which in all obtained control in 2,256 out of the 5,596 communes. The other parties came nowhere near them. Out of the total number of municipal councillors elected—131,625—43,274 were Christian Democrats, 3,883 specifically Communists, 5,045 specifically Socialists, and 43,866 belonged to the 'Left-wing blocs' which operated in favour of the big Left-wing parties—making a total of 96,068 councillors for the mass parties. The Liberal Party as such obtained 2,317 and the centre blocs 8,511. In the main cities, the Socialists obtained the majority in Milan and the Communists in Turin, Genoa, Bologna, and Florence. Even in Rome the 'popular bloc' was victorious. It should be noted that in the elections held on 9 November, covering most of the large cities, the Communists did better than the Socialists, a fact which caused serious debate among the Socialist leaders.

The Political Elections of June 1946. The political elections which took place on 2 June 1946 merely confirmed this state of affairs.

The Christian Democrats, with over 8 million votes, obtained 35·2 per cent of the total, the Socialists 20·7 per cent, and the Communists 19 per cent. Thus some 75 per cent of the total votes went to the three mass parties, which secured respectively 207, 115, and 104 deputies in the Constituent Assembly, together making a total of 426 out of 556.

It must be remembered that these were the first political elections to be held after many years. (For, as I said earlier, the electoral law of 1928 had deprived the voter of even the formal possibility of exercising that choice which is the very essence of the electoral system. Under that law he was confined to voting 'yes' or 'no' for a list of 400 'nominated deputies'—note the word 'nominated', not 'candidates'—to the Fascist Grand Council, chosen from among the 800 names proposed by the National Confederation of Syndicates and some other official organizations. With the establishment in 1939 of the Chamber of Fasces and Corporations, consisting automatically of members of the National Council of the Fascist Party and of the National Council of Corporations, the last vestiges of formal popular consultation were abolished.) The new elections passed off quite peacefully, though party struggle was fierce and passions ran high, especially because voting was not only for the Constituent Assembly but also for the referendum on the institutional question of republic or monarchy, which aroused even stronger feelings. A very high proportion of the electorate—89·1 per cent—voted.

The general election confirmed, at least in the North and Centre, the indications furnished by the municipal elections as to the relative strength of the main parties in the different regions, as can be seen from the following table showing the number of seats obtained.

Region	Christian Democrat	Socialist	Communist
Piedmont	16	13	9
Lombardy	30	24	14
Trentino	3	1	—
Veneto	28	16	7
Liguria	6	5	5
Emilia	10	13	16
Tuscany	11	8	13
Umbria	3	2	3
Marche	5	3	3

It was only south of Rome province that a difference could be observed between the results of the political and the municipal elections. In the former, the Christian Democrat party was everywhere the most successful, beginning with Rome itself, the only exception being Basilicata, where it polled practically level with Socialists and Communists. This was not the case, as we have seen, in the municipal elections; but, as I mentioned, in these elections, in the South much more than in the Centre or the North lists were put forward which had no connection with the main party groupings. In the political elections, at least a proportion of these votes clearly went to the Christian Democrats.

For the other parties the results were something of a débâcle. The Liberals, who had dominated Italian political life before 1919, obtained forty-one deputies. The Action Party, which had only just got over an internal crisis in the previous February, got seven, or nine including the two representatives of the Sard Action Party.

Thus within two months the municipal and political elections put the whole Italian political situation in a new light, inasmuch as the fiction concerning the equality of the parties, which had formed the necessary basis of the CNLs' policy, was completely exploded. Faced with the reality of the popular vote, the party positions became clearly differentiated. It was because of this that De Gasperi, the Christian Democrat leader who became Prime

E

Minister in December 1945 after the fall of the Parri Government, was able to maintain his position.

The crisis of Socialism and some other parties. Thus there were now three main parties in Italian political life, those of the Christian Democrats, the Socialists, and the Communists.

Difficulties now began to arise for several of the parties, apart from the Christian Democrats and Communists. Some of them disappeared altogether from the scene. The Action Party, already split in February 1946, was dissolved in 1947. Some of the others underwent crises which divided and weakened them, and this is what happened to one of the big 'mass' parties, the Socialists.

As early as July 1945, when the Socialist Party's national council met in Rome, a sharp division had arisen between the two trends which henceforward were to characterize the party's internal life. One of these trends was represented by Nenni, who based his policy on the existing agreement with the Communists. The reason given for this attitude was always the same: the Socialist Party must not detach itself from its original basis; that basis was the working-class masses, and if they were to detect any opposition between the Socialists and Communists which might harm their own interests, they would desert the Socialists for the Communists. The ideal thing, it was argued, would be to form a single workers' party.

In opposition to this policy another trend developed and became increasingly detached from the Nenni line. This second trend wished to preserve the party's complete political independence in order to avoid its being dragged in the Communist wake. It demanded political autonomy for the party.

But this was not all. Certain Socialists such as Saragat, the leader of the opposition trend who was later to become the first President of the Constituent Assembly, cherished in the back of their minds an ideal which could really only be described as liberal, even from the doctrinal standpoint. The feeling for personal freedom was very strong in Saragat; his Socialism was strongly tinged with liberalism; and he was a resolute opponent of Communism.

Following the discussions in the national council, at the party's first post-war Congress, held in Florence in April 1946, a compromise solution was reached, though only after lively discussion during which the divergences of view became increasingly marked.

But the basic problem still remained; and eventually, in January 1947, Saragat and his followers left the Socialist Party and formed a new party of their own, the *Partito Socialista dei Lavoratori Italiani* (Socialist Party of the Italian Workers, or PSLI.)

In January 1948 another important personality, Ivan Matteo Lombardo, left Nenni's party and in February 1948, together with Ignazio Silone, Aldo Garosci, and others, formed the *Unione dei Socialisti* (Socialists' Union). Finally, in May 1948, another leading figure, Romita, Minister of the Interior in the De Gasperi Government, also quitted the Socialist Party. This meant that throughout the previous three years there had been some manifestation or other of the crisis at work within the Socialist Party, and always for the same reason: opposition to a policy too closely linked to that of the Communist Party. A new Socialist grouping formed around Romita, known as the 'autonomists'.

At this point some attempts were made to arrive at unification of the various Socialist parties and movements outside the Nenni Socialist Party. But a crisis developed within Saragat's party, resulting in a Centre-Left split and the eventual formation in December 1949, of yet a third Italian Socialist Party, the *Partito Socialista Unificato* (Unified Socialist Party, or PSU).

What was the meaning of all these crises?

In point of fact, the same need which had inspired the political thought and practice of a century ago was making itself felt anew today. A century ago, especially in France, the watchword of the liberals was the 'juste milieu', an avoidance of extremes—whether of reactionaries—the 'ultras'—or the 'reds', who in those days were simply radicals or republicans. The same need now made its appearance again in the shape of various attempts to establish a 'third force'.

I shall not go into the reasons here which made such attempts difficult, for that would involve analysing the whole present-day political situation, so very different, from the internal and international points of view, from that of 1830. We need only recall the characteristics of political life today, all tending to render 'third force' parties much weaker than the big 'mass' parties.

But, be that as it may, this crisis had developed within Italian Socialism, and the whole complex force was weakened by these divisions. Split into three parts, the Socialist Party could no longer fulfil the role for which at the beginning of 1945 it had seemed destined. On the one hand, Nenni's party drew ever nearer to the Communist Party, and the Communists seemed the more likely of the two to prevail. On the other hand, in Saragat's party the opposition to Communism merely increased as time went on.

But the Socialist Party was not the only one to find itself in difficulties. The Liberal Party, too, suffered various crises. A whole group representing its left-wing trend ('left', naturally, only in relation to the other trends within the party) broke away. The 'Uomo Qualunque' party, whose origins were closely related to the particular political situation of 1945–6, found itself undermined by internal disputes and in the 1948 elections collapsed altogether.

Two parties, however, seemed above crises, or at any rate violent crises bringing serious consequences: neither the Christian Democrats nor the Communists had to submit to the kind of crisis that harassed the other parties. The reasons for this seem too clear to need much stressing. In the case of the Communist Party they are obvious. In the case of Christian Democracy, though there were often considerable divergences of view within the party, the common link of Catholicism was strong enough to prevent a crisis of widespread or long-term significance.

The Referendum. On the same day on which the first general election was held, 2 June 1946, a referendum also took place to decide on the institutional question. In it the people were asked which they preferred, a monarchy or a republic.

Three parties, the Communist, Socialist, and Action Parties, were definitely and openly republican; and there is no need to explain the attitude of a fourth, the Republican Party.

The position of the Christian Democrats was somewhat different. Basically, the fate of the monarchy lay in their hands. But at the party's congress in Rome at the end of April 1946 a large majority came out in favour of a republic, though its members were not put under any obligation to vote that way. Northern representatives were almost all for the republic, while those of the South wanted to retain the monarchy; and a good many Christian Democrats, especially in the South, did in fact vote for the monarchy. The Liberal Party, though itself mainly monarchist, also left its members free to vote as they wished.

Thus the parties' positions were already clearly defined when, on 9 May 1946, King Victor Emmanuel III abdicated in favour of his son Umberto, then Lieutenant-General of the Kingdom. This was undoubtedly a clever move in view of the referendum; but it came too late. Had it occurred in 1943, the old King's abdication might have produced very different results.

The result of the referendum showed 12,717,923 votes in favour of the republic as against 10,719,284 for the monarchy: a majority of some 2 million, or 54 per cent of the votes, according to the official figures given by the Court of Cassation. So the Italian Republic came into being. The first President, appointed on 28 June 1946, was Enrico De Nicola. He was succeeded on 11 May 1948 by Luigi Einaudi.

The political and municipal elections had already shown clearly the tendency in the South in favour of the Right-wing or Centre parties, and this trend was repeated in the case of the referendum. The mainly monarchist regions were in the South, and in the Naples area, the Abruzzi, Apulia, Basilicata, Sicily, and Sardinia the majority of votes went to the monarchy. The same was true of Rome, though only by a narrow margin. The monarchists had based their hopes largely on these regions; they expected to obtain a sufficiently large majority there to counterbalance the republican majority which they realized was inevitable in the Centre and North. In this their hopes were only partially fulfilled, for the South did indeed vote monarchist, but the majority in favour of it there was considerably lower than had been expected.

In the North, even Piedmont, the cradle of the House of Savoy, produced a republican majority (of 57·1 per cent, according to the *Annuario Statistico*). The other regions were even more pronouncedly republican, showing the following percentages in favour of the republic: the Veneto 59·3, Lombardy 64·1, Liguria 69, Emilia 77, Tuscany 71·6, the Marche 70·1, and Umbria 71·9. The regions with massive republican majorities were thus the same as those which in the political and municipal elections had voted predominantly for the Left-wing parties. But the highest percentage for the republic—85 per cent—was in Trentino, a region with a clear Christian Democrat majority. The highest percentage of votes for the monarchy was in Naples—Caserta (78·9 per cent).

Thus the institutional question was settled on 2 June. It remained to be seen how the Constituent Assembly would organize the country. I do not propose here to discuss the Constitution of the Italian Republic, but will instead confine myself to analysing the relations between the various political forces as reflected in the debate on the Constitution.

II POLITICS AFTER THE ELECTION OF JUNE 1946

Following on the election of June 1946, the political situation was such as to make a coalition government inevitable. The Christian Democrat party had 207 deputies, the Socialist Party 115, and the Communist Party 104; in other words, among the 556 deputies forming the Constituent Assembly no single party was strong enough to form a government on its own.

The Government formed in July 1946, still under De Gasperi's Premiership, was therefore based on a coalition of the main parties, the Christian Democrats, Socialists, Communists, Republican Party, and for a short time a single Liberal (Epicarmo Corbino). Its structure was governed by the continuance of the agreement between the Christian Democrats and the Left. The policy of the Communists was, indeed, quite clear: to participate in the Government, never to stay outside of it or of public office, and to maintain its presence everywhere. The programme of Communist policy was one of collaboration between the 'big mass parties'.

This time, it is true, Togliatti was not in the Government himself, but Nenni, the head of the Socialist Party, was. After the completion of the peace treaty negotiations in Paris, De Gasperi on 18 October gave up the Ministry of Foreign Affairs to Nenni, who in the meantime had become Vice-President of the Council.

So matters stood when the Constituent Assembly began to discuss the Constitution. As I said, I do not intend to go into details about the Constitution, but will merely record that the compromise agreement, if I may so describe it, between the big parties—including the Christian Democrat and Communist parties—managed to survive for a time. Proof of this can be seen in the debates on the Constitution.

The article of the Constitution which aroused the most discussion in the Assembly, and for which Communist agreement was most important, was Article 7. It stated that: 'The State and the Catholic Church are, each in its own sphere, independent and sovereign. Their relations are regulated by the Lateran Pacts.

Modifications to these Pacts, when accepted by both parties, do not require any procedure of constitutional revision.' This meant that where the Vatican and the Government were in agreement about a modification it would not be necessary to resort to the procedure of constitutional revision.

What was the political significance of this article? It consecrated both the agreement between the State and the Church and also, by implication, the Concordat, on which the Church set great store.

The representatives of all the parties were agreed in declaring that there was no intention of raising the religious question. No one wanted to revive the kind of anti-clericalism that had prevailed in the nineteenth and early twentieth centuries. Even in 1944 and 1945, the parties had been at pains to avoid raising any discussion of the problem of relations between State and Church so as not to disturb the moral unity of the Italian people. Thus no one had any intention at present of denouncing the Lateran Agreements.

Nevertheless, the Republicans, the Action Party, the Socialists, and the Labour Democrats were opposed to the insertion in the Constitution of a treaty of international character, a proceeding contrary to regular constitutional practice. 'We have no intention of raising the religious question,' they declared, 'but we cannot allow a treaty of international character to be mentioned in the Constitution'—especially since certain clauses of the Concordat raised various particular questions; Article 5 of the Concordat, for example, seemed to be in contrast to other provisions of the Constitution. It stated: 'No ecclesiastic can be given, or remain in, an employment or office under the Italian State, or in public organizations dependent on it, without the consent of the diocesan bishop. Withdrawal of such consent deprives the ecclesiastic of the possibility of continuing to exercise such employment or office. In any case apostate priests or priests who have undergone censure cannot be taken on or retained in any teaching post, office, or employment in which they come into immediate contact with the public.'

De Gasperi, however, asked that the article should be voted as it stood. He expressed himself in favour of complete respect for religious minorities and moreover drew attention—and this is important—to the political implications of the article. This article, he said, pledged the clergy to loyalty towards the Republic. 'My friends, we in Italy are not so solidified, so crystallized in the form of the régime as to be able to abandon too readily pledges of this kind, so solemnly undertaken. . . . By giving a contrary vote . . . we add yet another difficulty to those we already have, and that will certainly not help to strengthen the republican régime.' One gets the impression, the historian Jemolo comments, that should the article not be approved the Christian Democrats might yield to the monarchists' request that the whole Constitution be submitted to a popular referendum. The monarchists hoped in this way to reopen the institutional question, which they could not resign themselves to regarding as definitely closed. They had, indeed, at once appealed against the referendum of 2 June, but the Court of Cassation had rejected their appeal.

Togliatti declared that some revision of certain clauses of the Pacts, undertaken at a suitable time and in suitable ways, might be both desirable and possible. But, he added, in view of certain facts—that the Vatican made it a condition of peace in the religious sphere that constitutional recognition should be given to the principle of the Concordat; that the Communists were aware of their responsibilities, and the working classes did not want religious disagreements or internal dissensions for reasons of religion; and, finally, that the Communists wanted to avoid conflicts between the Communist and Socialist masses and the Catholic workers—in view of all these facts, the Communists would vote in favour of the article.

Thus the article was approved on 25 March 1947. It was approved with the support of the Communists, who on this occasion took a different line from the Socialists. The unity of action pact binding the two parties failed to operate in this instance.

Break-up of the Coalition Government. But the period of coalition Government and of tripartite rule was drawing to a close. On his return from a visit to the United States at the end of January 1947 De Gasperi resigned and formed a new Cabinet, still based on the three big parties; but the Left had to yield up two of the most important ministries, the Ministry of Foreign Affairs, where Count Sforza, a Republican, replaced the Socialist Party leader Nenni, and the Ministry of Finance, where a Christian Democrat, Campilli, took over from the Communist Scoccimarro. The split in the Socialist Party in January weakened Nenni's party considerably, especially from the parliamentary angle, for out of 115 Socialist deputies 52 joined Saragat's party.

The situation became daily more delicate for the three-party coalition. Consequently at the end of May 1947 De Gasperi reached an important decision: he dissolved the Government, and in the new one, his fourth Ministry, the Socialists and Communists were excluded. The new Cabinet was composed mainly of Christian Democrats with the collaboration of a Liberal —Einaudi, as Deputy Prime Minister and Budget Minister—and a Republican, Count Sforza, who, however, did not represent their parties officially but participated in the Government in the capacity of 'experts'.

Considerations of internal order undoubtedly influenced De Gasperi in this change of policy; for though the Communists had been taking part in the Government, opposition to the Christian Democrats had been on the increase in the country. But at this point the international situation became a decisive factor in the internal struggle between the parties. Foreign policy has always, within certain limits, influenced domestic policy and vice versa. A country's life cannot be divided into two spheres independent of each other. But the extent to which they influence each other varies.

It is typical of the times in which we live that international problems often play a decisive role in domestic politics today. At the basis of all internal disputes, not only in Italy but elsewhere, lies the acute divergence of attitudes towards the great overall problems and, in particular, the question of choice between the USA and the USSR. In this as in other things the situation differed greatly from that of 1919. Now there was steadily growing tension in the international situation: a major crisis was developing between the USSR and the USA, leading eventually to the 'cold war' and the Marshall Plan.

The corresponding tension within Italy became increasingly acute and culminated in the debate on the Atlantic Pact which took place in the Chamber from 11 to 18 March 1949, during which the Communists and Socialists launched a full-scale attack on the Pact. From then onwards the 'Atlantic' policy became the most constant and acute subject of disagreement.

The international situation was the most important factor in causing the downfall of the coalition Governments. These 'compromise' Governments were feasible in a given international situation at a time of relative calm; but it became quite impossible to sustain such a coalition between Christian Democrats and

E*

Communists (and the Nenni Socialists refused to detach themselves from the latter) in the changed international situation when calm was succeeded by the cold war. In this respect political developments in Italy show several similarities with those in other Western European countries, and no longer follow a purely Italian line. Towards the middle of December 1947 De Gasperi made some further changes in the Government, which now consisted of Christian Democrats in collaboration with the Liberals, the Republicans, and Saragat's PSLI. Saragat and Pacciardi, a Republican, became Deputy Prime Ministers. This Government of collaboration between the Christian Democrats and the Liberal and Centre-Left parties was formed in anticipation of the general election of April 1948.

The General Election of April 1948. The elections of 18 April 1948 completely altered the parliamentary situation. In 1946 the Christian Democrats had 207 deputies; on 18 April 1948 they secured 306 out of 574, in other words an absolute majority. In 1946 the Socialists and Communists had, respectively, 115 and 104 deputies; now the 'Democratic Popular Front' in which the two parties combined for purposes of the election obtained only 183. This altered situation made possible the formation of an exclusively Christian Democrat Government.

In the elections for the Senate, the Christian Democrats secured the election of 131 candidates out of a total of 237, while the Popular Front got 72. The Christian Democrats did not, however, have a majority in the Senate because in addition to the 237 elected Senators there were also 107 Senators 'by right' (for various reasons), and among the latter only 18 were Christian Democrats, whereas the Socialists had 11 and the Communists 31. Consequently out of a total of 344 Senators the Christian Democrats had 149 and the Popular Front 114.

This overwhelming victory of the Christian Democrats surpassed even its leaders' highest hopes. How was it achieved?

Two months before the election, on 15 February 1948, municipal elections were held in Pescara in which the Left-wing parties were victorious. They at once raised cries of jubilation, saying that Pescara was the forerunner of their imminent victory in April. But their triumph was short-lived: the Pescara victory turned out to have just the opposite effect, for it alarmed public opinion and so contributed to strengthening Christian Democracy.

The elections of April 1948 were, in fact, fought on the issue of Communism versus anti-Communism, which the Christian Democrats had made the platform of their electoral campaign.

The international situation also afforded considerable help to the Christian Democrats—and indeed to anti-Communist standpoints in general, though, as we shall see, this worked out entirely to the advantage of the Christian Democrats.

At the end of February events in Czechoslovakia accentuated fears of a Russian advance in the West. On the other hand, on 20 March 1948 the French Foreign Minister, M. Bidault, issued a declaration to De Gasperi in which the United States, France, and Britain pledged themselves to restore the Free Territory of Trieste to Italy. This was very important for Italy, where the newspapers of 21 March bore huge headlines on their front pages saying: 'The Allies Recognize Italy's Claim to the Free Territory of Trieste.' Trieste was a name that meant much to Italians alike in 1914 and in 1948.

Thus the general situation could be summed up as one of alarm at the Russian advance and fear of seeing Togliatti or, if not him, Nenni as head of the Government. All this operated in favour of Christian Democracy, whose poll rose from the 8 million-odd of 1946 to 12,708,263, or from 35·2 to 48·5 per cent of the total.

These results are worth analysing, for they afford a means of understanding the position of the political forces in Italy. As a matter of fact, the Left did not sustain very serious losses. In 1946 the Socialist Party obtained 4,765,665 votes and the Communist Party 4,358,243; the two parties together thus secured over 9 million votes. In 1948 the 'Democratic Popular Front', i.e. the Nenni Socialists and the Communists, got only 8,137,468 votes, thus apparently losing, at first sight, nearly a million votes.

But it must be remembered that in 1946 the Socialist Party was still united, whereas now the PSLI and the Socialists' Union had left it; and these two groups presented a joint list called 'Socialist Unity' which won considerable success, obtaining 1,856,287 votes and 33 deputies.

True, the Socialist Unity list was also supported by some who had not voted Socialist in 1946, for a certain number of voters who were not avowed Socialists saw in that list the possibility of a 'third force' which might avoid reducing the struggle to the sole alternative of Christian Democracy versus Communism. Nevertheless it was still true that a good proportion of the votes for Socialist Unity came from people who in 1946 had voted for the then united Socialist Party. It was certainly a set-back; but it did not necessarily mean that the Left had lost a great deal of ground since 1946.

The real loss on the part of the Left lay, rather, in the fact that despite the increase in the total number of voters since 1946—an increase of 1,854,385—they had barely succeeded in maintaining their position, whereas their rivals had made a formidable advance. In such a case, failure to advance is tantamount to losing. Election forecasts had predicted a big success for the Left, and it had not been thought possible that the Christian Democrats would get an absolute majority: this just goes to confirm the nature of the losses which the Left in fact sustained.

The other parties paid the price of the Christian Democrats' resounding victory. The Republicans' vote fell from 1,003,086 (1946) to 651,394 and their number of deputies from 23 to 9. The Liberals had formed a joint bloc—the 'National Bloc'—with 'Uomo Qualunque', thinking in this way to widen their electoral basis considerably; but the bloc only got 1,004,032 votes, as against 2,770,058 won by the two separate lists in 1946 (in point of fact, after the disputes within 'Uomo Qualunque' some of those who had supported that party in 1946 did not now vote for the National Bloc, which obtained 18 deputies instead of the 71—41 + 30—secured by the two separate lists in 1946).

The results in some individual constituencies demonstrate even more clearly the outstanding fact of the erosion of the smaller parties lying midway between Christian Democracy and the Left.

Take, for example, the constituency of Rome and the adjoining provinces, where in 1946 the Christian Democrats got 451,330 votes (11 Deputies), the Socialists 149,132 (3 Deputies), and the Communists 197,235 (4 Deputies). In 1948 the Christian Democrats made a great advance, obtaining 859,102 votes and 20 Deputies, while the Popular Front got 450,490 with 10 Deputies. This was a resounding defeat for the Popular Front as compared with the Christian Democrats; but in absolute terms the Front actually improved its position. The real losers were the smaller parties. For in 1946, out of the 29 Deputies elected in the constituency, 11 were Christian Democrats, 3 Socialists, and 4

Communists, together totalling 18, while the remainder were divided among the other parties—Liberals, UQ, Republicans etc. Now, however, out of 34 deputies to be elected, 30 went either to the Christian Democrats or the Popular Front, leaving only 4 for the other parties.

The same thing happened in the municipal elections in Rome. In 1946, the 'popular bloc' of Left-wing candidates obtained 188,599 votes, while the Christian Democrats got 102,252; on 12 October 1947 the bloc's vote rose to 208,566, whereas that of the Christian Democrats leapt to 204,297. The former did not actually lose, in fact it made some gains, but the latter gained much more.

It was the same in the constituency of Naples-Caserta. In 1946 this constituency had 11 CD Deputies, 2 Socialists, and 2 Communists, while the remaining 12 were of various parties. In 1948, 17 Deputies were Christian Democrats, seven of the Popular Front (which made a quite considerable advance), and only 7 from the other parties. Thus in 1946 15 seats went to the 'mass' parties and 12 to the others, whereas the ratio in 1948 was 24 to 7.

As we shall see, the Popular Front lost ground in the North but advanced in the South. This advance was not such as to counterbalance the losses in the North, but on the whole, taking into account the split in the Socialist Party, it cannot be said that the Left-wing forces had really lost ground as compared with 1946.

One factor in the Christian Democrats' victory was the large number of votes which had previously gone to the Liberals and other parties and now moved over to Christian Democracy. This was a typical feature of the 1948 elections. Confronted with the alternative of Christian Democracy or Communism, alarmed at the turn of events both at home (with strikes etc.) and abroad (the Czechoslovak affair), and fearful of a possible victory for the Popular Front, a good number of voters who were not in fact Christian Democrats, and who in 1946 had voted for the Liberals or other parties of the Centre or even the Right, could see no other safe course but to vote for the lists of Christian Democracy, the strongest of the anti-Communist parties.

In this way, the anti-Communist reaction of the great majority of the population operated in favour of Christian Democracy. The political struggle reduced itself more and more to a struggle between Christian Democracy and the Popular Front. We have already observed this fact in the particular areas of Rome and Naples; let us now consider it in the country as a whole. In 1946 the Christian Democrats had 207 deputies, the Left 219, together making a total of 426 out of 556, while the remaining 130 seats went to the other parties. In 1948, the Christian Democrats got 306 deputies, the Popular Front 183, totalling 489 out of 574. The other parties secured only 85 seats. The situation as a whole was quite clear-cut.

It must be borne in mind that Christian Democracy could rely on the support of certain forces that were able to exercise a powerful influence. Foremost among them was Catholic Action, which organized the so-called 'civic committees' (*comitati civici*), aimed at establishing a united Catholic and anti-Communist electoral body and persuading the electorate to vote *en masse*—for, naturally, Christian Democracy. The percentage of voters was in fact very high, reaching 92·1 per cent of the total electorate and thus surpassing the already very high figure of 89·1 achieved in the 1946 elections. It would be hard to imagine a higher percentage of voters in free elections; and the increase in the percentage operated definitely in the Christian Democrats' favour.

From all this we can see the difference between the effect of the Catholic forces today and in 1920, and between the policy of the present-day leaders and those of the past. As I said earlier, in 1919–20 Catholic Action was not very strong. Moreover, Don Sturzo's policy had aroused many doubts in ecclesiastical circles. Today, however, side by side with Christian Democracy there existed another force, that of Catholic Action, whose tremendous importance could not be ignored, and which gave the party its full support in the political struggle, especially at significant junctures. And the support of Catholic Action meant the determined and official support of the clergy as well.

Christian Democracy was therefore in a position to form a government alone, since it had an absolute majority in the Chamber. But De Gasperi remained faithful to the so-called 'formula of 18 April', that is to say, to a Government including as well representatives of the Liberal, Republican, and Saragat Socialist parties.

Any estimate of the political future as it appeared in 1948 would fall outside the scope of this book. But it may, instead, be worth while in conclusion to examine the regional distribution, both geographical and social, of the political forces at the time of the April 1948 elections.

III DISTRIBUTION OF POLITICAL FORCES IN POST-WAR ITALY

Before examining the relevant statistics, it should first be pointed out that for various reasons no exact comparison can be made between the 1946 election results and those of 1948.

First, as a result of changes in the electoral law, the number of deputies to be elected was not the same—in 1948 the total was 574, as compared with 556 in 1946. Moreover, in 1946 a quite considerable number of deputies—80—were elected to the *collegio unico nazionale* (combined national constituency), whereas in 1948 their number fell to 23 (these seats will of course be omitted from our regional calculations). Consequently the number of candidates in each local constituency increased. In that of Milan-Pavia, for example, 34 deputies were to be elected in 1946, 36 in 1948.

Secondly, some changes took place in the party formations. In 1946, the Socialist Party was still united and presented itself under its own lists, independent of those of the Communist Party. By 1948, however, a whole section of the Socialist Party had split away to form the new Socialist Workers' Party under Saragat, while other Socialists such as Lombardo, Silone, etc. had combined to form the Socialist Unity group. Moreover, in 1948, the Nenni Socialists fought the elections as a joint bloc with the Communists, and the Liberals did the same in combination with Giannini's 'Uomo Qualunque'.

Thus in any comparison between 1946 and 1948 there is bound to be an element of approximation and inaccuracy. Nevertheless certain conclusions can be reached which, while they cannot be 100 per cent mathematically correct, have a value as political indications.

In Piedmont, in the elections of 18 April 1948 (except for the Val d'Aosta, where the political set-up was different, but where the Christian Democrats were also more successful than in 1946) Christian Democracy obtained 1,116,318 votes as compared with 801,326 in 1946 and secured 22 deputies (16 in 1946). The Democratic Popular Front obtained 746,648 votes and 14 deputies, whereas in 1946 the Socialists and Communists standing separately secured 1,052,732 votes and 22 deputies. This was a considerable decline. Five deputies (267,593 votes) were elected for Socialist Unity.

Piedmont is the most highly industrialized region of Italy after Lombardy and Liguria. According to the pre-war (1936) census figures, 35·5 per cent of the population there was then employed in industry and 42·3 per cent in agriculture. The corresponding figures for Lombardy were 47·5 and 28·6 per cent, for Liguria 38 and 25·3, and for Tuscany 30·2 and 47·6[1]. Thus Piedmont can be described as a region with a strong concentration of industry and with large factories (e.g. Fiat in Turin), where the working classes have ever since 1919 represented one of the most solid bases of the Socialist and Communist movements. But in spite of this, the 1948 results showed a definite loss for the Left. On the other hand reformist, moderate, and anti-Communist Socialism represented by Saragat's party obtained a considerable success there, securing five deputies.

The same is true of Lombardy, the wealthiest and most highly industrialized region of Italy. In the four constituencies comprised within it, Christian Democracy obtained 2,071,261 votes and 46 deputies, as against 1,375,525 votes and 30 deputies in 1946. The Popular Front secured 1,314,439 votes and 27 deputies, whereas in 1946 the Socialist and Communists obtained 1,805,635 votes and 38 deputies. Socialist Unity got 373,254 votes and 6 deputies. Thus, as in Piedmont, the Popular Front lost ground here In only one constituency, that of Mantua-Cremona, did it continue to poll more votes than the Christian Democrats, maintaining the same number of deputies as in 1946 (five, equalling the Christian Democrats); this area is more agricultural than industrial, and the problem of the agricultural labourers is particularly acute there today, as it was in 1919. On the other hand, in the mountainous or hilly regions of Como, Sondrio, and Varese, where small-scale landownership predominates, the Christian Democrats obtained an overwhelming majority. Their majority was even more impressive in Brescia-Bergamo, which gave the party the highest percentage of votes in all Italy (66·8 per cent), whereas the Popular Front there obtained only 21·9 per cent of the votes and 4 deputies as against the Christian Democrats' 14. In the

[1] More recent figures would of course show a considerable shift from agriculture to industry. (*Translator's note*).

Veneto, the firmest stronghold of Christian Democracy, the party secured 38 deputies (28 in March 1946), whereas the number for the Popular Front fell to 14 (the Socialists and Communists had 23 in 1946); Socialist Unity got six deputies. This again represented a definite decline for the Popular Front.

In the Trentino, the ratio of Christian Democracy to the Popular Front was five to one. In Liguria, a region of strong industrial concentration, Christian Democracy secured 9 deputies (6 in 1946), the Popular Front 8, and Socialist Unity 2 (the Socialist and Communists had 10 in 1946). There the Left parties succeeded better in defending their 1946 position.

Northern Italy as a whole, excluding Emilia, showed the following results. The number of Christian Democrat deputies rose from 83 in 1946 to 120 in 1948 or, including the deputy for Val d'Aosta, a single-member constituency, 121. The party had obtained 3,738,210 votes in 1946 and now got 5,491,956. The Popular Front secured 64 deputies; in 1946 the Socialists had 59, the Communists 35; Socialist Unity now obtained 19. In 1946 the Socialists secured 2,654,341 votes, the Communists 1,772,077, making a total of 4,426,418. In 1948, the Popular Front got 3,138,529 votes, Socialist Unity 1,067,794.

The larger number of voters (10,610,948 in 1948, as against 9,840,411 in 1946) plainly operated in favour of Christian Democracy. Moreover the Left-wing parties not only failed to maintain their earlier position but also lost ground considerably. The split of 1947 in the Socialist Party undoubtedly had some effect; but it must also be added that in North Italy the tendency towards the extreme Left reached its highest point between 1945 and 1946 and the two parties representing it, rather than increasing their strength, now encountered a check.

Only in Emilia-Romagna did the Popular Front succeed in surpassing the Christian Democrats. It secured 23 deputies, as against 29 Socialist and Communist deputies in 1946; four seats now went to Socialist Unity. In 1946, the Socialists and Communists together polled 1,318,498 votes; in 1948 their poll was 1,126,450. Subtracting the 196,720 votes obtained by Socialist Unity, it will be seen that the Left-wing parties maintained their position, although even here the Christian Democrats made a definite advance (they got 724,486 votes and 14 deputies, as against 468,978 votes and 10 deputies in 1946).

The same can be said of Tuscany and Umbria. The Christian

Democrats made considerable progress—in Tuscany they secured 16 deputies (11 in 1946) and in Umbria 5 (3 in 1946); but the Popular Front still retained the lead which the Socialists and Communists had in 1946. In Tuscany the Front secured 20 deputies (21 in 1946), in Umbria 6 (5 in 1946). Yet Umbria was at that time one of the least industrialized regions of Italy, the ratio between industry and agriculture being 20·5 to 64·6 per cent.

It is also worth noting that while in Piedmont, Liguria, Lombardy, the Veneto, and even in Emilia the moderate, reformist, Socialists of Socialist Unity met with considerable success, in Tuscany and Umbria not a single one of the party's candidates was elected. This confirms what was said earlier about the 1946 elections: in the North a large proportion of Socialist opinion was unwilling to accept extremist programmes or to collaborate with the Communists, and the split in the Socialist Party consequently caused appreciable losses for the Left-wing bloc in 1948. But in Central Italy, or at any rate in Tuscany and Umbria, reformist Socialism had from the very beginning little significance, and the general trend was much more definitely towards the Left (in 1946 the Communists in fact secured more votes and deputies than the Socialists), with the result that the internal crisis of Socialism produced less marked repercussions there.

In the Marche, and in the whole of Italy south of Tuscany and Umbria, the Christian Democrats secured a majority and in some instances an overwhelming one (e.g. 9 deputies, as against 3 for the Popular Front, in Sardinia; 11 to 3 in the constituency of Benevento-Avellino-Salerno). Here too one or two comments are called for. While in North Italy, except for Emilia, the Popular Front not only remained below Christian Democracy but also, in an absolute sense, lost ground as compared with the Socialist-Communist results of 1946, in Italy south of Tuscany and Umbria, though it still remained far below Christian Democracy, the Popular Front actually advanced by comparison with 1946.

In the constituency of Rome and the neighbouring provinces Christian Democracy advanced from 11 to 20 deputies, but the Popular Front also improved its position, with 10 deputies as against 4 Communists and 3 Socialists in 1946. In Naples-Caserta, the Christian Democrats got 17 deputies (11 in 1946) but the Popular Front also advanced, securing 7 (2 Socialist and 2 Communist in 1946). Both these results showed an advance of the Left in relation to 1946.

In Southern Italy as a whole, Christian Democracy advanced from 1,699,408 votes and 48 deputies in 1946 to 2,901,271 votes and 79 deputies in 1948. But while in 1946 the Socialists and Communists got 1,015,729 votes and 24 deputies, in 1948 the Popular Front secured 1,370,689 votes and 36 deputies. The same thing occurred in Sicily and Sardinia, where the Christian Democrats secured 37 deputies (24 in 1946) and the Popular Front 14 (11 in 1946).

Thus in North Italy (including Emilia) the number of Christian Democrat deputies rose from 93 to 135 while those of the Popular Front fell from 123 to 87; Socialist Unity secured 23. Even taking into account these 23 arising out of the Socialist split, there still remained a definite decline in the Communist and Socialist forces in the North.

In Central Italy Christian Democracy secured 50 deputies (30 in 1946), the Popular Front 42 (39 in 1946), and Socialist Unity 2. Here consequently, the Left improved its position both in Umbria (one deputy more than in 1946) and in Rome (3 more), though in Tuscany it lost one deputy.

In Southern Italy and the Islands, as we have seen, Christian Democracy made considerable advances, but the Left too improved its position perceptibly.

These facts confirm the statement made by Togliatti to the Communist Party congress in January 1948, when he said that the South of Italy now represented 20 per cent of the party's total strength, whereas in 1946 it had accounted for only 16 per cent. All this explains how it was that the Socialist Party proved the major loser in 1948—plus the fact that because of the more compact organization of the Communist Party the electoral 'bloc' benefited that party more than the Socialists, for, as I explained earlier, blocs tend to favour the stronger and more highly organized party. When the parliamentary groups were formed in the Chamber and the Popular Front divided into two separate groups (which, however, continued to remain united in their political attitude and in parliamentary debates), the Communist group numbered 132 deputies instead of the 104 it had in 1946, while the Nenni Socialist Party numbered only 48. In 1946 it had 115, falling to 63 after Saragat and his followers split off in January 1947.

Taken as a whole, the above analysis leads to the following conclusion. The strongest base of the Left (including therein both the Nenni Socialists and the Communists) was still the North of Italy. This was due largely to the fact that the big industrial concerns were situated in the North, where the workers formed a compact body and in consequence possessed a more immediate and effective capacity for joint action such as strikes.

But, granting that, it must be added that it would be wrong to consider only the North and Centre of Italy in estimating the strength of the Left. It would be a serious mistake to see only the industrial workers behind the Red Flag. The workers were not all Communists or Nenni Socialists; there were Reformist Socialists, Christian Democrats, and so on among them too. The trade union organization, the General Confederation of Labour, whose most solid and best organized support was still to be found among the industrial workers, was in practice dominated by the Communists; but in 1948-9 the Christian Democrats, Republicans, and Saragat Socialists left the CGIL and formed two separate trade union organizations, the Free Italian General Confederation of Workers, established by the Christian Democrats in October 1948, and the Italian Labour Federation, set up in June 1949 by the Republicans and Saragat Socialists. This not only meant the break-up of unity in the labour field but also demonstrated the existence among the workers of often quite considerable minority groups which did not belong to the extreme Left.

In the rural areas, on the other hand, and especially in regions where large-scale landownership predominated, where day-labourers or crop-sharers (as in Tuscany) were numerous, and in regions where small-scale farming was so impoverished as barely to allow the farmer a decent livelihood, a notable advance of Communism could be observed. These were, moreover, the very regions where moderate Socialism had no solid long-standing basis or tradition; and in such regions there was no half-way solution but an abrupt move over straight from the Catholic to the Communist Party, It was, in fact, the same old story of land hunger that had influenced the situation in 1919.

In considering the Communists' efforts to penetrate the rural areas, we may recall that, among the various essays which Gramsci wrote during the long years of that imprisonment which eventually caused his death, was a study dealing with the problem of Italian unity, in which he maintained that the mistake of those who had created a unified Italy lay in their failure to bring the people of the countryside into the revolution. Historically, this theory cannot be accepted, for it would mean transferring to the nineteenth century the situation of today; but politically it is highly significant. It shows how the Communists turned their attention towards the peasants who, as I said earlier, in 1919–20 remained almost entirely outside the influence of the Socialist Party.

We now pass on from the Popular Front to the Christian Democrats and their success in the elections. Here the problem is more complex.

First of all, it is obvious that the victory of 18 April, in the general conditions, both internal and international, which I have briefly described, indubitably gave the Christian Democrat Party an exceptional weight in Parliament. It was the strongest party in Italy (and this was why the Socialists and Communists formed their bloc); after 18 April it had an absolute majority in Parliament, thus increasing its already considerable strength.

The Christian Democrats secured the support in the elections of a good number of voters who would normally have voted for the Liberal or similar lists. Such voters came mainly from the *bourgeoisie*.

The true Christian Democrat Party as such was variously composed from the point of view of social structure. It included on the one hand workers, especially in agriculture, small farmers, office workers, and professional men, and on the other hand large landowners and big industrialists—a cross-section, in fact of all strata of the *bourgeoisie*, as well as manual workers and in particular peasants. The party leaders themselves might be of the right, the centre, or the left; and its followers included representatives of the most widely differing social background and interests. The cohesive factor, and a very powerful one, was religion. The regions where Christian Democracy was overwhelmingly predominant were those in which Catholicism was traditionally very strong: for example, in the North, the Veneto, Trentino, the province of Bergamo, etc.

Such was the situation of the big parties after the election of 18 April 1948. The other parties, which became increasingly aware of the pressure of the 'mass' parties and which had lost a good deal of ground since 1946, were, so to speak, more 'localized'. The Republicans found their strongest support in Romagna and the Marche and in and around Rome, in other words in areas and circles which by long tradition from the time of the unification had been republican. The Liberals, who in former times had dominated the whole country, were now successful only in the South and the Islands. In the South, too, the Monarchists obtained some success, with fourteen deputies, while the neo-Fascist *Movimento Sociale Italiano* (MSI) secured six.

The moderate-reformist Socialism of Saragat, Lombardo, and Silone, on the other hand, found its chief stronghold in the North, with a new outlying nucleus of support in Eastern Sicily (Catania etc.). It had little success in the Centre and the South. Here too, as with the Republicans though in less clear-cut fashion, tradition played a part—the tradition of Reformist Socialism of the pre-1914 era, which had had its basis in North Italy.

In addition, these indications confirm the historic fact that Italian Socialism before 1914 had concentrated its efforts on the industrial and agricultural working classes of the North (especially in Emilia and Lower Lombardy) and neglected the South. The existence of a Reformist Socialist trend in Eastern Sicily today is due to the fact that Catania has a Socialist tradition of its own, going back to 1891 and the efforts of De Felice. Elsewhere, the tradition of Reformist Socialism was practically non-existent outside the North, and therefore it was easy for the appeal of the extreme Left to the masses to exercise a stronger attraction. The aim of the Communists after 1948 was to conquer the agricultural South.

3 THE ECONOMIC SITUATION

THE ECONOMIC AND FINANCIAL SITUATION can be dealt with only briefly here, taking as our point of departure the position as it was at the end of the war. What were the economic results of the war for Italy?

I THE ECONOMIC AND FINANCIAL CONSEQUENCES OF THE WAR

The effects of war damage have been estimated at around 7,000,000 million lire, or about one-fifth of the national wealth. Damage was unevenly divided; some towns were hard hit, especially in the densely-populated areas (e.g. Naples, Cagliari, Foggia, Turin, Milan, Genoa, etc.), while others, such as Rome, remained almost untouched. In the regions where fighting went on over a long period, along the Gustav Line between the South and Centre and the Gothic Line from the Centre to the North, even small villages were almost totally destroyed. Fortunately the major part of Italian industry, situated in the North, was saved. Despite damage from bombing, requisitioning, and the removal of machinery to Germany, industry in the main was unharmed. In the case of the textile industry, the Italians managed to keep large supplies of raw materials out of German hands, with the result that as soon as the war was over factories were able to start working again and even to export their goods.

Nevertheless industry had to overcome many difficulties, for it had been impossible to modernize buildings or plants or even to keep them in good running order, as for instance with the hydro-electrical installations. In general, industrial plant at the end of the war was, from the technical standpoint, old-fashioned and worn out, and hence more costly to run by comparison with that of other countries.

Agriculture, too, was for various reasons in a state of crisis. The country's agricultural wealth had diminished considerably. There was a shortage of fertilizers. In some areas where land reclamation had been carried out under Fascism—on the whole a positive achievement of the régime—war damage and failure to maintain drainage systems threatened to wreck all that had been accomplished, for regular maintenance was essential in order to keep healthy these areas formerly infested by malaria, such as the Pontine Marshes, south of Rome, one of the finest achievements in land reclamation. Further difficulties arose through the Government's mistaken policy concerning food supplies during the war. The result was a shortage of rationed foodstuffs—bread and other essentials—and the development of the black market, while at the same time agricultural production fell, especially that of essential foodstuffs such as wheat, which at official prices no longer represented a sufficiently remunerative crop to cultivate. Total wheat production in 1938 had amounted to 80 million quintals; in 1945 it was only 43 million. The average yield per hectare in 1938 was sixteen quintals; in 1945 it fell to thirteen quintals. Domestic production of wheat was therefore insufficient for the people's needs, and wheat is the very basis of the Italians' diet.

The transport system was also seriously damaged in the war. The merchant navy was of course very hard hit. But the railways too, the fundamental transport system inside the country itself, also suffered tremendous damage. On the main lines (Rome-Genoa-Turin, Rome-Florence-Bologna-Milan, Turin-Milan-Venice, Naples-Reggio Calabria, Naples-Foggia) miles of track were destroyed or torn up and sent to Germany (this last representing 36 per cent of the total), bridges were blown up, etc. The first trains from Rome to North Italy only began running again after tremendous efforts in the autumn of 1945. In addition, 80 per cent of the railway carriages and 60 per cent of the trucks had been destroyed, damaged, or taken to Germany, as well as more than half of all the steam and electric locomotives (56 and 60 per cent respectively).

Nevertheless it was in the field of transport that reconstruction came about most rapidly and effectively, and by 1946, thanks to a truly admirable effort on the part of the Italians, the railways were running practically normally.

The financial situation also presented great problems. The war had inevitably made necessary an increase in note circulation, though this was at first not excessive. Later on, as a result of the exceptional situation after the armistice, note circulation increased enormously. In the North, the Germans, after taking over all the gold in the coffers of the Bank of Italy, imposed a monthly increase of circulation. The Allies did the same in the South, where the Am-lira was introduced. Thus circulation rose from 22,495 million lire as at 31 December 1938 to 79,402 million at the end of 1942, 181,471 million at the end of 1943, and 319,634 million at the end of 1944.

The deficit in the State Budget rose steeply as a result of falling revenue from taxation: for now, as in 1915–18, the taxation policy was ill-organized and inadequate, and there was further confusion and disorganization as a result of the general situation in the country between 1943 and 1945. In 1938–9 the net deficit was 12,000 million; in 1942–3 it rose to 86,000 million and in 1945–6 to 380,000 million. The internal public debt, amounting to 145,000 million at the end of June 1939, reached 1,066,600 million at the end of June 1946.

This meant the beginning of inflation and, of course, a rise in prices, which was at first a good deal more marked in the South and Centre, where production is lower than in the North.

II ECONOMIC DEVELOPMENT: 1945–9

Such was the point of departure in 1945. Two main stages can be distinguished in economic development between then and 1949, the first lasting till September 1947 and the second after that date.

The Inflationary Stage. The first stage can in turn be sub-divided into two periods. The first, running from May 1945 to April 1946, was a period of relative financial stability. The increase in note circulation and the rise in prices continued, but still only to a limited extent. But the causes were already emerging which were eventually to produce the second stage, when inflation became pronounced. The State Budget had to meet huge expenditure for the most urgent needs of reconstruction, e.g. the railways, and its deficit rapidly increased. To remedy this, in view of the inadequacy of taxation, the Treasury was compelled more and more to have recourse to the Bank of Italy—which meant authorizing fresh note issues. In Italy there was no currency devaluation as there was in France or Belgium; but it was frequently talked of, and the very threat, though never carried out, had a deplorable effect in itself, and a great many notes were put back into circulation, at any rate in the towns. Thus the speed of note circulation increased almost daily. There was hardly any saving but a strong tendency to spend. The demand for consumer goods was high, whereas production was still a long way from resuming its normal rhythm.

So we move into the second period, running from May 1946 to September 1947. This was a period of definite inflation. Circulation rose from 394,700 million lire at 30 June 1946 to 577,600 million at 30 June 1947. Wholesale prices followed the same trend. Taking a basis of 1938 = 100, they showed the following increases:

May 1946	2,582
December 1946	3,677
March 1947	4,139
June 1947	5,329
September 1947	6,202

The rapid rise in the cost of living between 1946 and 1947 naturally brought about a rise in wages (taking 1938 = 100, the figure for May 1946 was 1,544, that for September 1947, 4,670). In this latter period the cost of living figure was 5,334 (1938 = 100). Industry had extensive recourse to credit, thus contributing to the increase and speed of circulation.

Efforts towards financial stabilization. This rising inflationary curve was checked thanks to the new financial policy introduced by Luigi Einaudi, who was both Deputy Prime Minister and Budget Minister in the De Gasperi Cabinet. Einaudi's main object was the defence of the lira, for inflation meant a headlong rush into the abyss. The measures he introduced on 22 August 1947 aimed at restricting the granting of bank credit to industry and trade. The result was that the huge stocks of goods accumulated in the warehouses in anticipation of a further fall in the value of the lira could no longer be maintained but had to be realized at least in part. Some of the credits sought by industry and trade had been used to finance this speculative piling-up of stocks, which were now thrown on the market with a corresponding effect on prices. A further contribution towards bringing down prices came through the policy of the Minister for Foreign Trade, Merzagora, in furthering large imports of foodstuffs. This meant the end of the black market and the beginning of a definite fall in prices, though retail prices took much longer than wholesale to come down. The speed of note circulation diminished, while saving increased, as was shown by the sharp rise in bank deposits towards the end of 1947 and even more in 1948.

All this signified a change in the psychological situation: expectation of a constantly increasing devaluation of the lira gave place instead to expectation of a further fall in prices. And since national production, both in agriculture and in industry, rose steadily between 1946 and 1948, a quite different phase from that of 1945–7 now opened. Note circulation was still on the increase (it reached 896,500 million at 30 June 1949) and so too was the public debt (2,146,800 million at that date); but these facts no longer had the same repercussions as in 1946–7.

The State Budget reached its highest deficit in the financial year July 1947–June 1948 (net deficit, 719,400 million), after which it gradually improved. The net deficit for 1948–9 fell to 503,000 million, that for 1949–50 to 207,000 million. Thus the second stage in Italy's economic and financial policy, inaugurated in the summer of 1947, can be described as one of monetary stabilization.

Economic Difficulties. Inflation had been successfully checked, but this did not mean that the economic situation had ceased to present serious problems. By 1949 the national income had reached the level of 1938, but the average *per capita* income was still below that of 1938, taking into account the increase in the population (from 43,776,000 in 1938 to 45,871,000 in 1948). The ostentatious wealth of certain 'new rich' elements in the big towns gave a deceptive impression. The great mass of the people, including not only industrial workers and peasants but office workers as well, were still compelled to subsist at a too low level of consumption often falling below the essential needs, and in primitive living conditions.

In the South, in particular, there were conditions of poverty which the occupation of land by the peasants in the autumn of 1949 brought home to all. The problem of the South moved into the foreground of Government planning—the problem of a large part of the population inexorably increasing yet with no corresponding increase in the means of livelihood.

General economic conditions (of production etc.) were still by no means easy. Italian industry had its periods of immediate postwar prosperity, due in part to the favourable international situation. Production rose between 1947 and 1948. The Central Institute of Statistics, taking 1938 = 100 as basis, shows a figure of 87 for 1947, 95 for 1948, while the Industrial Confederation gives a lower figure—75 for 1947, 82 for 1948. But in any case there was a definite advance. Two periods, in 1946 and the first half of 1947, also proved favourable for export trade as a result of the international political situation.

But things still remained difficult. Costs were higher in Italy than in other countries and this militated against successful competition on international markets. Many reasons contributed to place Italy at a disadvantage, among them the state of her industrial plant, often worn out or out of date and in need of renewal; the excess of manpower over and above the actual needs of production (and, as we shall see, the impossibility of reducing it in view of high unemployment); and the high cost of money or, in the last analysis, shortage of capital. To this must be added the burden of taxation, especially for small and medium-scale industries, a burden which tended to become more acute as a result of the Government's sterner fiscal policy.

The international situation in 1948-9, including the devaluation of sterling and consequently of other currencies as well, did little to further Italy's possibilities of export trade. The foreign market was increasingly difficult for her, while the home market was too weak to allow of full development of industrial production. As long as a whole area of Italy, the South, remained in the condition of a 'depressed area', Italian industry could reckon on only a limited expansion of the home market.

Agriculture. In agriculture, too, there was a steady increase in production, the Central Institute of Statistics figures showing 77·2 for 1947, 84 for 1948 (1938 = 100; the figure for 1945 was 60·1).

But from the point of view of foreign trade a fundamental fact must be remembered, which I mentioned in connection with an earlier period, that of 1919, namely, that Italy's agricultural export trade was a trade in luxury goods, or at any rate goods that were not prime necessities. She had to import wheat while her export wares were early vegetables, oranges, wine, etc. Consequently in periods of general crisis her exports inevitably fell, while her imports, consisting of foodstuffs or essential raw materials, could only be reduced within certain limits. It is possible to dispense with early vegetables and oranges but not with coal, cotton, or oil. And in fact Italy's exports of fruit and vegetables, which in 1938 represented 17·4 per cent of the total, fell in 1948 to 12·2 per cent.

The English market, for example, as a result of the Labour Government's economic policy and austerity régime could not then offer Italian producers the same possibilities as in normal times.

Moreover, it must be remembered that the big markets for Italian agricultural produce used to be in Central Europe. In 1945 those markets had vanished, and their revival was bound to be slow, even if political reasons did not prevent trade with them altogether. In this disappearance of former markets the situation resembled that after the First World War.

III UNEMPLOYMENT AND THE POPULATION PROBLEM

All these difficulties find expression in the unemployment figures showing the numbers of industrial and agricultural workers unable to find work. The average monthly figures for the first post-war years, according to the Ministry of Labour, were as follows:

1946	1,654,872
1947	2,025,140
1948	2,142,474
1949 September	1,722,575

This extremely serious problem of unemployment brings us logically to the fundamental fact which has weighed upon the whole of Italy's economic life—the population problem.

In 1870 the population of Italy was 27 million; in 1920, 36 million; in 1948, 46 million. An average rate of increase of 400,000–450,000 must be reckoned with (in 1948 it was over 500,000).

The problem is, in fact, how to provide for the subsistence and improved living conditions, especially in the South, of a still growing population, in a territory of limited resources.

Up to 1914 there was, as we saw earlier, the possibility of emigration. But now emigration had been greatly reduced owing to the laws governing it in various countries. In 1906–10 the number of emigrants per annum averaged 651,288; the number emigrating in 1947 was less than 160,000, of whom 60,000 went to the American continent; the figure rose to 280,000 in 1948. Agreements were concluded after the war with Belgium, France, and Argentina, but they did not always produce good results. For example, the results of the agreement with Argentina fell far below the hopes at first entertained.

It should be remembered that emigration had its heyday in a period (at the end of the nineteenth and beginning of the twentieth century) characterized by the stability of currencies and rates of exchange. But after the last war sharp variations in the rates of exchange and the value of money became almost the normal thing. What were the effects of this on emigration?

The answer is simple. In many cases the emigrant went out to seek work in distant countries in order to be able to provide the bare necessities for his family left behind in Italy. Take the case of the Italians emigrating to Argentina: following the devaluation of the Argentine currency, his wage, translated into lire, suffered a sudden and considerable reduction (quite apart from difficulties of transfer).

Take the Italian miners in Holland, in Limburg. Up to 20 September 1949, these miners got such good wages, paid in Dutch currency, that, given the favourable rate of exchange, they were able to send their families in Italy a quite respectable sum. After 20 September, the same wages had only two-thirds of their former value because the Dutch florin followed the example of the pound sterling in devaluing: thus the sum the miners sent home fell by a third. This kind of experience can have profound psychological repercussions.

Thus the problem of population increase is a major one in Italy and has its effects in every sphere.

CONCLUSION

And now, if we look at this last period as a whole, we reach the unescapable conclusion that the Italian State has overcome a formidable crisis.

It is worth remembering that the State is still relatively young, lacking the traditions of a unity going back through the centuries. Yet it has managed to overcome the serious crisis that threw the country into turmoil between 1943 and 1945. Notwithstanding defeat and the long period when the country was divided in two, notwithstanding shocks of every kind, moral, political, and economic, national unity emerged victorious from the test.

In this State which has known how to preserve its unity despite upheavals, and which since the war has revealed a quite astonishing capacity for recovery, the political struggle has taken on a different pattern from that which prevailed before the First World War. Here, as elsewhere, the masses have come into their own, and that has meant that the political party now plays a much more organized, continuous, and extensive role than did the classic parties of the late-nineteenth and early twentieth centuries. The era of large parties with a rigid structure has come to succeed the classic liberal era when party organization was weak and political personalities predominated.

From this point of view, and from the angle of domestic politics, the feature which most sharply differentiates the Italy of today from the Italy of the 1870s is the role of the Catholics.

Italy had been familiar with Socialism as an organized political force since the end of the nineteenth century. The urge towards the Left was not typical of Italy alone, for in this she shared in a trend which was general throughout Europe. In the same way, Communism is obviously not an exclusively Italian phenomenon even when confined to a Western European context.

The intervention of the Catholics in politics, on the other hand, marks a sharp distinction between the Italy of today and of 1900. And this is something that has not happened, or has happened only to a much lesser degree, in other countries, where the political strength of the Catholic parties may certainly be greater now than it used to be but without signifying so violent a contrast between the present and the past. After 1870, and up to the beginning of this century, the formula for Italian Catholics was *'né eletti, né elettori'* ('Neither elected nor electors'), in other words official abstension from the public life of the Italian State, which had been established not only apart from, but also in opposition to, the political power of the Papacy. When we recall that old formula and remember the active role of Christian Democracy and Catholic Action today, we realize at once how a new element has emerged in the life of this Italian State which has come successfully through its tribulations.

BIBLIOGRAPHY

BIBLIOGRAPHY[1]

1. WAR AND POST-WAR

A. *Diplomatic History.* A. Solmi, 'L'intervento italiano nella conflagrazione europa', in *Nuova Antologia*, LV, 1920; Id., 'Le origini del patto di Londra', in *Politica*, VI, 1923; G. Salvemini, *Dal Patto di Londra alla pace di Roma*, Turin 1925; M. Toscano, *Il patto di Londra*, Pavia 1931; F. Ruffini, 'Il potere temporale negli scopi di guerra degli ex imperi centrali', in *Nuova Antologia*, LVI, 1921; E. Vercesi, *Il Vaticano, l'Italia e la guerra*, Milan 1925; A. Palmieri, 'La spartizione dell'Asia Minore. La politica degli Alleati e l'Italia', in *Politica*, XI, 1928.

B. *Military Operations.* See especially A. Valori, *La guerra italo-austriaca*, 2nd ed., Bologna 1925; A. Tosti, *La guerra italo-austriaca*, Milan 1925; A. Gatti, *La parte dell'Italia*, Milan 1926; L. Segato, *L'Italia nella guerra mondiale*, 2 vols., Milan 1927; R. Bencivenga, *Saggio critico sulla nostra guerra*, Bari 1930; P. Maravigna, *Le undici offensive dell'Isonzo*, Rome 1928; *La guerra italiana nei giudizi stranieri*, preface by B. Mussolini to A. Alberti, Rome 1933.

C. *Internal History.* F. Meda, *I cattolici italiani nella guerra*, Milan 1921; A. Malatesta, *I socialisti italiani durante la guerra*, Milan 1926; A. Oberdorfer, *Il socialismo del dopoguerra a Trieste*, Florence 1922; G. De Rossi, *Il partito popolare italiano dalle origini al Congresso di Napoli*, Rome 1920; M. Missiroli, *Polemica liberale*, Bologna 1919; G. Ambrosini, *Partiti politici e gruppi parlamentari dopo la proporzionale*, Florence 1923 (see also U. Giusti, *Partiti politici e gruppi parlamentari dopo la proporzionale*, Florence 1921); A. Ferrari, 'Partiti ed uomini politici italiani nella guerra mondiale', in *Nuova rivista storica*, XIV, 1930.

D. *Economic and Social History.* See the volumes in the *Economic and Social History of the World War*, published under the auspices of the

---

[1] This bibliography, reprinted here with a few minor emendations, first appeared as the final part ('War and Post-war') of a bibliographical study which Professor Chabod wrote for the section on Italy in Vol. XIX of the *Enciclopedia italiana di lettere, scienze ed arti* (Rome 1933), p. 916 (reprinted ibid. 1949).

Carnegie Foundation; cf. also L. Einaudi, *La condotta economica e gli effetti sociali della guerra italiana*, Bari 1933. Also useful is E. Lémonon, *L'Italie d'après guerre* (1915–1921), Paris 1923. For the Fiume affair see A. Marpicati, *Fiume*, Florence 1931; S. Gigante, *Storia del comune di Fiume*, Florence 1928.

2. FASCISM

A. *General Works.* For the historical development of Fascism see in particular G. Volpe, in *Enciclopedia Italiana*, vol. XIV, pp. 851–78 (also published separately as Appendix in B. Mussolini, *La dottrina del Fascismo*, Milan-Rome 1932); Id., *Lo sviluppo storico del fascismo*, Palermo 1928; Id., *Guerra, dopoguerra, fascismo*, Venice 1928; G. Gentile, *Origini e dottrina del fascismo*, Rome 1929; Id., *Che cosa è il fascismo*, Florence 1925; F. Ercole, *Le origini dell'Italia fascista*, Rome 1925; Id., *Dal nazionalismo al fascismo*, Florence 1928; Id., 'Dal Risorgimento al fascismo', in *Annali istruzione media*, VIII, 1932. See also *Le origini e lo sviluppo del fascismo: dall' intervento alla marcia su Roma*, Rome 1928, ed. Partito Nazionale Fascista; G. Pini and F. Bresadola, *Storia del fascismo*, Rome 1928; G. A. Chiurco, *Storia della rivoluzione fascista*, 5 vols., Florence 1929, useful for the chronological aspect; A. Pagliaro, *Il fascismo: commento alla dottrina*, Rome 1933; M. Missiroli, *L'Italia d'oggi*, Bologna 1932; and the various studies collected in *La civiltà fascista*, introduction by B. Mussolini, edited by G. L. Pomba, Turin 1928.

Among the various biographies of Mussolini see M. Sarfatti, *Dux*, Milan 1926.

B. *The Fascist State.* A. Rocco, *La trasformazione dello stato. Dallo stato liberale allo stato fascista*, Rome 1927 (and C. Saltelli, *Potere esecutivo e norme giuridiche*, Rome 1926; N. Orsi, *Fascismo e legislazione fascista*, Milan 1928); *Il Gran Consiglio nei primi cinque anni dell'era fascista*, ed. PNF, Rome 1927; S. Panunzio, *Lo stato fascista*, Bologna 1925; G. Bortolotto, *Lo stato fascista e la nazione*, Rome 1931; Id., *Governanti e governati del nostro tempo*, Milan 1933.

C. *Financial Policy and Corporative Organisation.* L. Gangemi, *La politica economica e finanziaria del governo fascista nel periodo dei pieni poteri*, Bologna 1924; G. Volpi di Misurata, *Finanza fascista*, Rome 1928; A. De' Stefani, *La ricostruzione finanziaria*, Bologna 1926; C. Costamagna, *Diritto corporativo italiano*, Turin 1927; U. Spirito, *I fondamenti dell'economia corporativa*, Milan 1932; G. Bortolotto, *Lo stato e la dottrina corporativa*, 2 vols., Bologna 1932. On educational policy, see G. Gentile, *La riforma della scuola in Italia*, 2nd ed., Milan 1933.

D. *Opposition in the Early Period.* See L. Salvatorelli, *Nazional-*

fascismo, Turin 1923; G. Amendola, *Una battaglia liberale*, Turin 1924; I. Bonomi, *Dieci anni di politica italiana*, Milan 1923; Id., *Dal socialismo al fascismo*, Rome 1924.

E. *Foreign Policy*. A. Solmi, *Italia e Francia nei problemi attuali della politica europea*, Milan 1931. See also F. Coppola, *La rivoluzione fascista e la politica mondiale*, Rome 1924; G. Ambrosini, *L'Italia nel Mediterraneo*, Foligno 1927; R. Cantalupo, *L'Italia musulmana*, Rome 1928; C. Camoglio, *La politica estera fascista*, Rome 1931; A. Carena, *La politica estera del fascismo*, Rome 1928; Id., *La politica estera nel Mediterraneo orientale*, Rome 1931; U. Nani, *Italia e Jugoslavia* (1918–1928), Milan 1928; C. Curcio, 'L'Italia e l'Europa. Lincamenti dello sviluppo della politica italiana,' in *Raccolta di studi politici e giuridici*, I, Rome 1932; G. Volpe, in *Fra storia e politica*, Rome 1924.

ADDITIONAL BIBLIOGRAPHY[1]

1. General Works

G. Perticone, *La politica italiana nell'ultimo trentennio*, 3 vols., Rome, Ed. Leonardo, 1945 (vol. I covers the crisis of democracy, vol. II the period of the Fascist dictatorship, vol. III the years 1943–5); L. Salvatorelli and G. Mira, *Storia del fascismo. L'Italia dal 1919 al 1945*, Rome, Ed. Novissima, 1952, revised ed. under title *Storia d'Italia nel periodo fascista*, Turin, Einaudi, 1956; G. Carocci, *Storia del fascismo*, Milan, Garzanti, 1959; D. Mack Smith, *Italy. A Modern History*, The University of Michigan Press, Ann Arbor, 1959 (Italian translation under title *Storia d'Italia dal 1861 al 1958*, Laterza, Bari, 1959—cf. esp. Chs. IX–XII, pp. 477–762); *Storia d'Italia*, ed. N. Valeri, UTET, Turin, vol. V: *Dalla crisi del primo dopoguerra alla fondazione della Repubblica*, ed. by F. Catalano, 1960 (with full selected bibliography). G. A. Borgese, *Golia. Marcia del Fascismo*, Milan, Mondadori, 1946 (original ed., *Goliath*, New York, Viking Press, 1937) is of a literary and psychological rather than a historiographical character. Fascist works on the period of the régime include, in addition to those already cited in Chabod's bibliography (G. A. Chiurco, G. Volpe, F. Ercole, etc.), A. Tamaro, *Vent'anni di storia, 1922–1943*, Rome, Tosi, 1953; Id., *Due anni di storia 1943–1945*, 3 vols., Rome, Tosi, 1948–50.

For the essential international political background we confine ourselves to indicating the following recent general surveys: L. Salvatorelli, *Storia del novecento*, Milan, Mondadori, 1957; M. Crouzet, *L'époque contemporaine*, Paris, Presses Universitaires de France, 1957, Italian translation, Florence, Sansoni, 1959; M. Baumont, *La faillite de la paix* (1918–39), 2 vols., Paris, Presses Universitaires de France, 1951; *The Era of Violence*, 1898–1945, ed. D. Thomson, Cambridge University Press, 1960 (Cambridge Modern History, vol. XII); P. Renouvin, *Histoire des relations internationales. Les crises du XX⁰ siècle*, Paris 1957.

2. From the First World War to the Post-War Settlement

For bibliographical information, see essay by F. Curato, 'La storiografia delle origini della prima guerra mondiale', in *Questioni di storia contemporanea*, ed. by E. Rota, Milan, Marzorati, 1952, vol. I, pp. 393–530; also L. Valiani's documented survey, 'Recenti pubblicazioni sulla

---

[1] The following bibliographical note, compiled under the editorship of Sergio Caprioglio, makes no attempt to include all published works on the subject. Its aim is to provide a comprehensive survey of the works of historical criticism and the political publications dealing with Italian history from the First World War to the Liberation (with an Appendix covering the years 1945–48). Particular care has been taken to indicate works of a basic character (bibliographies, surveys, etc.) such as may serve the reader as a guide to the extensive existing literature on modern Italy.

prima guerra mondiale', in *Rivista storica italiana*, a. LXXII, 1960, fasc. III, pp. 445–79. No overall study exists on Italy's participation in the First World War; an acute survey of the period, P. Pieri's 'L'Italia nella prima guerra mondiale', is to be found in Vol. IV, pp. 680 et seq., of *Storia d'Italia*, ed. N. Valeri, 5 vols., Turin, UTET, 1959–60. On internal political aspects of Italian intervention see the essay (with good bibliography) by E. R. Rosen, 'Italiens Kriegseintritt im Jahre 1915 als innenpolitisches Problem der Giolitti-Aera. Ein Beitrag zur Vorgeschichte des Faschismus', in *Historische Zeitschrift*, no. 187/2, April 1959, pp. 289–363. On diplomatic aspects, see *Documenti diplomatici italiani*, series VI, 1918–22 (4 November 1918–17 January 1919), ed. R. Mosca; M. Toscano, *Il Patto di Londra. Storia diplomatica dell' intervento italiano* (1914–1915), 2nd ed., Bologna, Zanichelli, 1934; E. Serra, *Camille Barrère e l'Intesa italo-francese*, Milan, Giuffrè, 1950; cf. also G. Salvemini, 'Giolitti e il Patto di Londra', in *Quaderni di cultura e storia sociale*, 1953, nos. 7 and 8/9; 'Ancora su Giolitti e il Patto di Londra', letters by L. Salvatorelli and C. Spellanzon, in *Quaderni*, cit., 1953, no. 10; G. Natale, 'Le "giornate radiose" del maggio 1915', in *Quaderni*, cit., 1953, no. 11. On economic and social aspects, see A. Caracciolo, 'L'intervento italiano in guerra e la crisi politica del 1914–15', in *Società*, a. X, no. 5, October 1954, pp. 809–26, no. 6, December 1954, pp. 986–1012. For the interventionist standpoint see the extensive work, part-history part-memoirs, of A. Albertini, *Venti anni di vita politica*, part II, *L'Italia nella guerra mondiale*, 3 vols., Bologna, Zanichelli, 1951–53. On the state of mind of those who fought in the war, especially interventionist officers, see A. Omodeo, *Momenti della vita di guerra. (Dai diari e dalle lettere dei caduti)*, Bari, Laterza, 1934; a psychologically honest picture of life at the front is given in E. Lussu, *Un anno sull'altipiano*, new ed., Turin, Einaudi, 1960. On the Peace Conference of Paris basic works are R. Albrecht-Carrié, *Italy at the Paris Peace Conference*, New York, Columbia University Press, 1938; and F. S. Marston, *The Peace Conference of 1919. Organization and Procedure*, London, Oxford University Press, 1944 (with full bibliography); among works of Italian authors are S. Crespi, *Alla difesa dell' Italia in guerra e a Versailles*, Milan, Mondadori, 1937; A. Torre, *Versailles. Storia della Conferenza della Pace*, Milan, ISPI, 1940; F. Curato, *La Conferenza della Pace* (1919 1920), 2 vols., Milan, ISPI, 1942; and, in particular, the two volumes of A. Aldrovandi Marescotti, *Guerra diplomatica* (1914–1919), Milan, Mondadori, 1936; and *Nuovi ricordi*, Milan, Mondadori, 1938. For the democratic trends see L. Bissolati, *La politica estera dell'Italia dal 1897 al 1920*, Milan, Treves, 1923; G. Salvemini, *Dal Patto di Londra alla Pace di Roma. Documenti della politica che non fu fatta*, Turin, Gobetti, 1925. On D'Annunzio's Fiume venture and relations with Yugoslavia, see P. Alatri's detailed analysis,

Nitti, *D'Annunzio e la questione adriatica* (1919–1920), Milan, Feltrinelli, 1959; cf. also A. Giannini, *Documenti per la storia fra l'Italia e la Jugoslavia*, Rome, Istituto per l'Oriente, 1934; G. Ferrero, *Da Fiume a Roma*. *Storia di quattro anni* (1919–1923), Milan, Athena, 1945; P. Badoglio, *Rivelazioni su Fiume*, Rome, De Luigi, 1946; A. Caviglia, *Il Complotto di Fiume*, Milan, Garzanti, 1948; C. Sforza, *Jugoslavia*, Milan, Rizzoli, 1948; L. Federzoni, *Il Trattato di Rapallo*, Bologna, Zanichelli, 1921. Among collected speeches, memoirs, etc., are: G. Giolitti, *Memorie della mia vita*, 2 vols., Milan, Treves, 1922, 3rd ed., 1945; Id., *Discorsi parlamentari*, 4 vols., Rome, Tipografia della Camera dei Deputati, 1953–56 (v. in particular vols. III and IV, covering the years 1909–25); Id., *Discorsi extraparlamentari*, Turin, Einaudi, 1952 (with a long introductory essay by N. Valeri); A. Salandra, *La neutralità* (1914), Milan, Mondadori, 1928; Id., *L'intervento* (1915), Milan, Mondadori, 1930; Id., *Memorie politiche* (1916–1925), Milan, Garzanti, 1951; V. E. Orlando, *Discorsi per la pace e per la guerra*, ed. A. Giannini, Foligno, Campitelli, 1923; Id., *Memorie* (1915–1919), ed. R. Mosca, Milan, Rizzoli, 1960; T. Tittoni and V. Scialoja, *L'Italia alla conferenza della pace*, speeches and documents, ed. by A. Giannini, Rome, Libreria di Scienze e Lettere, 1921; F. S. Nitti, *Rivelazioni. Dramatis personae*, Naples, Edizioni Scientifiche Italiane, 1948; Id., *Scritti politici*, vols. I and II, Bari, Laterza, 1959 and 1961; M. Soleri, *Memorie*, Turin, Einaudi, 1949 (with preface by L. Einaudi); O. Malagodi, *Conversazioni della guerra* (1914–1918), ed. B. Vigezzi, 2 vols., Milan/Naples, Ricciardi, 1960. For democratic opinion on the problems of the peace, see, in addition to the works by Bissolati and Salvemini already cited, C. Sforza, *Pensiero e azione di una politica estera italiana*, speeches and writings of the years 1920–1, ed. A. Cappa, Bari, Laterza, 1923; Id., *L'Italia dal 1914 al 1944 quale io la vidi*, Rome, Mondadori, 1944. For nationalist opinion, see F. Coppola's three volumes in the 'Biblioteca' series of the review *Politica: La pace democratica*, *La fine dell'Intesa* and *La liquidazione della vittoria*, Bologna, n.d.; of E. Corradini's works v. esp. *L'unità e la potenza della nazione*, Florence, Vallecchi, 1922; *Scritti politici* (1902–1923), Florence, Vallecchi, n.d. (but 1923), and the anthology edited by G. Bellonci, *La rinascita nazionale*, Florence, Le Monnier, 1929; by M. Rocca, cf. *Il Trattato di Rapallo*, Milan 1921.

3. Benito Mussolini

Mussolini's collected writings, *Opera omnia di Benito Mussolini*, ed. E. and D. Susmel, Florence, La Fenice, 1951 ff. (in course of publication; by 1962 32 vols. had appeared). Biographies: Y. De Begnac, *Vita di Benito Mussolini*, 3 vols., Milan, Mondadori, 1936–40 (the main biography of Mussolini published under the Fascist régime); G. Megaro, *Mussolini in the Making*, London/New York 1938, Italian translation

Mussolini dal mito alla realtà, Milan, IEI, 1947 (deals with early period); G. Dorso, *Mussolini alla conquista del potere*, Turin, Einaudi, 1949; P. Monelli, *Mussolini piccolo borghese*, Milan, Garzanti, 1950, 4th ed. 1954 (a study of Mussolini the man, from a non-apologetic angle); P. Alatri, *Benito Mussolini* (*Note biografiche e bibliografiche*) in *Questioni di storia contemporanea*, ed. E. Rota, Milan, Marzorati, vol. III, pp. 759-96; G. Pini and D. Susmel, *Mussolini: L'uomo e l'opera*, 4 vols., Florence, La Fenice, 1954-56 (a Fascist attempt at dispassionateness).

4. *The Post-1918 Crisis and the Origins of Fascism*

A. *Bibliographies and surveys*: N. Valeri, 'Premessa ad una storia dell' Italia nel post-Risorgimento', in G. Pepe, F. Chabod, N. Valeri, D. Demarco, G. Luzzatto, *Orientamenti per la storia d'Italia nel Risorgimento*, Bari, Laterza, 1952, pp. 53-85; Id., 'Sulle origini del fascismo', in *Questioni di Storia contemporanea*, cit., 1953, vol. III, pp. 733-57; P. Alatri, 'Interventismo e fascismo nella recente storiografia', in *Le origini del fascismo*, Rome, ed. Riuniti, 1956, pp. 482-552; L. Valiani, 'Il movimento socialista in Italia dalle origini al 1921. Studi e ricerche nel ventennio 1937-1957', in *Questioni di storia del socialismo*, Turin, Einaudi, 1958 (v. esp. pp. 114-19 and, for bibliographical information, pp. 162-67); G. De Rosa, 'Considerazioni storiografiche sulla crisi dello Stato prefascista e sull'antifascismo', in *Il movimento di Liberazione in Italia*, no. 57, October-December 1959, fasc. 4, pp. 19-79.

B. *General Works*: A. Tasca, *La naissance du fascisme. L'Italie de 1918 à 1922*, Paris, Gallimard, 1938, Italian edition under title *Nascita e avvento del fascismo. L'Italia dal 1918 al 1922*, Florence, La Nuova Italia, 1950 (this edition contains extensive bibliographical notes not included in the original French edition); G. Salvemini, *L'Italia economica dal 1919 al 1922*, Milan, Giuffrè, 1950; P. Alatri, *Le origini del fascismo*, Rome, ed. Riuniti, 1956 (collected articles and essays previously published in the periodicals *Belfagor* and *Il Contemporaneo*, and in *Questioni di storia contemporanea*, vol. III); N. Valeri, *Da Giolitti a Mussolini. Momenti della crisi del liberalismo*, Florence, Parenti, 1956; A. Frassati, *Giolitti*, Milan 1959; N. Valeri, L. Salvatorelli, F. Schiavetti, A. Garosci, A. Spinelli, N. Chiaramonte, F. Parri, U. La Malfa, *Lezioni sull'antifascismo*, Bari, Laterza, 1960 (cf. in particular Lectures I, II, and III); and F. Delzell, 'Origini della resistenza antifascista in Italia', in *Il movimento di Liberazione in Italia*, no. 61, October/December 1960, fasc. 4, pp.3-43 (general survey of the policy of the anti-Fascist parties and groups between 1922 and 1926). A useful anthology, edited by N. Valeri, is entitled *La lotta politica in Italia dall'Unità al 1925. Idee e documenti*, Florence, Le Monnier, 1946, new ed. 1958.

C. Parties in the post-war crisis

The Fascist Party. In addition to the references given in Chabod's bibliography, see the following works by first-hand witnesses: D. Grandi, *Le origini del fascismo e la missione del fascismo*, Bologna, Cappelli, 1922 (one of the series 'Il fascismo e i partiti politici' in the 'Biblioteca di studi sociali' ed. by R. Mondolfo); G. Acerbo, *I primi tre anni della rivoluzione fascista*, Rome 1923; P. Gorgolini, *Il fascismo nella vita italiana*, with preface by B. Mussolini, Turin, ed. 'Italianissima', 1922; E. Paposogli, *Fascismo*, Florence, Vallecchi, 1923; *Panorami di realizzazione del fascismo*, Rome, Castaldi, 1942 (the two latter volumes contain extensive documentation on the activities of the Fascist squads); P. Pantaleo, *Il fascismo cremonese*, Cremona 1931; R. Farinacci, *Squadrismo. Dal mio diario della vigilia* (1919–1922), Rome, Ardita, 1933; Id., *Storia della rivoluzione fascista*, Cremona anno XVI (1938) (see vols. I and II; the real author of the book was P. Pantaleo); L. Balbo, *Diario 1922*, Milan, Mondadori, 1932.

Liberals and Democrats. The view taken of Fascism by the progressive wing of Italian Liberalism is to be found in the works of A. Amendola, P. Gobetti, L. Salvatorelli, and G. Dorso. By Amendola, see his speeches, *Una battaglia liberale. Discorsi politici* (1919–1923), Turin, Gobetti, 1924 (republished in *La nuova democrazia*, Milan/Naples, Ricciardi, 1951); *La democrazia italiana contro il fascismo 1922–1924*, Milan/Naples 1960 and the collection of letters recently published by his wife, E. Kühn Amendola, *Vita con Giovanni Amendola, Epistolario* (1903–26), Florence, Parenti, 1961. On Amendola see essay by G. Carocci, *Giovanni Amendola nella crisi dello Stato italiano* (1911–1925), Milan, Feltrinelli, 1956; also F. Rizzo, *Giovanni Amendola e la crisi della democrazia*, Rome, Centro Editoriale dell'Osservatore, 1956. The works of P. Gobetti, L. Salvatorelli, and G. Dorso come under the heading of historical and ideological criticism rather than of political propaganda in the strict sense. For Gobetti's standpoint, see *La rivoluzione liberale. Saggio sulla politica in Italia*, Bologna, Cappelli, 1924, new ed. Turin, Einaudi, 1948, and the *Antologia della Rivoluzione liberale*, ed. P. Valeri, Turin, De Silva, 1948. The complete edition of Gobetti's works is in course of publication by Einaudi; vol. I, which appeared in 1960, edited by P. Spriano, contains the political writings (*Scritti politici*). Similarly Feltrinelli is engaged in republishing the periodicals edited by Gobetti. On Gobetti see, among others, G. Carocci, 'Piero Gobetti nella storia del pensiero italiano', in *Belfagor*, a. VI, no. 2, 31 March 1951, pp. 129–48; N. Sapegno, 'Figure del primo antifascismo. L'insegnamento di P. Gobetti', in *Rinascita*, a. III, no. 7, July 1946, pp. 157–63; P. Spriano, introduction to the collected *Scritti politici* published by Einaudi (pp. xvii–l). By L. Salvatorelli, see especially, *Nazionalfascismo*, Turin, Gobetti, 1923; by G. Dorso, *La rivoluzione meridionale*, Turin, Gobetti, 1925, new ed. Rome, Einaudi, 1945; also on the relations between the South and Fascism, see T. Fiore, *Un popolo di formiche*, Bari, Laterza, 1951 (collected letters to P. Gobetti in 1925). On Sardinia, see E. Lussu, *Marcia su Roma e dintorni*, Rome, Einaudi, 1945, new ed. Milan/Rome, Ed. 'Avanti!', 1957. Lastly, see M. Missiroli, *Il fascismo e la crisi italiana*, Bologna, Cappelli, 1921; Id., *Una battaglia perduta*, Milan, Corbaccio, 1924. A photographic reproduction of *Non Mollare*, the first clandestine anti-Fascist newspaper (1925), was made in 1955; and an anthology compiled from the weekly periodical *Il Caffè* (1924-5), including articles by Bauer, Calamandrei, etc., appeared under the editorship of B. Ceva in 1961 (Milan, Lerici).

The Socialists. For a critical survey of the post-war situation from the Socialist angle see P. Nenni, *Storia di quattro anni* (1919-1922), Milan, Quarto Stato, 1927, new ed. Rome, Einaudi, 1946; Id., *Six ans de guerre civile en Italie*, Paris, Valois, 1930, Italian translation, Milan, Rizzoli, 1945. For the attitude of Reformist Socialism towards Fascism see vols. V and VI of the correspondence of F. Turati with A. Kuliscioff, *Dopoguerra e fascismo*, 1919-22 and *Il Delitto Matteotti e l'Aventino*, 1923-25, Turin, Einaudi, 1953 and 1959. In the series 'Il fascismo e i partiti politici', ed. by R. Mondolfo for the 'Biblioteca di studi sociali' of Cappelli, Bologna, see R. Mondolfo, *Per la comprensione storica del fascismo*, 1922; G. Zibordi, *Critica socialista del fascismo*, 1922. An extensive documentation on Fascist acts of violence is to be found in *Fascismo. Inchiesta sulle gesta dei fascisti in Italia*, Milan, ed. 'Avanti!', 1921, 2nd ed. 1922. On G. Matteotti and his anti-Fascist activities cf. *Reliquie*, Milan, Dall'Oglio, 1925, new ed. 1946; *Giacomo Matteotti contro il fascismo*, anthology ed. by A. Pagliuca, Milan/Rome, Ed. 'Avanti!', 1954. The publishing firm of Einaudi is preparing to bring out a complete edition of Matteotti's works. On Matteotti himself, in addition to the contemporary volume by P. Gobetti, *Matteotti*, Turin, Gobetti, 1924, new ed. Milan, Gentile, 1945, cf. A. Schiavi, *La vita e l'opera di Giacomo Matteotti*, Rome, Opere Nuove, 1957. Other works on the post-1918 crisis seen from the angle of individual authors include A. Labriola, *Le due polemiche. Fascismo e riformismo* (*Note*), Naples, Morano, 1924; Id., *Polemica antifascista*, Naples, Ceccoli, 1925; and the volume by the former Socialist I. Bonomi, *Dal socialismo al fascismo*, Rome, Formiggini, 1925, new ed. Milan, Garzanti, 1946 (cf. also Id., *La politica italiana dopo Vittorio Veneto*, Turin, Einaudi, 1953).

The Popolari. On the origins and birth of the Partito Popolare, see the general works by S. Jacini, E. Pratt Howard, De Rosa and Candeloro. A full survey of the studies on the subject is contained in the essay by L. Ambrosoli, 'Problemi della storia del Partito Popolare Italiano', in *Rivista storica del socialismo*, a. I, fasc. 4, October-December, 1958, pp. 443-62. For the Popolari's interpretation of the Fascist phenomenon, cf. esp. L. Sturzo, *La libertà in Italia*, Turin, Gobetti, 1925, and also Don Sturzo's writings and speeches contained in his *Popolarismo e fascismo*, Turin, Gobetti, 1924, and in *Pensiero antifascista*, Turin, Gobetti, 1925. All this material is now collected in L. Sturzo, *Il Partito popolare italiano*, 3 vols., Bologna, Zanichelli, 1956-7. Cf. also C. Degli Occhi, *Che cosa ho pensato del fascismo quando ero popolare*, Bologna, Cappelli, 1923.

The Communists. An extensive bibliography of the publications concerning the Communist Party, edited by S. Merli, appears in the *Annali* of the G. G. Feltrinelli Institute in Milan, vol. III, 1960. For the history of the Communist Party, cf. the following general works: 'Trenta anni di vita e di lotte del PCI', in *Quaderni di Rinascita*, no. 2, Rome 1951; P. Togliatti, *Il Partito comunista italiano*, Milan, Nuova Accademia, 1958; also the biographical notes *Conversando con Togliatti*, ed. M. and M. Ferrara, Rome, Cultura Sociale, 1954; definitely polemical points of view are expressed in G. Galli, *Storia del Partito comunista italiano*, Milan, Schwarz, 1958 (the first edition was of 1953, ed. F. Bellini and G. Galli) and A. Tasca, 'I primi dieci anni del PCI', in *Il Mondo*, 18-25 August, 1-8 and 15-22 September 1953. See also P. Togliatti, 'La formazione del gruppo dirigente del PCI nel 1923-24', in *Annali*, cit., pp. 388-529. On the origins, cf. P. Gobetti, 'Storia dei comunisti torinesi scritta da un liberale', in *Coscienza liberale e classe operaia*, Turin, Einaudi, 1951, pp. 217 et seq.; P. Spriano, *Torino operaia nella grande guerra* (1914-18), Turin, Einaudi, 1959; A. Romano, 'Antonio Gramsci tra la guerra e la rivoluzione', in *Rivista storica del socialismo*, a. I, fasc. 4, October-December 1958, pp. 405-32. In 1954 the publisher Einaudi embarked on the publication of A. Gramsci's works of the period before his arrest; cf., in chronological order, *Scritti giovanili* (1914-1918), 1958; *Sotto la Mole* (1916-1920), 1960; *L'Ordine Nuovo* (1919-1920), 1954. An anthology from the periodical *L'Ordine Nuovo* is in preparation, edited by P. Spriano, to be published by Einaudi. On Gramsci himself, and on his ideas at that time, cf. *Studi gramsciani*, records of a conference held in Rome on 11-13 January 1958, Rome, ed. Riuniti, 1958, and *La città futura*, Milan, Feltrinelli, 1959 (with frequent references to the subject of factory councils and Gramsci's views on them), also P. Togliatti, *Gramsci*, Florence, Parenti, 1955 (collected essays). The biography by L. Lombardo Radice and G. Carbone, *Vita di Antonio Gramsci*, Rome 1951, is now inadequate. Among first-hand accounts, of especial importance is that of M. Montagnana, *Ricordi di un operaio torinese*, Rome, Rinascita, 1952; cf. also B. Santhià, *Con Gramsci all'Ordine Nuovo*, Rome, ed. Riuniti, 1956.

Anarchists. By the chief exponent of the Italian anarchist movement, E. Malatesta, cf. his *Scritti*, ed. L. Fabbri, Geneva, ed. 'Il Risveglio', 3 vols., 1934-6 (the collection covers the years 1919-32). On Malatesta's attitude to Fascism, cf. L. Fabbri, *Malatesta. L'uomo e il pensiero*, Naples, Ed. RL, 1951 (esp. pp. 223-37). See also L. Fabbri, *Controrivoluzione preventiva*, Bologna, Cappelli, 1922; the memoirs of A.

Borghi, *Mezzo secolo di anarchia* (1898–1935), preface by G. Salvemini, Naples, ESI, 1954 (esp. pp. 223–300); and P. Masini, *Anarchici e comunisti nel movimento dei Consigli a Torino*, Turin 1951.

5. *Italy under Fascism*

A. *Economic and Social Problems.* There is no general work on the situation of the working classes under Fascism and the economic and and social policy of the régime. For the necessary statistical information, see R. Bachi, *L'Italia economica, Annuario della vita commerciale, industriale ecc.*, Città di Castello 1919–21; G. Mortara, *Prospettive economiche* (1921–1937), 16 vols., Città di Castello 1921–37, and *l'Annuario statistico italiano*. In the *Annali di statistica*, series VIII, vol. IX, Rome 1957, cf. 'Indagine statistica sullo sviluppo del reddito nazionale dell'Italia dal 1861 al 1946' (with bibliography). Among studies on particular subjects, cf. L. Rosenstock-Franck, *L'économie corporative fasciste en doctrine et en fait*, Paris; Id., *Les étapes de l'économie fasciste italienne*, Paris 1939; C. Pellizzi, *Una rivoluzione mancata*, Milan, Longanesi, 1949; P. Grifone, *Il capitale finanziario in Italia*, Turin, Einaudi, 1946; G. Salvemini, *Sotto la scure del fascismo*, Turin, De Silva, 1948 (first appeared in 1931; it examines the policy of the Fascist syndicates); F. Guarneri, *Battaglie economiche fra le due grandi guerre*, Milan, Garzanti, 1953; G. Gualerni, *La politica industriale fascista*, Milan 1956; E. Rossi, *Lo Stato industriale*, Bari, Laterza, 1953; Id., *I padroni del vapore*, 1955; D. Guerin, *Fascismo e gran capitale*, Milan, Schwarz, 1956; L. Valiani, 'Il movimento sindacale sotto il fascismo, 1929–1939', in *Dall'antifascismo alla Resistenza*, Milan, Feltrinelli, 1959, pp. 39–70; S. Merli, 'Corporativismo e illusioni riformistiche nei primi anni del regime', in *Rivista storica del socialismo*, a. II, fasc. 5, January–March 1959, pp. 121–37.

B. *Religious Policy.* On relations between the Church and Fascism, and on the Lateran Pacts, cf. the relevant sections in A. C. Jemolo's standard work, *Stato e Chiesa in Italia negli ultimi cento anni*, Turin, Einaudi, 1949, 4th ed. 1955 (esp. Chs. VI and VII, pp. 485–686, with bibliography), and the very full account in Salvatorelli and Mira, *Storia d'Italia nel periodo fascista*, cited above (esp. pp. 419–505); also M. Missiroli, *Date a Cesare. La politica religiosa di Mussolini*. Rome [1929]; V. E. Orlando, *Su alcuni miei rapporti di governo con la Santa Sede*, Naples 1930, 2nd ed. Milan/Rome 1944; L. Salvatorelli, *La politica della Santa Sede dopo la guerra* [1937]; Id., *Pio XI e la sua eredità pontificale*, Turin, Einaudi, 1939. On the position of the Communists in 1929 concerning the problem of relations between State and Church, cf. essay by P. Togliatti, 'Fine della questione romana', in *Rinascita*, June 1948 (the essay is of 1929).

C. *Foreign Policy*. Italian Ministry of Foreign Affairs, *I documenti diplomatici italiani*, series VII (ed. R. Moscati), vols. I, II, III (covering the years 1922–25), series VIII (ed. M. Toscano), vols. XII, XIII (1939), series XI (ed. M. Toscano), vols. I, II (1939), Rome 1952 et seq. On the first phases of Fascist foreign policy, cf. R. Moscati, 'La politica estera del fascismo. L'esordia del primo ministero Mussolini', in *Studi politici*, September 1953–February 1954; Id., 'La politica estera fascista nel 1924–25', in *Rivista storica italiana*, 1959. The latest general study is E. Di Nolfo, *Mussolini e la politica estera italiana (1919–1933)*, Padua, Cedam, 1960; M. Missiroli, *La politica estera. Dalla marcia su Roma a Monaco*, Milan 1939; on the characteristics of the Duce's foreign policy, cf. G. Salvemini, *Mussolini diplomatico (1922–1932)*, Bari, Laterza, 1952 (the 1st ed. is of 1932); M. Donosti, *Mussolini e l'Europa. La politica estera fascista*, Rome, Ed. Leonardo, 1945; L. Salvatorelli, *Il fascismo nella politica internazionale*, Modena/Rome 1946. On Fascist policy at Geneva, cf. E. Reale, *La politique fasciste et la Société des Nations*, Paris 1932; Id., *La politique étrangère du fascisme dès les accords de Rome à la proclamation de l'Empire*, Paris 1938; also S. Trentin, *Le fascisme à Genève*, Paris 1932. For Mussolini's attitude to Austria, cf. J. Braunthal, *La Tragedia dell'Austria*, Florence, La Nuova Italia, 1955. Among memoirs, cf. those of A. Salandra (Italian delegate at Geneva), *Memorie politiche*, Milan, Garzanti, 1951, and R. Guariglia, *Ricordi (1922–1946)*, Naples 1950. On the Abyssinian venture, cf. P. Badoglio, *La guerra d'Etiopia*, Milan, Mondadori, 1936; E. Del Bono, *La conquista dell'Impero*, Rome 1936; R. Graziani, *Fronte Sud*, Milan, Mondadori, 1939.

D. *The Police Régime*. For testimonies of anti-Fascists imprisoned during the régime, cf. *Carceri, esperienze e documenti*, special number of *Il Ponte*, anno V, March 1949. A. Gramsci's *Lettere dal carcere*, Turin, Einaudi, 1947 (vol. I of the *Opere* of A. Gramsci) occupy a special place of their own. Cf. also C. Levi, *Cristo si è fermato a Eboli*, Turin, Einaudi, 1947; M. Giua, *Ricordi di un ex detenuto politico (1935–1943)*, Turin, Chiantore, 1945; B. Ceva, 1930. *Retroscena di un dramma*, Milan, Ceschina, 1945; A. Gavagnin, *Una lettera al re*, new ed., Milan/Rome, Ed. 'Avanti!', 1960; A. Colombi, *Nelle mani del nemico*, Rome, Ed. Rinascita, 1950; F. F. Nitti, *Le nostre prigioni e la nostra evasione*, Naples, ESI, 1946 (1st ed. is of 1930); A. Jacometti, *Ventotene*, Verona, Mondadori, 1947; B. Allason, *Memorie di un'antifascista (1919–1940)*, Rome/Florence/Milan, Ed. U, n. d. (but 1946); R. Morandi, *Lettere al fratello (1937–1943)*, Turin, Einaudi, 1959. On the police régime established under Fascism, cf. *La pupilla del regime*, Modena, Guanda, 1956; *Una spia del regime*, Milan, Feltrinelli, 1955, both ed. by E. Rossi; G. Leto, *OVRA, fascismo, antifascismo*, Bologna, Cappelli, 1951.

E. *Fascism and Culture.* Cf. F. Flora, *Ritratto di un ventennio*, Naples 1944; L. Lombardo Radice, *Fascismo e anticomunismo. Appunti e ricordi* (1935–1945), Turin, Einaudi, 1946; E. Garin, *Cronache di filosofia italiana* (1900–1943), Bari, Laterza, 1955; E. R. Papa, *Storia di due manifesti. Il fascismo e la cultura italiana*, Milan, Feltrinelli, 1958; V. Gerratana, introduction to G. Pintor, *Il sangue d'Europa*, Turin, Einaudi, 1950. On the Fascist 'way of life', cf. special number of *Il Ponte, Trent' anni dopo*, October 1952.

6. *Opposition in Exile*

A. *Bibliographies and Surveys.* M. Cantarella, 'Guida bibliografica degli scrittori italiani in esilio (1925–1945)' in *Belfagor*, a. IV, no. 3, 31 May 1949, pp. 338–50; G. S. Spinetti, *Bibliografia degli esuli politici sotto il fascismo*, Rome, Ed. di Solidarismo, 1959 (contains many references but is inaccurate); a vast *Guida bibliografica dell'antifascismo e della Resistenza* is in preparation under the auspices of the R. Morandi Institute; M. Bendiscioli, 'Presupposti metodologici della ricostruzione storica della Resistenza', in *Il movimento di Liberazione in Italia*, no. 52–53, July–December 1948, fasc. 3–4, pp. 72–92; G. De Rosa, 'Considerazioni storiografiche sulla crisi dello Stato prefascista e sull' antifascismo', in *Il movimento di Liberazione in Italia*, no. 57, October–December 1959, fasc. 4, pp. 17–79.

B. *General Works.* A. Gar[osci], 'L'emigrazione politica italiana durante il fascismo', article in the *Enciclopedia italiana di lettere, scienze ed arti*, second supplement (1938–48), Rome 1949, vol. 1, pp. 114–16; C. F. Delzell, 'Il fuoruscitismo italiano dal 1922 al 1943', in *Il movimento di Liberazione in Italia*, March 1953, pp. 3–37; A. Garosci, *Storia dei fuorusciti*, Bari, Laterza, 1953 (a basic work, containing extensive bibliographical notes); L. Salvatorelli, 'L'opposizione democratica durante il fascismo', in *Il secondo Risorgimento*, Istituto Poligrafico dello Stato, 1955, pp. 97–180; N. Valeri, L. Salvatorelli, F. Schiavetti, A. Garosci, A. Spinelli, N. Chiaramonte, F. Parri, U. La Malfa, *Lezioni sull'antifascismo*, Bari, Laterza, 1960 (v. esp. Lectures IV, V, and VI; selected bibliography at end of each lecture).

C. *Parties and Movements among the anti-Fascist Emigrés*

Giustizia e Libertà. For the history of the 'Giustizia e Libertà' movement, founded in 1929 and associated with the names of the Rosselli brothers, Salvemini, and P. Gobetti, cf. esp. C. Rosselli, *Socialismo liberale*, Paris, Ed. GL, n. d. (but 1930), new Italian edn. Rome/Florence/Milan, Ed. U, 1945; *Oggi in Spagna, domani in Italia*, preface by G. Salvemini, Paris, Ed. GL, 1939; *Scritti politici e autobiografici*, preface by G. Salvemini, Naples, Polis, 1944. Articles by Carlo

Rosselli also appeared in the periodical *La Libertà*, the weekly *Giustizia e Libertà*, and the *Quaderni di Giustizia e Libertà*; the latter, originally published in Paris between March 1932 and January 1935, have been reprinted in facsimile (Turin, Bottega d'Erasmo, 1959). A complete edition of Carlo Rosselli's works, edited by A. Garosci, is in preparation, to be published by Einaudi. For Rosselli's life, and also for the story of the 'Giustizia e Libertà' movement, see A. Garosci, *La vita di Carlo Rosselli*, 2 vols., Rome/Florence/Milan, Ed. U, n. d. (but 1946—a basic work), to be supplemented by A. Levi, *Ricordo dei fratelli Rosselli*, Florence, La Nuova Italia, 1947. By Salvemini, in addition to the works already cited, see *The Fascist Dictatorship in Italy*, New York, H. Holt, 1927, enlarged ed. London, Cape, 1928, Italian translation, New York, Libreria del 'Nuovo Mondo', 1929; *La terreur fasciste* (1922–1926), Paris, Gallimard, 1930; and, in collaboration with G. La Piana, *What to do with Italy*, New York, Duell Sloan and Pearce, 1943, Italian translation, *La sorte dell'Italia*, Rome/Florence/Milan, Ed. U, 1945. Among accounts by members of the 'Giustizia e Libertà' movement the most important is Salvemini's *Memorie di un fuoruscito* (Milan, Feltrinelli, 1960). On the ventures of Bassanesi and De Bosis, inspired by 'Giustizia e Libertà', cf. L. de Bosis, *Storia della mia morte e ultimi scritti*, preface by G. Salvemini, Turin, De Silva, 1948; on De Rosa's attempt on Prince Umberto in Brussels, cf. *Le procès De Rosa. Dépositions, plaidoiries et jugement*, Paris, Valois, 1930. A. Garosci gives a short biographical profile of De Rosa in *No al fascismo*, Turin, Einaudi, 1957, pp. 129–58. Cf. also E. Lussu, *La catena*, Rome/Florence/Milan, Ed. U, 1945; Id., *Diplomazia clandestina* (14 Giugno 1940—25 Luglio 1943), Florence, La Nuova Italia, 1956; J. Lussu, *Fronti e frontiere*, Bergamo, Ed. U, 1945; F. F. Nitti, *Le nostre prigioni e la nostra evasione*, Naples, ESI, 1946; A. Gavagnin, *Vent'anni di resistenza al fascismo*, Turin, Einaudi, 1957 (Gavagnin was head of the 'Giovane Italia' group, an organization which preceded 'Giustizia e Libertà'). A valuable anthology including writings by U. Calosso, A. Garosci, G. Salvemini, C. Rosselli, E. Rossi, etc., edited by E. Rossi, appears under the title of *No al fascismo*, already cited. For changes in the movement after 1936 and for the birth of a 'post-Fascist anti-Fascism' in Italy, cf. A. Capitini, 'Liberalsocialismo nel 1937', in *Mercurio*, 1945; Id., 'Un'esperienza religiosa dell'antifascismo', in *Il movimento di Liberazione in Italia*, no. 33, November 1954, pp. 60–64; also G. Calogero, *Difesa del liberalsocialismo*, Rome, De Luigi, 1945.

Socialists. There is no general study of Socialist emigration or, more particularly, of the reconstruction and activity of the Socialist Party abroad. This gap is partially filled by vol. II of the *Storia dell'Avanti!*, by G. Arfè, Milan/Rome, Ed. 'Avanti!', 1959, dealing with the years of exile (1927–40). On F. Turati's escape from Italy, cf. C. Rosselli, *Come Turati lasciò l'Italia* (published in *La Libertà* [Paris], 14 April 1932 and reprinted in C. Rosselli, *Scritti politici e autobiografici*, pp. 17-27). On Turati's exile in Paris, cf. A. Schiavi, *Esilio e morte di F. Turati*, Rome, Opere Nuove, 1956. Collections of writings by Socialists in exile are few in number and hitherto very incomplete; among them cf. C. Treves, *Il fascismo nella letteratura antifascista dell'esilio*, Rome, Opere Nuove, 1953 (covering 1928-33); B. Buozzi, *Scritti dell'esilio*, Rome, Opere Nuove, 1958. On Buozzi cf. the biography by G. Castagno, *B. Buozzi*, Milan/Rome, Ed. 'Avanti!', 1955. Information on the activities of the Socialist émigrés is also to be found in the memoirs of V. Modigliani, *Esilio*, Milan, Garzanti, 1946; P. Nenni, *Pagine di diario*, Garzanti, 1947; Id., *Taccuino 1942*, Milan/Rome, Ed. 'Avanti!', 1954; A. Balabanoff, *Ricordi di una socialista*, Rome, De Luigi, 1946; P. Treves, *Quello che ci ha fatto Mussolini*, Rome, Einaudi, 1945 (English ed. *Italy, Yesterday, Today, Tomorrow*, London 1940). Among the anti-Fascists who stayed on in Italy and grew to maturity after Fascism came into power, an outstanding name is that of R. Morandi, who abandoned his youthful republicanism for Socialism during the dictatorship; a complete collection of his writings is now available, *Opere di Rodolfo Morandi*, Turin, Einaudi, 1958 ff: of particular interest are vols. I, *La democrazia del socialismo* (1923-1937), III, *Lettere al fratello* (1937-1943), and IV, *Lotta di popolo* (1937-1945). On Morandi, cf. essay by S. Merli, 'La formazione culturale e politica di Rodolfo Morandi (1923-1933)', in *Rivista storica del socialismo*, a. I, no. 3, July-September 1958, pp. 169-209, and chronology in the volume *La democrazia del socialismo* (1923-1937), pp. XVII-LXXIV.

Communists. Documentation on the history of the Communist Party during the period of the dictatorship and of clandestine activity in Italy is still scarce. For those years the student should refer to the general works cited above, especially to Part II of *Quaderni di Rinascita*, no. 2 (*Il partito comunista nel periodo della organizzazione del regime fascista*, 1923-29), and to *Conversando con Togliatti*. A very important source is the periodical *Lo Stato operaio*, the theoretical organ of the Italian Communist Party in exile, which appeared in Paris from 1927 onwards. For relations with the Communist International, cf. a very useful collection of documents edited by J. Degras, *The Communist International 1919-1943. Documents*, vol. II, 1923-28, London, Oxford University Press, 1960. On the position of the Communists in relation to Fascism in the first years of the clandestine struggle, cf. Ercoli [P. Togliatti], 'A proposito del fascismo', in *Società*, a. VII, no. 4, December 1952, pp. 591-613 (an essay which appeared in 1928 in the Russian edition of the periodical *Communist International*).

For this period cf. also D. Zucàro, *Vita del carcere di Antonio Gramsci*, Milan/Rome, Ed. 'Avanti!', 1954. Between 1947 and 1951 Einaudi published Gramsci's letters and writings while in prison (*Opere di Antonio Gramsci*). For further information see the Bibliographical Note on Gramsci by G. Carbone, in *Società*, 1951, no. 1, and the bibliography attached to C. L. Ottino's *Concetti fondamentali della teoria politica di A. Gramsci*, Milan, Feltrinelli, 1956, pp. 148–51.

Catholics. The activities of anti-Fascist Catholics are especially associated with the names of Don Luigi Sturzo, F. L. Ferrari, and G. Donati. By Don Sturzo, see *La mia battaglia a New York*, Milan, Garzanti, 1949; Id., *Italy and Fascism*, London, Faber and Gwyer, 1926; Id., *L'Italia e i nuovi ordini internazionali*, Rome, Einaudi, 1944; by F. L. Ferrari, cf. *Le régime fasciste italien*, Paris, Spes, 1928; by G. Donati, cf. *Scritti politici*, 2 vols., Rome, Ed. Cinque Lune, 1956.

7. *The Spanish War and the Exiles*

A balanced introduction to the problems of the Spanish civil war will be found in G. Brenan, *The Spanish Labyrinth. An Account of the Social and Political Background of the Civil War*, Cambridge University Press, 1960 (1st ed. 1943; with full selected bibliography). For other works by non-Italians (essays, memoirs, etc.) see bibliographical guide by G. Rovida, 'La guerra civile spagnola. Problemi storici e orientamenti bibliografici', in *Rivista storica del socialismo*, a. II, no. 6, April–June 1959, pp. 265–94. The most recent and complete account of the civil war is H. Thomas, *The Spanish Civil War*, London, Eyre and Spottiswoode, 1961 (also in Italian translation). On the participation of Italian exiles in the war and in the international brigades, cf. R. Pacciardi, *Il battaglione Garibaldi*, new ed., Rome, 'La lanterna', 1945; L. Longo, *Le brigate internazionali in Spagna*, Rome, Ed. Riuniti, 1956; L. Valiani, *Le brigate internazionali in Spagna*, in *Dall'antifascismo alla Resistenza*, Milan, Feltrinelli, 1959, pp. 71–87; for the Socialists, cf. P. Nenni, *Spagna*, Milan/Rome, Ed. 'Avanti!', 1958 (collected articles, notes, etc.); for 'Giustizia e Libertà', cf. C. Rosselli, *Oggi in Spagna, domani in Italia*, Paris, Ed. GL, 1938; F. F. Nitti, *Il maggiore è un rosso*, Milan/Rome, Ed. 'Avanti!', 1955; for the Communists, cf. Ercoli [Togliatti], 'Sulle particolarità della rivoluzione spagnola', in *Stato Operaio*, November 1936; for the anarchists, cf. C. Berneri, *Guerre de classe en Espagne*, Paris 1938. For the attitude of intellectuals to the war, cf. C. Garosci, *Gli intellettuali e la guerra di Spagna*, Turin, Einaudi, 1959 (with full bibliography). For the official point of view of the Italian Government, cf. A. Bollati—G. Del Bono, *La guerra civile in Spagna*, Turin, Einaudi, 1937–39; F. Belforte, *La guerra civile in Spagna*, Milan, ISPI, 1938–9, 4 vols.; for international repercussions, see R. Cantalupo, *Fu la Spagna*, Milan, Mondadori, 1948.

8. *The Second World War and the Resistance*

A. *Bibliographies and Surveys*. F. Ravà and G. Spini, 'Fonti documentarie e memorialistiche per la storia della crisi dello Stato italiano

(1940-1945)', in *Rivista storica italiana*, a. LXI, 1949, fasc. 3, pp. 401-31, fasc. 4, pp. 574-602; *Saggio bibliografico sulla seconda guerra mondiale*, Rome, ed. Ufficio storico del Ministero della Difesa, 1949 (*Supplemento*, 1951); M. Toscano, *Fonti documentarie e memorialistiche per la storia diplomatica della seconda guerra mondiale*, in *Questioni di storia contemporanea*, cited above, vol. I, pp. 531-92.

B. *General Works*. G. Gigli, *La seconda guerra mondiale*, Bari, Laterza, 1951; R. Battaglia, *La seconda guerra mondiale*, Rome, Ed. Riuniti, 1960 (with selected bibliography). On the German-Italian alliance, or rather the alliance between the Nazi and Fascist régimes (the Axis), cf. E. Wiskemann, *The Rome-Berlin Axis: A History of the Relations between Hitler and Mussolini*, London, Oxford University Press, 1949 (Italian translation, 1955). On the 'Pact of Steel', cf. M. Toscano, *Le origini diplomatiche del patto d'acciaio*, Florence, Sansoni, 2nd rev. ed. 1956. Among memoirs and diaries, cf. in particular G. Ciano, *Diario* 1937-38, Bologna, Cappelli, 1948; Id., *Diario*, I (1939-40), II (1941-43), Milan/Rome, Rizzoli, 5th ed. 1950; C. Favagrossa, *Perché perdemmo la guerra*, Milan, Rizzoli, 1946; M. Roatta, *Otto milioni di baionette*. *L'esercito italiano in guerra dal 1940 al 1944*, Milan, Rizzoli, 1946; U. Cavallero, *Comando supremo*, Bologna, Cappelli, 1946; P. Badoglio, *L'Italia nella seconda guerra mondiale*, Milan, Mondadori, 1946; Hitler-Mussolini, *Lettere e documenti*, Milan, Rizzoli, 1946 (contains an incomplete collection of the letters exchanged between Hitler and Mussolini from 1939 to 1943); *L'Europa verso la catastrofe. 184 colloqui con Mussolini, Hitler, Franco, etc. . . . verbalizzati da G. Ciano*, Milan, Mondadori, 1948; M. Magistrati, *L'Italia a Berlino* (1938-39), Milan, Mondadori, 1956.

9. *The Armed Resistance* (1943-5)

A. *Bibliography and Surveys*. *Bibliografiia storica nazionale*, 1943-6, Rome, ed. Giunta centrale per gli Studi storici, 1949 (cf. nos. 3863-4016, pp. 173-79, covering the Resistance); *Resistenza. Panorama bibliografico*, ed. A. Bartolini, G. Mazzon, L. Mercuri, Trapani, 1957; 'La storiografia della Resistenza e i suoi problemi metodologici', records of a Study Conference, Milan, 14 December 1952, in *Il movimento di Liberazione in Italia*, no. 22, January 1953; R. Battaglia, 'La storiografia della Resistenza. Dalla memorialistica al saggio storico', in *Il movimento di Liberazione in Italia*, no. 57, October-December 1959, fasc. 4, pp. 80-131; *La Resistenza in Italia, 25 luglio 1943-25 aprile 1945*, bibliographical essay ed. by L. Conti, Milan, Feltrinelli, 1961 (contains a vast list of newspapers and manifestoes printed in the maquis).

B. *General Works*. L. Longo, *Un popolo alla macchia*, Milan, Mondadori, 1947 (with bibliography); M. Niccoli, *La Resistenza italiana*, article in the *Enciclopedia italiana di lettere, scienze ed arti*, second supplement (1938–48), Rome 1949, vol. II, pp. 686–91; G. Vaccarino, 'Le mouvement de Libération nationale en Italie (1943–1945)' in *Cahiers d'Histoire de la guerre*, no. 3, Paris, February 1950, pp. 77–112; R. Battaglia, *Storia della Resistenza italiana* (8 *settembre* 1943–25 *aprile* 1945), Turin, Einaudi, 1953 (with extensive selected bibliography); M. Salvadori, *Brief History of the Patriot Movement in Italy*, 1943–1945, Chicago, Clements & Sons, 1954, It. revised translation, Venice, Neri Pozza, 1955; R. Battaglia and G. Garritano, *Breve storia della Resistenza italiana*, Turin 1955; R. Carli Ballola, *Storia della Resistenza*, Rome/Milan, Ed. 'Avanti!', 1957. For the Fascist point of view on the years 1943–5 and the history of the Salò Republic, cf. E. Cione, *Storia della Repubblica sociale italiana*, Caserta, Ed. 'Il cenacolo,' 1948; A. Tamaro, *Due anni di storia*, 1943–1945, 3 vols., Rome, Tosi, 1948–50.

C. *Political and Ideological Aspects of the Resistance*. A. Galante Garrone, 'Aspetti politici della guerra partigiana in Italia', in *L'Acropoli*, vol. II, no. 16, April 1946, pp. 149–64; R. Battaglia, 'Il problema politico della Resistenza', in *Società*, a. IV, no. 1, January-February 1948, pp. 64–87; Id., 'Il significato nazionale della Resistenza', in *Società*, a. VI, no. 2, June 1950, pp. 193–211; M. Bendiscioli, *La Resistenza: gli aspetti politici*, in *Il secondo Risorgimento*, op. cit., pp. 293–366 (with full bibliography); L. Valiani, *Il problema politico della Nazione italiana*, in *Dieci anni dopo* (1945–1955). *Saggi sulla vita democratica italiana*, Bari 1955, pp. 3–112; C. Pavone, 'Le idee della Resistenza. Antifascisti e fascisti di fronte alla tradizione del Risorgimento', in *Passato e Presente*, no. 7, January-February 1959, pp. 850–918; L. Valiani, *La Resistenza e la questione istituzionale*, in *Dall'antifascismo alla Resistenza*, op. cit., 1959, pp. 100–51.

D. *The CNLs and the anti-Fascist Parties*. For the part played by the CNLs cf. P. Calamandrei, 'Funzione rivoluzionaria dei Comitati di Liberazione', in *Il Ponte*, a. I, no. 2, May 1945; M. Delle Piane, *Funzione storica dei Comitati di Liberazione Nazionale*, Florence 1946; I. Bonomi, *Diario di un anno* (2 *giugno* 1943–10 *giugno* 1944), Milan, Garzanti, 1947; F. Catalano, *Storia del CLNAI*, Bari, Laterza, 1956 (basic, with full bibliographical appendix). On the reorganization of the anti-Fascist parties in 1942–3, cf. *La crisi italiana del 1943 e gli inizi della Resistenza*, records of Second Congress of Studies on the History of the Liberation Movement, in *Il movimento di Liberazione in Italia*, 1955, nos. 33–35, fasc. 1–2. On the earliest risings among the workers, cf. G. Vaccarino, *Gli scioperi del marzo 1943*, in *Aspetti della Resistenza in Piemonte*, Turin 1950, pp. 3–40. On political life in the South after 8 September 1943, cf. A. Degli Espinosa, *Il Regno del Sud 1943–1944*, Rome 1946; new ed. Florence 1955.

BIBLIOGRAPHY

Communist Party. Cf. P. Togliatti, *Per la salvezza del nostro paese,* Turin, Einaudi, 1946 (articles, speeches, etc., from 1941 to 1945); *Il Partito comunista contro la guerra, contro il fascismo, per la libertà, per la democrazia, per l'indipendenza d'Italia,* report of the Party Directorate to the 5th Congress, Rome, L'Unità, 1945; L. Longo, *Sulla via dell'insurrezione nazionale,* Rome, Cultura Sociale, 1954; P. Secchia, *I comunisti e l'insurrezione* (1943–1945), Rome, Cultura Sociale, 1954; 25 *aprile* 1945, special number of *Rinascita,* a. XII, no. 4, April 1955, on the tenth anniversary of the Resistance.

Action Party. Cf. A. Monti, *Realtà del Partito d'Azione,* Turin, Einaudi, 1945; G. Pischel, *Che cosa è il Partito d'Azione. Dottrina ed esperienza storica di un nuovo Partito e sue direttive per l'avvenire,* Milan, A. Tarantola, 1945; L. Valiani, *Tutte le strade conducono a Roma,* Florence, La Nuova Italia, 1947; *Una lotta nel suo corso. Lettere e documenti politici e militari della Resistenza e della Liberazione,* ed. S. Contini Bonacossi and L. Collobi Ragghianti, Venice, Neri Pozza, 1954; C. L. Ragghianti, *Disegno della Liberazione italiana,* Pisa, Nistri-Lischi, 1954; A. Omodeo, *Libertà e storia. Scritti e discorsi politici,* introduction by A. Galante Garrone, Turin, Einaudi, 1960.

Socialist Party. Cf. *Politica del Partito socialista,* n. p., Ed. 'Avanti!', n. d. Part of the same documentary material appears in *Cinque anni di politica unitaria. Documenti del P.S.I. dal* 1943 *al* 1948, a. II, nos. 1–2, 1948; R. Morandi, *Lotta di popolo* (1937–1945), Turin, Einaudi, 1958.

Liberal Party. Cf. B. Croce, *Pagine politiche. Luglio–dicembre* 1944, Bari, Laterza, 1945; Id., *Quando l'Italia era tagliata in due (settembre* 1943–*giugno* 1944), Bari, Laterza, 1946; M. Soleri, *Memorie,* op. cit. (esp. pp. 230–335).

Christian Democracy. Cf. A. Marazza, 'La democrazia cristiana nella lotta', in *Mercurio,* a. II, no. 16, December 1945; G. Rossini, *Il fascismo e la Resistenza,* Rome, Ed. Cinque Lune, 1955.

Regular Army. Cf. esp. R. Cadorna, *La riscossa. Dal* 25 *luglio alla liberazione,* Milan, Rizzoli, 1948; A. Trabucchi, *I vinti hanno sempre torto,* Turin, De Silva, 1947; C. Primieri, *La Resistenza. Il contributo delle forze armate alla Liberazione,* in *Il secondo Risorgimento,* op. cit., pp. 181–261.

E. *The Partisan War in the Various Regions.* Cf. C. Barbagallo, *Napoli contro il terrore nazista,* Naples, Maone, n.d. (but 1943); 25 *aprile. La Resistenza in Piemonte,* ed. ANPI, Turin, Orma, 1946; A. Azzari, *L'Ossola nella Resistenza italiana,* Domodossola, La Cartografica Antonioli, 1954; A. Malgeri, *L'occupazione di Milano e la liberazione,* Milan, Ed. Associati, 1947; essays by M. Giovana on the Resistance in Piedmont from 1943 to the Liberation, in *Il movimento di Liberazione in Italia* (no. 38–9, September–November 1955, pp. 3–30; no. 41, March 1956, pp. 3–36; no. 44–5, September–November 1956, pp. 3–19; no.

48, July-September 1957, pp. 3-30; no. 49, October-December 1957, pp. 3-29); R. Luraghi, *Il movimento operaio torinese durante la Resistenza*, Turin, Einaudi, 1958; R. Cessi, *La Resistenza nel Bellunese*, n.p., Ed. Riuniti, 1960. For relations between the partisan movement and the Allies, cf. N. Kogan, *Italy and the Allies*, Cambridge, Mass., Harvard University Press, 1956, and, in particular, C. R. S. Harris, *Allied Military Administration of Italy, 1943-1945*, London, HMSO, 1957; also reports of F. Parri and F. Venturi, *La Resistenza italiana e gli Alleati*, to the Second International Congress on the History of the European Resistance Movements (Milan, 26-29 March 1961; v. also reports given at the same Congress by N. Kogan, W. Deakin, and E. Boltin).

F. *Diaries and First-Hand Accounts*. D. Livio Bianco, 'Venti mesi di guerra partigiana nel Cuneese', in *Nuovi Quaderni di Giustizia e Libertà*, no. 5-6, January-August 1945, pp. 13-98; new ed., Cuneo, Panfilo, 1945, and Turin, Einaudi, 1954 (under title *Guerra partigiana*); P. Levi Cavaglione, *Guerriglia nei Castelli Romani*, Rome, Einaudi, 1945; G. B. Lazagna [Carlo], *Ponte rotto. Storia della divisione garibaldina 'Pinan Cichero'*, Genoa, Ed. del Partigiano, 1946; G. Pesce, *Soldati senza uniforme* (*Diario di un gappista*), Rome, Cultura Sociale, 1950; A. Gobetti, *Diario partigiano*, Turin, Einaudi, 1956; P. Secchia and C. Moscatelli, *Il Monte Rosa è sceso a Milano. La Resistenza nel Biellese, nella Valsesia e nella Valdossola*, Turin, Einaudi, 1958.

G. *Anthologies. La résistance italienne*, Milan, ed. Corpo Volontari della Libertà, 1947 (with numerous photographs); L. Sturani, *Antologia della Resistenza*, Turin, Centro del Libro Popolare, 1951 (Part II, pp. 78-388, deals with the Armed Resistance); *Lettere di condannati a morte della Resistenza italiana*, ed. P. Malvezzi and G. Pirelli, Turin, Einaudi, 1952, 6th ed. 1955; P. Calamandrei, *Uomini e città della Resistenza*, Bari, Laterza, 1955; *Canti della Resistenza italiana*, Milan/Rome, Ed. 'Avanti!', 1960.

10. *From the Liberation to the Elections of* 18 *April* 1958

For this period we confine ourselves to indicating some works of a general character: *Dieci anni dopo* (1945-1955). *Saggi sulla vita democratica italiana*, Bari, Laterza, 1955; *Il secondo Risorgimento*, Rome, Istituto Poligrafico dello Stato, 1955 (*v.* esp. essays by P. Gentile, Ferrara and Mortati); M. and M. Ferrara, *Cronache di vita italiana 1944-1958*, Rome, Ed. Riuniti, 1960; on the political struggle in the immediate post-war period, the Constituent Assembly, and the birth of the Republic, cf. L. Valiani, *L'avvento di De Gasperi*, Turin, De Silva, 1949; R. Romita, *Dalla Monarchia alla Repubblica*, Pisa, Nistri-Lischi, 1959; G. Conti,

La Costituente, Rome, Ed. 'La Voce', 1947; *Commentario sistematico alla Costituzione italiana*, ed. P. Calamandrei and P. Levi, 2 vols., Florence, Barbèra, 1950; *Gli atti dell'Assemblea Costituente sull'art. 7*, ed. A. Capitini and P. Lacaita, Manduria-Perugia, Ed. Lacaita, 1959; L. Basso, *Il principe senza scettro. Democrazia e sovranità popolare nella Costituzione e nella realtà italiana*, Milan, Feltrinelli, 1958; on economic and social problems, cf. *Atti delle commissioni parlamentari d'inchiesta sulla disoccupazione e sulla miseria* and *Rapporto della Commissione economica del ministero per la Costituente* (reports and appendices); B. Manzocchi, *Lineamenti di politica economica in Italia (1945-1955)*, Rome, Ed. Riuniti, 1960; *I sindacati in Italia*, essays by G. Di Vittorio, G. Pastore, I. Viglianesi, etc., Bari, Laterza, 1955; E. Rossi, *Settimo: non rubare*, 4th ed., Bari, Laterza, 1954; Id., *Lo Stato industriale*, Bari, Laterza, 1953; on the elections and the parties, cf. F. Compagna and V. De Caprariis, *Geografia delle elezioni italiane dal 1946 al 1953*, Bologna, Ed. 'Il Mulino', 1954; the series of volumes on the history of the parties, issued under the auspices of the 'Nuova Accademia' publishing house, Milan; G. Galli, *La sinistra nel dopoguerra*, Bologna, Ed. 'Il Mulino', 1958; on the South, cf. E. Sereni, *Il Mezzogiorno all'opposizione*, Turin, Einaudi, 1948; F. Compagna. *La lotta politica italiana nel secondo dopoguerra e il Mezzogiorno*, Bari, Laterza, 1950; G. Amendola, *La democrazia nel Mezzogiorno*, Rome, Ed. Riuniti, 1957; M. Rossi-Doria, *Dieci anni di politica agraria nel Mezzogiorno*, Bari, Laterza, 1958; E. Sereni, *Vecchio e nuovo nelle campagne italiane*, Rome, Ed. Ruiniti, 1956; on relations between State and Church, cf. *Stato e Chiesa* (essays by Salvatorelli, Pettazzoni, Basile, Falconi, etc.), Bari, Laterza, 1957.

INDEX

Abruzzi, the, 126, 127
Abyssinian war, 7; why it was undertaken, 76-7; Italian reaction to, 77-9
Action Party, and Fascism, 8, 9; appearance of, 90, 91; its composition, 91-2; internal divergencies, 92-3; anti-monarchist, 93; and Italy's post-war future, 102; and the Resistance movement, 111-12; its political circular, 112; after the Liberation, 117; election results, 124, 126, 127, 129; dissolved, 130
Adriatic questions, 16, 31, 40, 41, 47
Agricultural labourers, their position in Italy, 27-9, 75; their land hunger, 28, 31; Fascism and, 50, 51; and Communism, 148-9
Agriculture, its post-war position, 1919, 26-9; 1945, 152, 156-7; in the economic crisis, 74-5
Albertini, Senator, 65, 69
Alexander, Field-Marshal, 99, 114, 115
Allied Military Government, 115, 117, 121
Allies, the, and Italian Resistance forces, 10, 109, 113-17; and the Italian theatre of war, 99, 100-1, 114; and Italy's post-war administration, 102, 103-4, 120
Ambrosio, General, 96
Amendola, Giovanni, 64, 68

Aosta, Duke of, 60-1
Apulia, 27, 119, 126, 127
Army, the, spirit of sedition in, 20, 60; its plight in 1919, 25-6, 31; causes of its defeats, 37; and Fascism, 60; and the King, 95; collapses after the armistice, 100; and the Resistance, 109
Atlantic Pact, 137
Austria, 16, 17-19, 79-80
Aventine secession, 64-5, 67

Badoglio, Marshal, his governments, 96, 102-5, 106; disagrees with the parties, 97-8; leaves Rome, 99
Balbo, Count Cesare, and Italian policy, 16-17
Balbo, Italo, 49, 51, 59, 60, 67
Basilicata, 126, 129
Benedict XV, Pope, 54, 88
Bianchi, Michele, 59
Bissolati, Leonida, 19, 35, 48
Blackshirts, 50, 59; become the MVSN, 67-8
Bologna, 27, 51, 59, 128
Bonomi, Ivanoe, 35, 48; becomes Prime Minister, 95, 116, 117, 118; his plan to overthrow Fascism, 97
Bourgeoisie, see Middle classes
Brindisi, 99, 102
Bureaucracy, an influence towards stability, 120-2

Cadorna, General, 114-15
Calabria, 28, 126, 127
Caporetto, 28, 37, 88, 96
Catania, 27, 150
Catholic Action, supports Christian Democracy, 11, 36-7, 142; the Church and, 71, 88, 89
Catholic Party, 11, 29; its beginnings, 35; in the 1919-20 elections, 36, 37-8; its organization, 38, 88-9; Giolitti and, 57; Mussolini and, 62, 63, 70-1
Catholicism, and Italian political life, 35, 54, 70-1, 90, 94, 149, 159-60
Cattani, Leone, 118-19
Cavour, Count Camillo, 34, 87
CGIL, 37, 38
Chamber of Deputies, 63, 65, 73
Chamber of Fasces and Corporations, 73, 128
Christian Democracy, 35, 37, 111; replaces Liberalism, 11-12; succeeds Partito Popolare, 89; and Italy's post-war future, 90, 94, 102, 112-13, 121; in the post-war elections, 125-6, 127-8, 128-30, 138; linked by Catholicism, 132; in the new Constituent Assembly, 134, 135, 136-8; its overwhelming victory, 138-42, 149; its geographical distribution, 143-8; its social structure, 139
Church, the, Fascism and, 54-5; accepts Mussolini's government, 70-1; opposes racial laws, 81-2; assists refugees, 106; and the new Constitution, 134-6
Ciano, Count, 82-3
Committees of National Liberation, 95; the political parties and, 93, 94, 112, 113, 117; in S. Italy, 101, 102; in Rome, 105-6;

Committees, cont.
and the Resistance, 110; their political difficulties, 112, 113-17; the allies and, 10, 114, 121; aims of, 118-19; and the post-war elections, 127, 129
Communism, its beginnings in Italy, 30-1; reaction against in 1948, 139, 141, 144; the rural areas and, 148-9
Communist Party, 11; splits from Socialists, 38, 40; suppressed by Fascists, 63, 68; its underground organization, 88, 89, 92, 94; and the future of Italy, 90-1, 94, 98, 102, 104; and the Resistance movement, 109, 111-12; in the post-war elections, 124, 125-8, 129, 138-42; attitude of Socialist party to, 130-2; in the new Constituent Assembly, 134-8; its geographical distribution, 143-8
Concordat, 1929, 11, 54, 82, 135
Congress of Leghorn, 68-9
Congress of Rome, 1921, 59
Constituent Assembly, 123, 128, 134-6
Corporative system, 71-5, 78-9
Cosenza Congress, 93
Cremona, 27, 29, 49
Crispi, Francesco, 17, 30
Croce, Benedetto, 69, 89, 90, 103
Currency difficulties, 153-4, 155, 156
Czechoslovakia, 18, 139, 141

Dalmatia, 16, 47
D'Annunzio, Gabriele, and Fiume, 20, 40, 59, 60
De Bono, Emilio, 59
De Gasperi, Alcide, 88; Prime Minister, 121, 129-30, 134, 135-6, 142

Democracy of Labour Party, 104-5
Democratic Popular Front, in the post-war elections, 138, 139, 140-2, 143; its geographical distribution, 143-8
De Nicola, Enrico, 133
De Vecchi, Cesare Maria, 59, 62
Dollfuss, Chancellor, 79, 80

Einaudi, Luigi, 23, 89, 133, 137, 154-5
Elections, municipal and political, 1946, 1948, 123-9, 138-42
Emigration, 22, 158
Emilia, Fascism in, 50, 51; and the post-war elections, 125, 126, 127, 129, 145, 146

Farinacci, Roberto, 48, 49, 60, 65
Fascism, its decline in popularity, 7-8, 83-4; the Resistance and, 8-10; its upsurge in 1920, 43, 47, 49-50; its foundation, 47; Mussolini and, 47-8; its early adherents, 48-9, 51-2, 59; clashes with Socialism, 49; its use of violence, 50, 59, 65, 69; causes of its success, 51-5, 56-61; its appeal to the *bourgeoisie*, 51-5; and class interests, 53-4; the older politicians and, 56-8; aims of its leaders, 58-9; its co-operative period, 62-3; opposition to, 64-5, 68-9; becomes a true dictatorship, 65; its new laws, 65-7, 72; backed by its own militia, 67-8, 95; period of consolidation, 69-76; foreign and Italian approval of, 69-70; produces the Labour Charter, 71-2; its last period, 76, 83-4; the effect of the Abyssinian war on,

Fascism, cont.
77-80; a tool of Nazism, 81; breaks with the Church, 81-2; breach with the people, 82-4, 87; political background of the struggle against, 88-94; its downfall, 94-6; and bureaucracy, 120; and elections, 123, 128
Fascist Grand Council, 63, 66-7, 73, 128
Fascist Republican Army, 113
Fascists, their first appearance, 40; clash with socialists, 49; and the Church, 54; their aims, 58-9, 60; change the electoral laws, 63-4; and the *rapprochement* with Germany, 80 ff.
Ferrara, 27, 49, 51
Fiume, 16, 20, 40, 47
Florence, 107-8, 128
France, 32, 79, 80, 87, 139
Free Italian General Confederation of Workers, 148
Freedom Volunteers' Corps, 114-15

GAP, 109
Garibaldi, Giuseppe, 20, 87
Garibaldi Brigades, 111
General Confederation of Industry, 43, 75
General Confederation of Labour, 28, 30, 31, 41, 49; post-war, 148
Genoa, 30, 118, 128
Gentiloni Pact, 35
Germany, the Resistance and, 9-10, 94, 108-9; Italian fear of, 17; anti-semitism in, 55; development of its SS, 67-8; influence of on Fascism, 78-9; and the Abyssinian war, 79; occupies Austria, 80-1; Mussolini and, 82-3;

Germany, cont.
  development of unity in, 87;
  her occupation of Italy, 96-7, 98, 100, 101
Giannini, Guglielmo, 119, 143
Giolitti, Giovanni, 22-3; his policy, 34-5, 39-40, 56-7; and the Catholic Party, 36; and D'Annunzio, 40; and the occupation of the factories, 41-2, 52; his fiscal measures, 53; and the rise of Fascism, 56-7, 59-60, 63, 68
Gobetti, Piero, 68, 92
Gramsci, Antonio, 30, 68, 148
Grandi, Count Dino, 49, 51, 60
Great Britain, 78, 79, 80, 139
Great War, 1914-18, 8; and Italy's internal life, 21-32; 1939-45, 8; absence of illusions in, 24; Italy enters, 84; lack of volunteers in, 87-8; the armistice and after, 98-101; damage caused by, 151
Guariglia, Raffaele, 79 and n.

Hapsburg Empire, collapse of, 15-16; question of its succession, 16-20
Hitler, Adolf, 79, 80

Independents, 124
Industry, in 1919, 29-30; and Fascism, 50, 55; in the economic crisis, 75; and the Abyssinian war, 78; war damage to, 151-2; post-war conditions, 154-5
Italian Corps of Liberation, 109
Italian High Command, and the armistice, 98
Italian Labour Federation, 148
Italian Republic, 88; establishment of, 122, 123; state of the parties in, 123ff.

Italian Social Republic, *see under* Salò
Italian Workers' Federation, 38, 49
Italy, post-war (1939-45) rebuilding of, 11-12, 159-60; her position in 1919, 15-16, 19; influence of Balbo on her policy, 16-17; develops nationalist feelings, 19-20, 21; social and political upheavals in during 1914-18 war, 21-32; her youth as a State, 22, 159; her comparative poverty, 22, 26; her belief in a short war, 22-3; currency difficulties in, 24-5, 153-4, 155, 156; largely an agricultural country in 1919, 26; the agrarian movement, 28-9; rise of Socialism in, 30-2; her politics before 1914, 33-5; emergence of inter-party politics, 35-9; post-war political crises, 39-42; improvement in her financial position, 42-3; fear of revolution in, 43, 52; and the Church, 54; her reaction to antisemitism, 55; fails to perceive the dangers of Fascism, 57-9; the economic crisis of the thirties, 72-3, 74-6; and the Abyssinian war, 76, 77-9; and Austrian independence, 79-80; development of unity in, 87; the political parties and her future, 90ff.; her wartime division, 101ff.; her first post-Fascist government, 104; political situation after the Liberation, 117ff.; moves towards conservatism, 121-2; becomes a Republic, 122, 133; geographical distribution of her parties, 124-50; the post-war coalition, 134-8; her inflationary period, 153-5; her population problems, 157-8

INDEX

Italy, Central, after the armistice, 105-7, 108; after the Liberation, 111; and the post-war elections, 126, 129, 146, 147
— North, 28; the Resistance movement in, 9-10, 108; the centre of industry, 29-30; after the armistice, 100-1; after the Liberation, 118; and the post-war elections, 125, 126-7, 129, 133, 141, 145, 146, 147-8, 150
— South, the Resistance movement in, 9; Communism in, 11; the agricultural labourer in, 27-8; after the armistice, 100-1, 102; and the post-war elections, 126, 127, 129, 141, 146, 147; and the monarchy, 133, 150; post-war economic conditions, 155-6

Jews, laws against, 55, 67, 81, 84
Justice and Liberty movement, 91, 93, 111, 117

Kingdom of Italy formed, 35
Kingdom of the South, 102 ff.

Labour Charter, 71-2
Land, its occupation in 1919, 28-9; reclamation of, 152
Landowners, and the agricultural labourer, 27, 30, 43, 50; and Fascism, 50, 55; in the economic crisis, 75; support Christian Democracy, 144
Lateran Pacts, 54, 70, 90; the new Constitution and, 134, 135-6
Left wing, in the post war elections, 124-8, 138-41, 145-7; its strongest base, 147-9
Liberal Party, 33, 34, 36, 57; Mussolini and, 62; opposes Fascism, 69, 89; and Italy's post-war future, 90, 94, 102, 112-13;

Liberal Party, cont.
and the post-war elections, 126, 127, 128, 129, 140, 141, 149-50; in De Gasperi's government, 132, 134, 137
Liberal Socialism, 91-2
Liguria, 111; and the post-war elections, 125, 127, 129, 144, 145, 146
Lombardo, Ivan Matteo, 131, 143, 150
Lombardy, 11, 87; and the post-war elections, 125, 127, 129, 144, 146

Marche, the, and the post-war elections, 125, 126, 127, 129, 149
Margherita, Queen, and Fascism, 61
Matteotti, Giacomo, his murder, 7, 60, 64
Mazzini, Giuseppe, 15, 16, 17, 33
Meda, Filippo, 35, 54
Middle classes, their attitude to Fascism, 8, 51-3, 55, 58, 60; fear of Communism, 11; the 1914-18 war and, 23-6, 31; the Socialist Party and, 32; and the occupation of the factories, 52; and Catholicism, 54; in the Resistance, 110; and Christian Democracy, 149
Miglioli, Guido, 29, 39, 71
Milan, 30, 41, 128; Fascism in, 47, 49; and the Pact of Steel, 82-3; and the Resistance, 109, 118
Millerand, Alexandre, 41
Modigliani, G. E., 32, 38, 64, 68
Monarchy, the, the political parties and, 33, 93, 104; the Vatican and, 54; Mussolini and, 62; Fascist leglislation and, 65-7; results of the Referendum, 132-3
Montezemolo, Colonel, 105, 106

Mussolini, Benito, 8; and the beginning of Fascism, 47-8; his character, 48, 60; and conciliation with the Church, 54 (*see also* Lateran Pacts); Giolitti and, 56, 59-60; establishes his organization, 62-3; becomes a true dictator, 65; the Grand Council and, 67; creates the militia, 67-8; and the Labour Charter, 71-2; and the economic crisis, 72-3; creates the Corporations, 73-4; and the Abyssinian war, 76, 77-8, 79; and Hitler's Germany, 79-81, 82; and the Pact of Steel, 82-3; the Second World War and, 84; his dismissal, 96; liberated by the Germans, 100

Naples, 9, 27, 119; its Liberation, 100; and the post-war elections, 126, 127, 141, 146
National Confederation of Syndicates, 128
National Council of Corporations, 73, 128
National Council of the Fascist Party, 128
Nationalists, 34, 47
Navy, Italian, 99-100
Nenni, Pietro, 118, 121; the split within his party, 130-1; in the Constituent Assembly, 134, 136
Nitti, Francesco Saverio, 20, 25, 40, 68

Orlando, Vittorio Emanuele, 16, 54

Pact of Steel, 82-3
Parri, Ferruccio, 11, 115, 121
Partito Popolare, 11, 29; *see also* Catholic Party
Pescara, 138

Piedmont, 27, 38, 87, 110, 111, 133; and the post-war elections, 11, 125, 127, 129, 143; its industrial character, 144
Pius XI, Pope, 70, 71, 81, 88
Pius XII, Pope, 106
Po Valley, 11, 27, 38; occupation of the land in, 28, 29, 43
Poland, 83
Popolo d'Italia, 47, 70
Press, the, 66, 67

Radicals, 34, 36
Reds, the, 28-9, 50
Reformist Socialists, 19, 35, 148, 150
Reggio Emilia Congress, 1912, 19, 48
Republicans, 124, 149; and the monarchy, 33, 132; in De Gasperi's government, 134, 135, 137
Resistance, Italian, its military and political source, 8-9, 100; and Fascism, 9; its significance, 9-10; the Action Party and, 92-3, 111; unites the anti-Fascist forces, 94, 123; and German occupation, 100; its character and composition, 108-10, 111; its political problems, 111-17; after the Liberation, 117; comes to a close, 121-2
Right wing, and the post-war elections, 126-7
Risorgimento, the, 8, 15, 16, 110
Romagna, 9, 50, 51, 149
Roman Question, 54, 90
Rome, and the Resistance, 9, 10, 105, 107; after the Liberation, 105, 118; centred on the Vatican, 118, 119-20; and the post-war elections, 126, 128, 129, 140, 141, 146

INDEX

Rome agreements (1935), 79
Rome-Berlin Axis, 80 ff.
Rome Government, and the CLNAI, 116-17
Rome, March on, 53, 55, 58-9
Romita, Giuseppe, 131
Rosselli, Carlo, 68, 81, 91
Russia, Italian fear of, 17; the working classes and, 30-1; the Socialist Party and, 38

Salandra, Antonio, 22, 34, 59, 69
Salerno, 102
Salò, Fascist Republic of, 10, 100, 101, 107
Salvemini, Gaetano, 7, 68, 120
SAP, 109
Saragat, Giuseppe, his Socialist party, 130-1, 136, 138, 143, 144, 150
Sard Action Party, 129
Sardinia, 87; and the post-war elections, 126, 127, 146, 147
Sforza, Count, 40, 68, 136, 137
Sicily, Allied landings in, 96; and the post-war elections, 126, 147, 150
Silone, Ignazio, 131, 143, 150
Socialism, its growth in Italy, 30-2, 91; believed to be anti-nationalist, 31-2, 38; Rosselli and, 91
Socialist Party, 11; before 1914, 33, 34-5; in the 1919-20 elections, 36-7, 38; its internal crises, 38-9, 91; calls for revolutionary action, 41; Mussolini and, 47-8; Fascist clashes with, 49, 63; Giolitti and, 57; its post-war revival 89; and Italy's future, 91, 102, 121; in the post-war elections, 124, 125-9, 138-41; its internal divisions, 130-2, 136, 139, 143, 146; in the Constituent Assembly, 134, 135,

Socialist Party, cont.
   136-8; its geographical distribution, 143-50
Socialist Party of the Italian Workers (PSLI), 131, 139, 143
Socialist Unity, 139-40, 143, 144
Socialists' Union, 131, 139
Sogno, Edgardo, 111
Soleri, Marcello, 42-3, 59, 89
Sonnino, Baron Sidney, and the Hapsburg Empire, 16, 18, 40
Sorel, Georges, 48
Soresina, 29
Spain, Italian intervention in, 78, 80, 82, 94
Stalin, Joseph, 10
Stresa agreements, 79
Strikes, 40-2, 52-3, 95, 109, 141
Sturzo, Don Luigi, 35, 68, 142; Giolitti and, 36, 39, 57; in exile, 70

Taxation, 23, 25, 153, 156
Taylor, General, 98-9
Togliatti, Palmiro, 104, 105, 134, 136, 147
Trade Unions, 36, 37, 148; Fascism and, 49-50; and the landowner, 50
Transport system, war damage to, 152
Treaty of London, 16, 19
Treaty of Rapallo, 40, 41, 47
Treaty of Rome (1924), 47
Trentino, and the post-war elections, 125, 126, 127, 129, 145, 149
Trento, 15, 17, 18
Treves, Claudio, 32, 35, 38, 64, 68
Trieste, 15, 17, 18, 139
Triple Alliance, 17, 18
Turati, Filippo, and Socialism, 30-1, 32, 34-5, 38; opposes Fascism, 64, 68

Turin, its industry, 30, 41, 43, 109, 118; and post-war elections, 128, 144
Tuscany, rise of Fascism in, 50, 51; and the post-war elections, 125, 126, 127, 129, 145-6

Umberto, Crown Prince (later Umberto II), 103, 105, 133
Umbria, and post-war elections, 125, 126, 127, 129, 145-6
Unemployment, among agricultural labourers, 27, 75; post-war figures, 157
Unified Socialist Party (PSU), 131
United States, 24, 25, 137, 139
'Uomo Qualunque,' 119, 126, 132, 140, 143
USSR, 103, 104, 137, 139

Vatican, the, reconciliation with, 7, 54; after the Liberation, 106; a source of authority, 107, 118; and the new Constitution, 134-5
Veneto, and post-war elections, 125, 126, 127, 129, 145, 146, 149
Vercelli, 27
Victor Emmanuel II, 87

Victor Emmanuel III, and the March on Rome, 59; and Fascism, 60-1, 65; the Liberals and, 89, 90; yields to public opinion, 95-6; dismisses Mussolini, 96-7; differences with the political parties, 97-8; leaves Rome, 99; and Badoglio, 102, 103; his abdication demanded, 103, 104; hands over to Umberto, 105, 133
Victor Emmanuel, Prince of Naples, 103
Voluntary Militia for National Safety (MVSN), 67-8

White Bolshevism, and the agrarian movement, 28-9
Wilson, General Maitland, 114, 118
Wilson, President, 19
Working classes, after the 1914-18 War, 25, 30; desire a political revolution, 30-1; Socialism and, 32; occupy the factories, 41, 52; percentage of Fascists, 1921, 51; their political opinions, 51, 148

Yugoslavia, 16, 19, 40, 47